The Swiss Corridor

Józef Garliński

The Swiss Corridor

Espionage networks in Switzerland
during World War II

J.M. Dent & Sons Ltd
London Melbourne Toronto

First published 1981
© text, Józef Garliński 1981

Printed in Great Britain by
Billing & Sons, Guildford, London, Oxford & Worcester
for J.M. Dent & Sons Ltd
Aldine House Welbeck Street London

This book is set in Linotron 202 Garamond by
Tradespools Ltd, Frome, Somerset

British Library Cataloguing in Publication Data

Garliński, Józef
   The Swiss corridor.
   1. World war, 1939–1945 – Secret service
   I. Title
   940.54'86

ISBN 0-460-04351-X

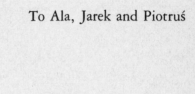

To Ala, Jarek and Piotruś

Contents

List of Plates

Acknowledgements for photographs

The photographs are by courtesy of: Drago Arsenijevic, Geneva
(11, 12, 14, 15–17); Berto-Verlag GmbH, Bonn (24, 25);
Bundesarchiv, Bern (34); Heinz Höhne, Grosshandsdorf,
Codeword: Director (18, 19, 21, 22, 31); Hans Rudolf Kurz, Bern
(1–8, 10, 29, 30, 35, 37); Libraire Académique Perrin, Paris
(33); McGraw-Hill, New York (20); Otto Pünter, Bern (13);
RIA Fotagentur, Zürich (9); Patrick Seale Books, London (32);
Ullstein GmbH Bilderdienst, Berlin (23, 26–8); Halina Wiśniowska, London (36).

The author is grateful to the following publishers and persons
who helped him in various ways when he was collecting the
photographs: S. Fischer Verlag (Frankfurt am Main), Hamish
Hamilton Ltd (London), E. Hine (Imperial War Museum,
London), Hutchinson Publishing Group Ltd (London), Karl
Lüönd (Tolhusen), Secker and Warburg Ltd (London), Weidenfeld and Nicolson Ltd (London).

Line Illustrations

x

Foreword

by Professor M.R.D. Foot

Much of the secret history of the last world war has been revealed, slice by slice, over the past fifteen years; we are now getting near the bone. Among the few big tangles hitherto unsusceptible to a rational account, the Swiss problems are among the most complex and the most important. Did the Russian-dominated intelligence circuit run by Sándor Radó ('Dora') from Geneva work with the connivance of the Swiss authorities? Exactly what were 'Dora's' relations with Rudolf Roessler ('Lucy') in Lucerne? Where on earth did 'Lucy' get his excellent information from—direct (but how?) from Hitler's war headquarters, or smuggled to him (but again, how?) from some source large, rich, cunning, and competent enough to unscramble the Germans' highly elaborate machine ciphers?

As a Pole, Dr Garliński has been brought up with problems of intelligence resistance and security from boyhood. As a Polish officer, he fought the Germans unavailingly in 1939, and—almost automatically—entered the Home Army. He took his first degree, in law, clandestinely, in the forbidden University of Warsaw. The German police caught up with him; he survived Auschwitz and Neuengamme. He did not care to return to a Poland gone communist, and made a fresh career among the Polish community in West London; but, as a Pole, he could not and cannot forget Poland's sufferings, during the war and since: the fourteen thousand arrested officers, for instance, who vanished into Soviet camps—over four thousand turned up dead in forest graves at Katyn, the rest just vanished.

He took—at first in his spare time, now as a career—to writing recent history. His *Poland, SOE and the Allies* broke important new ground. He then developed from his experiences at Auschwitz an impressive doctoral thesis at the London School of Economics, under the knowledgeable guidance of Professor Joll; this he turned into a remarkable book, *Fighting Auschwitz*. Then he wrote a study of the German revenge weapons, the V1 and V2, and a lucid layman's survey—called simply *Intercept*—of what the Poles, French and British did in turn to break the Germans' 'Enigma' ciphering system. This book is his fifth account in English of the crucial by-ways that helped to determine the course of the world war and the peace that followed it.

He takes care, even when handling highly sensational material, to stick to ascertained facts and to abjure sensationalism, a splendid contrast with some people who have gone into this corner of the market in historical fiction and try to present their wares as fact. His book will exasperate those few fanatics who still place their hopes in a Soviet paradise on earth; the rest of us can read in it a singularly honest attempt to grapple with a series of almost inextricably complicated problems of strategy and conduct. The Russians come out of it almost as badly as the Germans; the Americans and the British receive their share of blame as well. This is history as it was lived: unheroic, but, so far as the historian can see it, true.

M.R.D. Foot

Terms and Abbreviations

Abwehr	German military intelligence.
AK	*Armia Krajowa* (Home Army).
BP	Bletchley Park.
Bundesrat	Swiss government.
Bureau F	German intelligence agency in Bern.
Büro Ha	Private Swiss intelligence agency in Lucerne.
Comintern	Communist International (an organization set up in 1919 in Russia to bring about world-wide revolution).
Dora Group	Soviet intelligence outpost in Switzerland.
Enigma	German ciphering machine.
Gestapo	*Geheime Staatspolizei* (secret state police).
Kazi	code-name for a Czechoslovak intelligence station in Switzerland.
KPD	*Komunistische Partei Deutschland* (The German Communist Party).
Kripo	*Kriminalpolizei* (German criminal police).
Lucy Ring	code-name for an intelligence network in Switzerland built by Rudolf Roessler.
Luftwaffe	German Air Force.
Nachrichtendienst	Intelligence Service.
Nell	code-name for Swiss intelligence station in Lugano.
NKVD	*Narodny Komissariat Vnutrennych Dyel* (People's Commissariat of International Affairs: used for Soviet secret police).
NSDAP	*National Socialistische Deutsche Arbeiterpartei* (National-socialist German Workers' Party).
Obrona Naroda	Defence of the Nation (Czechoslovak military underground organization).

OKH	*Oberkommando des Heeres* (High Command of the German Army).
OKL	*Oberkommando der Luftwaffe* (High Command of the German Air Force).
OKM	*Oberkommando der Marine* (High Command of the German Navy).
OKW	*Oberkommando der Wehrmacht* (High Command of the German Armed Forces).
Operation Boehme	code-name for the German plan to invade Switzerland in 1943.
Operation Citadel	code-name for the German offensive in Russia in July 1943.
OSS	Office of Strategic Services.
Outpost S (later Wera)	code-name for the Polish secret liaison outpost in Bern.
Pfalz	code-name for the Swiss intelligence station in Basel.
Pilatus	code-name for *Büro Ha*.
Razvedupr	*Glovnoye Razvedyvatelnoye Upravlenie* (Soviet Military Intelligence).
Reichswehr	German army, without Air Force, after the Treaty of Versailles.
Rigi	code-name for the Swiss intelligence station in Lucerne.
Rocco	code-name for the anti-fascist group in Italy.
Roten Drei	Red Three (radio stations of *Dora Group* in Switzerland).
Rote Kapelle	The Red Orchestra (Soviet spy-ring in Western Europe).
RSHA	*Reichssicherheitshauptamt* (State security headquarters).
Salm	code-name for the Swiss intelligence station in Schaffhausen.
Schwarze Kapelle	The Black Orchestra (the name used by German security for the Anti-Hitler conspiracy in Germany).
SD	*Sicherheitsdienst* (security service).
SIS	Special or Secret Intelligence Service.

SOE	Special Operations Executive, a secret British organization set up to help the countries under German and Japanese occupation.
Speer	code-name for the Swiss intelligence station in St. Gallen.
SS	*Schutzstaffel* (German political-military protection units).
Tannenbaum	code-name for the German plan to invade Switzerland in 1940.
Ultra	code-name for intelligence unit which distributed *Enigma*-deciphered messages.
Uto	code-name for the Swiss intelligence station in Zürich.
Wehrmacht	German Armed Forces.
Wera	code-name for the Polish secret liaison outpost in Bern.
Wiking Linie	code-name for an intelligence network in Germany built by a Swiss officer, Max Waibel.

Introduction

While working on my last book on the extraordinary story of the German cipher machine called Enigma, I came across information about the intelligence services working in Switzerland during the last war. The subject attracted me, my publisher was encouraging, so I set to work knowing from the very beginning that it would be difficult and fraught with complications.

I also knew that the archives concerning intelligence are for the most part not yet open, and for this reason I would have to rely on witnesses, on fragmentary information and on the few original documents so far unused.

In these circumstances the composition of the book could not be too ambitious and I could not hope to cover the whole problem nor to exhaust the subject. I was forced to concentrate on the most important topics and present them in the plainest possible way. I gave most of my attention to Soviet Intelligence, with, beside it, British, German and American activities. I have devoted a lot of space to Switzerland herself and her intelligence, for the events described took place on her territory and her active neutrality played an important part during the last war. French, Polish, Italian, Czechoslovak and Austrian achievements have also been brought into the picture.

Every historical work has a primary objective, for the author is putting forward a point of view and not merely presenting facts. My aim is to inform a wider circle of readers, not only the specialists, of the ubiquity of foreign intelligence agencies. They are active everywhere in a state of readiness well in advance, many years before the expected military conflict. Their tentacles reach deep and wide, their agents always have excellent cover stories—sometimes they are recruited from among the citizens of the country which is being penetrated. They behave so because of their political convictions. Co-operation with enemy intelligence is not considered by them as treason.

We must hope that no new world-wide conflict will break out and that millions of people will not again be murdered cruelly and senselessly; but hope alone is not enough. We must be physically and morally prepared for such an eventuality, we must know from whence the threat comes and be prepared to defend ourselves. This state of readiness is today especially important, for the voices are multiplying which, consciously or unconsciously, are trying to bring about the complete moral and physical disarmament of the West. It will inevitably lead to war.

As usual in my work, I received help from many people. I am especially grateful to my friend, Professor Michael Foot, who not only indicated various sources and wrote an excellent foreword to my book, but also went through the script very thoroughly and made a long list of remarks, thanks to which I have avoided many errors.

I received quite priceless information from Halina Wiśniowska, who decided to break her long years of silence and granted me, the very first, several authorized interviews on the subject of her contact with Admiral Canaris and her collaboration with the Intelligence Service in Switzerland during the war. Thanks to this my book has been enriched by authentic and so-far unknown material of documentary value.

I was given a lot of help by Lieutenant Colonel Dr Hans Rudolf Kurz of Bern, who gave me several interviews and facilitated my access to the documents of Swiss Intelligence during the last war. He introduced me to the Director of the State Archives in Bern, Dr E. Tschabold, thanks to whom I was allowed to see some of the still secret documents which interested me.

In various ways, generally by an exchange of letters and by answering my questions, I was helped by the following persons: Stanisław Appenzeller (France), Anthony Brooks, Dr John W.M. Chapman, Captain Victor G. Farrell, Jarosław J. Garliński, Dr Lothar Kettenacker, Dr Józef Kiermisz (Israel), Colonel Maria Leśniakowa, Colonel Tadeusz Lisicki, Walter Meyer, Otto Pünter, Werner Rings (the last three from Switzerland), Professor Dr Jürgen Rohwer (Germany), Dr Xaver Schnieper (Switzerland), Anna Spławska and Sarah Tyacke. I am truly grateful to them all.

J.G. London, 1980.

Dramatis Personae

		Born	Died
1	Bolli (Schwarz), Margrit (*Rosa*), Dora Ring	15.12.1919	—
2	Böttcher, Paul (*Paul*), Dora Ring	?	
3	Canaris, Wilhelm, Head of the Abwehr, also Black Orchestra	1.1.1887	9.4.1945
4	Dulles, Welsh Allen, OSS	7.4.1893	29.1.1969
5	Dübendorfer, Rachel (*Sissy*), Dora Ring	?	1973
6	Foote, Alexander (*Jim*), Dora Ring	13.4.1905	1.8.1956
7	Gisevius, Hans Bernd (*Tiny*), Black Orchestra	1910	—
8	Guisan, Henri, C-in-C Swiss Army	1874	12.4.1960
9	Hamel, Edmond (*Eduard*), Dora Ring	2.4.1910	—
10	Hamel Olga (*Maude*), Dora Ring	29.11.1907	—
11	Harnack, Arvid, (*Arvid*), Red Orchestra	24.5.1901	22.12.1942
12	Hausamann, Hans, Büro Ha	1897	17.12.1974
13	Masson, Roger, Head of Swiss Intelligence	1.6.1894	22.3.1967
14	Mayr von Baldegg, (*Luise*) Bernhard, Swiss Intelligence	27.10.1909	—
15	Oster, Hans, Black Orchestra	9.8.1888	9.4.1945
16	Pünter, Otto (*Pakbo*), Pakbo Ring	4.4.1900	—
17	Radó, Helene (*Maria*), Dora Ring	18.6.1901	1.9.1958
18	Radó, Sándor (*Dora*), Dora Ring	5.11.1899	—
19	Roessler, Rudolf (*Lucy*), Lucy Ring	22.11.1897	October 1958
20	Schellenberg, Walter, RSHA	1910	31.3.1952
21	Schneider, Christian (*Taylor*), Lucy Ring	1896	1962
22	Schnieper, Xaver, Lucy Ring	6.1.1910	—
23	Schulze-Boysen, Harro (*Choro*), Red Orchestra	2.9.1909	22.12.1942
24	Stauffenberg, Claus Schenk von, Black Orchestra	1908	20.7.1944
25	Sukulov-Gurevich, Victor (*Captain Kent*), Red Orchestra	1911	—
26	Szymańska, Halina (*Krzywda*), Go-between, Canaris and British Intelligence	6.12.1906	—
27	Trepper, Leopold (*Gilbert, Grand Chef*), Red Orchestra	23.2.1904	
28	Waibel, Max, Swiss Intelligence	1901	21.1.1971
29	Wenzel, Johann (*Hermann*), Red Orchestra	1902	—

1 Secret Preparations

1

The young man crept up to the two-metre high barbed-wire fence and attempted to slip under it to the other side. But the wires were too close together, about twenty centimetres from one another and tightly strung. A different way had to be sought. The night was very dark, not a sound was to be heard, so the young man gripped his small bundle in his teeth and very carefully began to climb up the wires, ladder-like. At the top he leaned over to the far side, let his bundle fall as quietly as possible, freed his clothes from the barbs and jumped down. He picked up his bundle, took a few steps, thinking that the first part of his enterprise had been successful, when from a near-by bush a torch light shone and a shout in Russian rang out—'Halt, hands up!'

After a few days spent in a village shed guarded by soldiers of the *NKVD*, he was loaded on to a lorry and taken to the prison in Minsk, 300 kilometres to the east of the Ribbentrop-Molotov line drawn across Poland in the autumn of 1939. Here began severe night-time interrogation, in which he had very little chance. He had been caught in the act of crossing the frontier, in his bundle a small radio transmitter had been found and on his person a list of codes. His explanation that he had gone to look for his family broke down in the face of these very obvious signs of intention to spy. It was true that Hitler's Germany was an ally of the Soviet Union, but after all it does happen that friend watches the steps of closest friend. The officer in charge of the interrogation could also have suspected that the intelligence mission had been planned by the Polish Underground Movement under German occupation, but he dismissed this possibility. He knew that in the territories occupied by his own people a Polish Underground Movement operated, so why would they need to send someone from Warsaw to these parts? This must be an idea of the Germans, all the more so as several other, similar young men, caught in more or less the same circumstances, were already in the prison.

This appraisement was correct, but not altogether. The young man who was brought to his room each night had indeed been dispatched to the Soviet side by German Intelligence, but his story was more complicated than that. From the very first months of the occupation he had belonged to the Polish military underground in Warsaw, where, because of his linguistic abilities, he had worked in intelligence. At the beginning of 1941 this intelligence found out that the Germans were very discreetly looking for men who knew the Russian language well. Further information disclosed that they were being recruited to the spy school in Königsberg, where they were being taught the Morse code and how to work small short-range radio transmitters. Polish underground intelligence was very interested in this, for here was an opportunity to penetrate some German—and even perhaps Soviet—secrets, and so it decided to put forward very cautiously a few candidates of its own. This was the road trodden by the young man whose intelligence career ended the moment he crossed the German-Soviet demarcation line.

The interrogation was going very badly, accompanied by severe physical force, difficult to bear. However the mental strain must have been still worse. Every night, while he was being forced to confess, from the depths of the prison came the desperate cries of a woman, who had also found herself in the hands of the NKVD. The interrogating officer, obviously irritated by this, rifled his papers nervously, until one night, unable to stand any more, he turned in a rage to the man he was interrogating, as if seeking understanding from him: 'Oh, what a bitch, she has to scream, she won't let me work in peace.'

Each morning the prisoner returned to his cell with ever gloomier thoughts, when one day, just as he was walking back worn out, things suddenly changed. The walls shook, the earth trembled and the noise of very close detonations almost deafened him. The warder drove him to his cell at the double, slammed the door and left him alone. From outside came the loud echoes of further detonations, people could be heard running about in the corridor, the door was opened again and from every cell the prisoners were ordered out. They were hustled out into the yard, ordered to form fours, threatened with being shot at the least attempt at escape and were impelled through the town eastward. This was the result of a surprise German air-raid which partly destroyed the prison and forced it to be evacuated.

2

After leaving the town the column went on marching east, driven on by the shouts of the escort. Some of the weaker prisoners had already fallen out and been shot in the roadside ditch. In the air German planes circled, looking for targets to bomb, the column of prisoners was passed by cars and lorries full of Soviet officials fleeing in panic, and buildings were burning on both sides of the road.

In the evening the long drawn-out column was halted in a wood and the prisoners, in fours as they stood, were ordered to lie down. Every one lay motionless so as not to arouse the interest of the guards, but listened carefully, for from the head of the great human snake came disquieting sounds. Four shots in succession, a slight pause and again four similar sounds. There was no doubt about it, the *NKVD* was murdering the prone prisoners by shots in the back of the head.

The young man nudged his right-hand neighbour, they looked hard at each other; he turned to the left with the same slight wink. Night was drawing in, the regular series of shots was getting nearer and nearer. At a sign the four jumped up and dived into the wood. Shouts were heard from the guards, bullets whistled past but the prisoners pushed on, stumbling over roots and grazing themselves on branches. Some twenty minutes later they stopped, breathless: only the murmur of the trees was to be heard. They were free.

All the next day they were too scared to move out of cover and they began to make their way towards human habitations only when the sounds of fighting indicated that the front had moved eastward. With great caution they crossed territory which only a few days previously had been occupied by the Red Army and was now no-man's land, not as yet caught in the pincers of the German administration and police. They saw the primitive, hastily thrown up huts and hovels where the Red Army soldiers had huddled. Everywhere they were surprised to come upon miserable equipment thrown around in confusion. They were amazed by the hundreds of Soviet tanks and trucks whose shot-up hulks were piled up on both sides of the road, which was barely kept open for front-line transport. The signs of surprise, panic and of short, one-sided fighting were everywhere visible. They went into villages, asked for food and talked to the villagers. They were now on the Polish territory seized by Stalin in agreement with Hitler in 1939. On all sides they met with the same opinion: the Red Army had not expected the attack, it had been taken completely by surprise, the soldiers had shown no desire to fight, only fear of the German 'ally'. The whole

Soviet organization had gone to pieces at the first German attack. Several times the fugitives came across Soviet soldiers who had managed to keep out of German hands although they had not been able to retreat. They had been helped by the local population and were already dressed in civilian clothing, but they kept out of sight. The sound of pure Russian sometimes opened their mouths and they muttered a few words. Their broken sentences expressed complete dismay and bewilderment. They had not expected any attack, were not prepared for it and had not been given any warning. With threats of punishment their officers had forbidden them to repeat rumours of German armies massed on the other side of the frontier.[1]

The young man took in all this, looked around him and his amazement grew with every hour. He knew the German side fairly well, he had seen the methodical preparations, the large number of troops just over the frontier, and he could not understand how Soviet Intelligence could have been unaware of them. Had Soviet command and troops failed to see the obvious danger?

His amazement would have been a hundred times greater if, by some miracle, he had found himself in Moscow, able to penetrate the thick walls of the Kremlin and peer into the cabinet of the silent man who, for many years, quite alone, had controlled the fortunes of the huge empire.

This man had also not expected a German attack, had not believed in it, and all the intelligence reports and memoranda which had been sent to him he had completely ignored.[2]

2

One's first impressions driving into Switzerland are rather conflicting. The road is good and wide, as if leading through a large lowland country, while at the same time the mountain chains hem the traveller in on all sides and force upon him the realization that he is entering a country filled with natural barriers and obstacles.

This impression of lofty crags and natural granite boundaries increases if the traveller is a historian who, looking at this landscape, is aware that during the last war it was surrounded on all sides by modern forces which at any moment could have attacked. These forces were a powerful instrument in the hands of Hitler or his Italian ally— and the German Chancellor, although he very often wavered and changed his mind, returned later to his original ideas. One of his

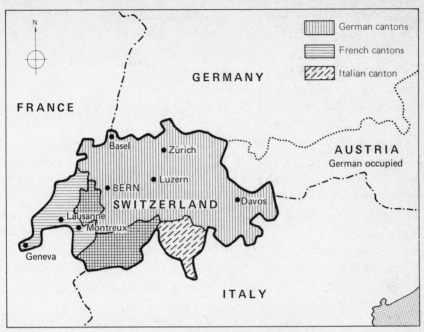

1 Map of Switzerland showing German, French and Italian cantons

obsessions was to unite all German-speaking people into one great thousand-year Reich and so he did not lose sight of German Switzerland. The German leader's mania was well known there and was taken very seriously; in the northern and north-eastern cantons everyone apprehensively awaited developments after the German attack on Poland and the partition of that country with Soviet Russia. The moment of greatest danger would come when the German panzer divisions made their first attempt to break through the French front, so on 10 May 1940 panic broke out in Switzerland. General Guderian's tanks broke through the defences and drove westwards in the region of Sedan, and the roads to the south were blocked by terrified people from the German cantons, who were further demoralized by an overt and whispered 'fifth-column' propaganda campaign. Everyone headed for Lausanne, Montreux and Geneva hoping that Hitler's rapacious grasp would not reach out for French-speaking Switzerland.[3]

There were other even more mundane reasons for expecting an invasion by foreign forces: exceptionally important lines of communication linking Nazi Germany with its Italian ally ran through

Switzerland, over its viaducts and through its tunnels. In the event of the war spreading, the road to the heartland of France lay through Switzerland, while Swiss factories produced a great many precision instruments of great value to the war effort. However, the fact that these lines of communication used tunnels and viaducts was also a drawback, since in time of war they could be blown up and within a few seconds routes through the narrow passes could be cut. The then German Ambassador in Bern, Otto Köcher, was of the opinion that the Swiss would be prepared to do this and would be able to put up a lengthy defence and that was what he told Berlin. Nevertheless, the little country's fortunes wavered and changed and at times hung by a hair. Full mobilization went ahead, and in May 1940 there were 450,000 soldiers under arms.[4] Swiss political and military leaders worked for and thought of only one thing: how best to act so that the hair did not break and that Switzerland should maintain its neutrality.

3

During the First World War Switzerland managed to retain its neutrality, but there was partial mobilization and a great deal of money was spent on defence. After the defeat of Germany, which had been the only country capable of posing a serious threat to the small democracy, Switzerland immediately reverted to a peacetime way of life, using every resource to rebuild industry and agriculture. There ensued complete demobilization and a return to the traditional Swiss idea of a 'militia on alert', which consists of every able-bodied man, who has undergone military training, keeping in his home a rifle and full equipment so that he can be called up within a matter of hours. This form of vigilance was retained, but all staffs, military offices and commands were drastically reduced in size. This affected, above all, military intelligence, of which only pitiable remnants remained.[5]

This state of affairs continued for a number of years until in 1933 the Nazis came to power in Germany. Once again Switzerland felt threatened, but in practice this threat was countered only in the form of discussions, debate and in a few changes of personnel, which, however, did not take place immediately. It was only in 1937 that a new man was appointed to head Military Intelligence, Section Five of the General Staff. This was Lieutenant-Colonel Roger Masson, a man full of energy, initiative and ideas. The situation when he took over was so miserable that he could not believe it. He had a department of five and an annual budget of 30,000 francs. At the same time Austria, hardly bigger than Switzerland, was spending on intelligence the equivalent of three million francs.[6]

In Germany a war industry was being rapidly developed and new military units were being formed; Hitler was conducting aggressive politics opposed by no one, and the outlines of a new war were becoming ever clearer, so Masson energetically set about his task. Within a year his budget was 50,000 francs and by 1939 it had risen to 320,000 francs. The staff had doubled from five to ten, but this manning level still precluded any major activity. It was only after the attack on Poland of 1 September 1939 and after Britain and France's declaration of war against Germany, and when Switzerland had mobilized, that things began to change. In November of that year Intelligence station no. 1 was set up in Lucerne under Captain Max Waibel and became a sort of control for six further similar units. The first of these was also located in Lucerne and was given the code-name *Rigi*, the second, code-name *Speer*, was in St. Gallen, the third in Basel, code-name *Pfalz*, the fourth in Zürich, code-name *Uto*, the fifth in Schaffhausen, code-name *Salm*, and the last one in Lugano, code-name *Nell*. They covered northern, southern and eastern Switzerland quite well, since it was from there that any real danger would come. Meanwhile the whole intelligence organization, hitherto known as Section Five of the General Staff, was given a new name, Sub-Group 1a (*Untergruppe* 1a), and then at the beginning of 1941 it was changed to Sub-Group 1b. It comprised military intelligence proper (*Nachrichtendienst*) and the security service (*Sicherheitsdienst*). It had a counter-intelligence role and concentrated on two main tasks: monitoring the activities of potential enemies who could threaten Switzerland's security and who were extending intelligence feelers on Swiss soil; and collecting information on the activities of friendly countries, who although not themselves a threat to Switzerland, had their own intelligence networks there and could jeopardize Swiss neutrality.[7]

After Austria had been incorporated into the Third Reich, Switzerland had only three neighbours and so its military intelligence was divided into three sections: Bureau D (Germany), Bureau F (France) and Bureau I (Italy). Colonel Masson, now in a position to insist on greater government assistance, fought for his views, and his department increased with every month. In 1943 his budget was already 600,000 francs and by 1944, 750,000 francs. The number of staff multiplied many times over and reached 120, not to mention agents and informers.[8]

All these preparations and the whole development of intelligence and counter-intelligence were directed solely towards peaceful ends and the maintenance of neutrality. The small country never had and never could have any aggressive intentions, but it was prepared to bear arms in its own defence against any enemy. The threat could come from the North and from the East, since that was where the German divisions lay, therefore it was essential to know what plans were being debated in the German staffs and above all in Hitler's closest circle. The slender material resources and the small staff did not allow large-scale activities. It was essential to reject all traditional and conventional methods and use improvisation and untried means in the search for secret and important information.

4

One of the Swiss Army's most active reserve officers was Captain Hans Hausamann, who had quite extensive business interests and thus contacts in a number of countries. When the Nazis came to power in Germany in 1933, he became involved in journalism, which at first consisted of collecting press cuttings in several languages on the political changes in Germany. The Captain was a Social Democrat and realized how necessary it was to oppose the rise of Hitlerism. In Teufen, where he had been living for many years, he set up an agency which has gone down in history as the *Büro Ha*.[9] He was helped in this by his position of press officer of the Swiss union of officers. A few years before the war his attention concentrated on quite open Nazi activities in Switzerland and at the deficiencies of the Swiss Army, which was poorly trained and completely unprepared for war. He wrote a pamphlet on the subject, publishing 5,000 copies of it at his own expense. It was not a popular subject, but the Captain was a determined man; he involved a number of people in the debate, obtained popular support from the inhabitants of the northern, most exposed cantons and also from the Social Democrats, and the poor state of affairs began to change.[10]

Lieutenant-Colonel Masson had known Hausamann for many years and had a very high opinion of him, so it gave him great pleasure to see the captain opening his office and carrying out this type of work. As an experienced man and head of Intelligence, the Colonel was convinced that Hausamann had gone very much further and that his press cutting service was only a cover for much more important and secret activities. The budget for Masson's department was so small that he had to look for very cheap or even free sources of information. He made secret contact with *Büro Ha*, which was quite independent of the General Staff and Intelligence, for Hausamann managed on his own without any government funds.[11]

After the outbreak of the war and the setting up in Lucerne of Intelligence Station no. 1, Hausamann transferred his office there, installing it in a private villa called 'Stutz' at Kastanienbaum, eight kilometres to the south of Lucerne, and gave it the code-name *Pilatus* after the mountain which dominates the city. Masson put the Captain in touch with Max Waibel (*Rigi*) and thus *Büro Ha* became definitely connected with military intelligence, although it still retained full independence. It had little money and, like Swiss military intelligence, was forced to look for contacts who were prepared to work for love. Hausamann used his former business friendships to recruit suitable people in Germany, Austria, France, Italy, Great Britain and Finland.[12]

In addition to these foreign sources, which penetrated deeply into the affairs of countries in some cases far distant from Switzerland, *Büro Ha* also took an interest in its own country, since a great many foreign intelligence organizations had their own stations and networks there. Particularly valuable in this field was a Czech Captain (later Colonel) Karel Sedlacek, who was in Zürich at the end of 1934 and set up a Czechoslovak Intelligence station under the code-name *Kazi*, installing a radio transmitter in the Consulate. He arrived disguised as a journalist called Thomas Selzinger representing the Prague paper *Narodni Listy*. He was no great man with the pen and had someone to write up his reports.[13] Sedlacek had extensive contacts amongst the diplomatic community, in particular Britons, Americans and Frenchmen; he also knew a number of eminent émigrés who had taken refuge in Switzerland and continued to take part in political activities. They were all busy setting up mysterious networks of secret contacts and collecting information. They knew a great deal and Sedlacek was able to learn much from them. He shared his results with Hausamann who passed them on to Captain Waibel. The German occupation of Bohemia and Moravia and the creation of an independent Slovakia altered Sedlacek's situation to the extent that he was now a political exile, although he was still an accredited journalist. His intelligence station continued to operate, but now he sent his reports not to Prague but to London.

After conquering Poland, Hitler turned his attention westwards, but he had to regroup his forces, move some of them over to the French front and await spring, thus both sides could carry on preparations for the decisive battle in relative peace. Switzerland also made the most of this period by training its army. Intelligence expanded and improved its secret contacts. It was precisely then that Hausamann made a new friendship which gave *Büro Ha* a completely new aspect. It was an apparently minor and unimportant contact made with a self-effacing man who was also living in Lucerne and who ran a small publishing firm. Only later did it transpire just what he was capable of and how significant was his influence on the last war. [14]

5

Rudolf Roessler, a small, grey, quiet and unobtrusive man in glasses, was a German émigré who had come to Switzerland before the war. He was born in Bavaria in 1897 into a German middle-class, Protestant, civil service family. His father was a senior official in the Ministry of Forests and Waterways; his elder brother and sister both received good educations and he himself showed great aptitude for the arts. He took part in the First World War as a young volunteer when he made many friends who later made careers in the Army. In the exceptionally difficult conditions of trench warfare he had a positive influence on those around him by virtue of his calmness, his knowledge of literature and his very balanced and remarkably mature personal philosophy. [15]

He survived the war and, like the whole generation of young Germans who could not accept defeat and the humiliation of their country, for a long time searched for a role to play in the new order. He chose journalism and for a number of years collaborated with several journals in southern Germany, working closely with the *Augsburg Post Zeitung*. The war had bred in him a horror of brutality and violence and he began to move from extreme right-wing views towards liberalism and pacifism. Together with the whole country he experienced the shock waves of economic ruin, inflation and decadence and he anxiously watched the rise of the 'brown shirts'. He continued to maintain contact with some of his wartime friends and drew their attention to the successes of Hitler's party; at the same time he was showing interest in theology and philosophy.[16]

In 1929 he extended his interests to the theatre, becoming secretary of a theatrical organization, and a little later he took over control of the journal *Das National Theater* in Berlin. His career as a journalist of wide interests was developing very successfully, while his wartime friends were progressing up the *Reichswehr*. He was proposed for membership of the very exclusive Berlin *Herrenklub*, where he obtained an additional important platform for his views and gave hundreds of lectures.

Roessler's fears turned out to be justified: Hitler's national socialist party, despite several failures, overcame every obstacle and in January 1933 came legally to power. The era of terror, concentration camps, murdering of opponents and lawlessness began. The young intellectual, despite his calm temperament and philosophical outlook on life, had difficulty in controlling himself at the sight of the dense ranks of brown shirts marching in a sea of flags and loud songs. Then, in mid-1933 in Berlin, he met a young Swiss of extreme-left-wing views called Xaver Schnieper, who was working on a doctorate in philosophy and whose father was an influential civil servant of the canton of Lucerne. They became friends and Schnieper suggested that Roessler come to Switzerland. It would be safer there and he could develop a far broader and outspoken form of journalism. It would be possible to fix immigration formalities with the help of Schnieper's father. It was an enticing proposition and in 1934 Roessler, together with his wife Olga, arrived in Switzerland and settled in the Lucerne suburb of Wesemlin. He received the right of asylum and a number of friends, mobilized by Schnieper, helped him financially to set up a small publishing firm, *Vita Nova Verlag*. After some time he succeeded in acquiring a number of famous writers, such as Nikolay Berdyayev, Paul Claudel and F.W. Förster. There was nothing secret about his work, which had no connection with any intelligence service or conspiracy, and Roessler devoted himself to it with great energy.[17] However he had not left Nazi Germany for safe Switzerland to become an ordinary émigré interested only in his own safety.

6

A few months passed and then, still in 1934, articles in German on Hitler and events in Germany signed *R.A. Hermes* began to appear in

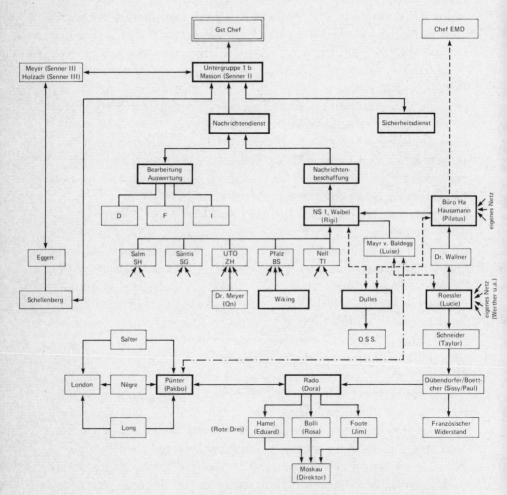

2 The Swiss Intelligence Service and its international connections during World War II. Diagram by Hans Rudolf Kurz with two corrections by Jósef Garliński: 1. A line of communication drawn between Pünter and Baldegg. 2. No direct conact between Pünter and the Director in Moscow.

Gst Chef: Chief of General Staff; *EMD Chef*: *Eidgenossisches*[18] *Militärdepartement Chef* (Swiss Government Military Department); *Nachrichtendienst*: Intelligence Service; *Sicherheitsdienst*: Security Service; *Nachrichtenbeschaffung*: Delivery of Intelligence; *Bearbeitung*: Analysis; *Auswertung*: Realization; *Eigenes Netz*: Own Network the Swiss press. The anonymous writer's public increased daily, since he wrote very interestingly, but above all he produced facts which shed new light on developments within the Third Reich. At first people did not want to believe his stories of arrests, concentration camps and increasing persecution of the Jews, but they began to change their minds when he foretold a number of events which turned out to be true. For instance he gave a month's notice that the German Army would break the conditions of the Versailles Treaty and occupy the demilitarized Rhineland, which in fact took place in March 1936[19] Further prognostications which also turned out to be true and further attacks on Nazism, also based on very accurate and convincing analyses of what had happened and would happen, turned *Hermes* into one of the foremost political commentators of the time. In Germany his articles were received with rage and the authorities there rapidly established that the secret *Hermes* and Rudolf Roessler were one and the same man. Since they could not reach him, they tried to hurt him in some other way and in 1937 he was deprived of his German citizenship.

Events in Europe were gathering momentum, Hitler was ever more actively pursuing his aggressive policies and eliminating the decisions of Versailles, while Roessler with every article was increasing his attacks and delving ever deeper into the internal affairs and plans of Nazi Germany. His analysis of these questions, based as it was on an excellent knowledge of the facts, invited the question: how did he come by this information, who was sending it to him and how? Many conjectures were made, but no one was able to give a positive answer. Meanwhile events were moving rapidly and by the summer of 1939 it was clear that a German attack on Poland could come at any time. Switzerland was by now on alert, its intelligence service was rapidly expanding and Dr Schnieper, who was already involved in its work, approached Roessler wondering whether he might like to help his new country. His knowledge of Nazi Germany and its various secrets was so important that it could be of use to the military authorities responsible for the security of the state. Roessler agreed. By this time he already had a great many friends amongst influential people, who also perhaps may have exerted a certain influence on him. One of them was Dr Bernhard Mayr von Baldegg, a reserve Captain who had professional contacts with Captain Waibel, who ran intelligence post no. 1 in Lucerne.[20]

Meanwhile Roessler, despite his secret sources of first class information, was not working for Intelligence and was only a well known journalist who, like all those in his profession, was in the business of obtaining important news as rapidly and discreetly as possible. Since, however, he had agreed to co-operate with the security authorities, he needed to be in touch with some Intelligence station and *Büro Ha* was selected. Security required that he have no direct contact with captain Hausamann and this condition was fulfilled so conscientiously that the two never met throughout the whole war, although they both lived in the same medium-sized town. Their contact was an Austrian living with Schnieper, Dr Franz Wallner, who also had been connected with *Büro Ha* from 1939. However, this contact was only one-way: from Roessler to Hausamann, never the reverse.[21]

The war broke out and the threat to Switzerland increased. It then transpired just how valuable was the contact with Rudolf Roessler. The information received by the *Büro Ha* from him was of the very highest quality and thus Swiss Intelligence knew precisely what was happening in Germany and what were the intentions of the German leaders. However he was not really a spy in the classic meaning of the word, since his reports did not contain bare facts and did not reveal their sources. They were more in the nature of academic papers based on a thorough knowledge of the subject and containing a great many interesting and nearly always accurate and well documented analyses. Yet the sources were never given and on this score Roessler was adamant. He provided material of the highest quality whose value was proved time and again, but he categorically refused to reveal his channels of information or the names of people and institutions which helped him.[22]

2 Foreign Intelligence Services

1

During the last world war 1,389 people were arrested in Switzerland for betraying military, political and economic secrets. Military courts passed 478 sentences, of which 283 were on Swiss nationals and 195 on foreigners. During the same period civil courts tried 387 people for spying: 245 Swiss and 142 foreigners. Treason was punished most severely and 33 death sentences were passed for it.[1]

These few statistics alone show clearly that in the small democracy of little more than $40,000\,km^2$, with a population of just under 6 million, a great many discreet and secret things took place during the last war. This was inevitable, since Switzerland's central position was an encouragement while her neutrality guaranteed a certain security. No foreigner, even if caught red-handed, was faced with the death penalty for spying, only prison. It was also almost certain that even the longest prison sentences would automatically be quashed when the war ended.

At the very beginning of hostilities, when Poland fell, the great powers continued to behave as if they were not threatened with total involvement in the new world-wide conflict. Great Britain and France declared war on Germany and mustered their armies on the Franco-German frontier, but showed no great eagerness to move. The Western Front remained silent, even when Germany's main strength was directed against Poland. Hitler continued to hold the initiative.

Intelligence matters were in much the same state. The British who were considered to be the leaders in this field, had a well developed network, but at that time were interested above all in German secret weapons. They had been on their track even before the war, and their interest grew several fold when, on 19 September 1939, still during the Polish campaign, Hitler gave a speech in Gdańsk making a clear reference to them.[2] Moreover, British Intelligence had world-wide responsibilities for an Empire stretching over several continents. Switzerland did attract attention, but only in a limited way and

15

mainly because the tracks of a number of foreign intelligence services crossed it. Great Britain was not interested in Swiss affairs and had never been an enemy of the small republic. As was usual, intelligence work centred around the legation in Bern, but before operations on the Eastern front there was little activity there.

France showed even less zeal in this direction, since Switzerland had also never been a target of serious French intelligence efforts. The First World War had exhausted the French nation, which had been bled too severely to have the will to make further sacrifices, and victory had taken away the desire for revenge. The French had made a supreme effort and built the Maginot Line behind which they felt safe and showed no desire to be aggressive.[3] The French embassy was preoccupied more with refugees, mainly Jews from German-occupied countries, than with the war itself.

If Great Britain and France, which had declared war on Germany, were showing no signs of action, then it was even less likely that the United States would move. She had intervened in the First World War, but had not joined the League of Nations and had withdrawn from European affairs. Anti-war feeling was widespread, the Congress expressed it and President Roosevelt, who had to protect his country against a new world war, was obliged to take this into account. It was also possible that there would be no need to intervene. The Germans, it was true, had defeated Poland, but in the West about 100 French divisions and the British Expeditionary Force faced them. Hitler's boasts that the war in the West would be as 'lightning' as in Poland would not necessarily be justified. The American embassy in Bern was, like the French, above all busy with political refugees.

2

The Germans, who were interested in Switzerland for various reasons, approached this question quite differently. Independently of Hitler's obsession with seeing all Germans in one country, Switzerland presented an interesting strategic and economic problem. The German commanders remembered the years 1914–18 and the terrible trench war, which France had succeeded in enduring. Now France was also protected by a line of modern fortifications, which might be a very different obstacle to overcome. However, these fortifications did not protect France along her Swiss border, so thought had to be given to the possible eventuality of invading a neutral country to attack her

16

Western neighbour from that side.

In addition to this possibility, the Germans were also concerned with transit rights and Swiss industry. On these questions they managed to come to an agreement, thus they could concentrate on espionage and Nazi propaganda in the German-speaking cantons. There it was legal to form any organization and so this work was undertaken with German precision and National Socialist enthusiasm. Suffice it to say that in 1939 in Zürich alone twenty-three German organizations were operating, with the *NSDAP* in the lead.[4] They were all very active, organizing meetings, demonstrations, joint dances and community singing, and they were noisy, confident and aggressive. Naturally these activities were all quite open, but with the aim of preparing the ground for future incorporation in the great Reich. Amidst these overt supporters of Hitler's ideas there were of course those on whom German espionage could rely to penetrate Switzerland for its own ends.

German Military Intelligence, called the *Abwehr*, whose head was Admiral Wilhelm Canaris, carried out espionage against Switzerland from Stuttgart. Its office there was divided into a number of departments of which one was devoted to sabotage. The offices in Munich and Karlsruhe were also turning their attention towards the small republic, where a great many German agents, around a thousand it was calculated, were operating. They were employed in gathering information about Swiss fortifications, the army, industry, political organizations, the press, émigrés and other countries' embassies.[5]

In addition to the *Abwehr* the German security office, *Reichssicherheitshauptamt* (*RSHA*), established in 1939, which always competed with Military Intelligence, was interested in Switzerland. Despite the greed of the Party, which wanted to have everything under its control, there were suspicions that Admiral Canaris had joined a group of senior officers who for years had been opposed to Nazism. This in fact was what the Admiral did during the Polish campaign, when he discovered that there was an extermination plan for the Polish upper classes which was being implemented as the *Wehrmacht* advanced.[6]

The *RSHA* had six departments, of which department VI dealt with intelligence abroad. It also operated out of Stuttgart which housed the headquarters of the *Sicherheitsdienst* (*SD*) belonging to *RSHA*. Furthermore, department IV of this organization, the infamous

17

Gestapo, also took an interest in Switzerland, for it followed the activities of Jews, freemasons, Marxists, Eastern 'sub-humans' and other groups, which Nazism considered its most fanatical opponents.[7]

By tradition, the German Embassy in Bern was also engaged in espionage, using the contacts of its consulates. The most active of these was the consulate attached to the embassy, in which was *Bureau F*, working quite openly and receiving clients, but in fact engaged in espionage. Other German consulates, in Basel, Geneva, Lausanne, Lugano, St. Gallen and in Zürich also carried out numerous intelligence tasks. They collected information about the terrain of Switzerland and everything that was happening there, they also took notice of the activities of the various embassies and legations as well as the groups of political refugees.[8]

The Italian dictator, Benito Mussolini, also showed an interest in Switzerland, especially the Italian-speaking part, since he too harboured an ambition of creating a great empire and wanted to unite all Italians in a single state. He was however in a completely different situation from Hitler—his country did not possess a strong and modern army and industry was unprepared for a long war—and he had to take care not to show too much aggressiveness which could have disastrous consequences. His recent conquest of Abyssinia and his further penetration into Libya had to be digested, as well as the wounds received in the civil war in Spain, and so Italy behaved with restraint and her intelligence activities in Switzerland were restricted to the normal work of the legation in Bern. In addition some very careful propaganda was carried on in the Italian cantons.[9]

Other European countries, such as Belgium, Holland, Denmark, Norway, Spain, Yugoslavia, Hungary and Greece, which had not yet been dragged into the war but which could be, tried to maintain their neutrality as carefully as possible, despite pressure from both sides. Therefore their espionage activities were very limited. Spain could have been the most aggressive, possessing as she did a political system similar to that in Germany and Italy and owing much of her internal structure to both dictatorships, but the Civil War had exhausted her to such an extent that she also tried to remain neutral. However, it was a neutrality coloured by no mean dose of sympathy both for Germany and Italy, and so Spanish Intelligence, whenever it could, helped those two countries.[10]

Amongst non-European countries the Chinese showed some

activity in Switzerland if only for the fact that they had for several years been fighting a war against the aggressor Japan, which was allied to Hitler, and they thus inclined towards the Allies. It was sometimes possible to obtain a great deal of interesting and valuable information from them.[11]

3

In Switzerland the legations of those countries which had been defeated or occupied by the Germans without a struggle were also operating. At this stage of the war this applied to Austria, Czechoslovakia and Poland. Austria had formally ceased to exist, since Hitler had brought about a 'voluntary' unification (*Anschluss*), although this had required German divisions to enter the country on 12 March 1938. Therefore, despite the sympathy felt for Austria's tragedy in various Swiss circles, she no longer could have any official diplomatic representation. All that remained were secret contacts between the Austrian resistance and Switzerland where several Austrian politicians had taken refuge and where courier routes from all over Europe crossed. At this stage of the war, when German might had not yet been shaken, the Austrian resistance movement had barely awoken.[12] In time, and as Nazism began to crumble, the underground movement in Austria increased until finally in December 1944 a Provisional National Committee was set up in secret. It was composed of Catholic representatives who had made contact with the Socialists and Communists. This Committee received the support of Austrian political refugees who had taken shelter in Switzerland and were operating there. Secret contact was made and couriers began to circulate between the occupied homeland and its politicians, as well as northern Italy where partisans operated. The Committee also looked for a route to the Western Allies and established contact with them.[13]

This question looked different from the Czechoslovak point of view. After the Munich conference when the leaders of the four powers (Chamberlain, Daladier, Hitler and Mussolini) decided that the Sudetenland would be incorporated into Germany, Czechoslovakia was considerably weakened and President Edward Beneš resigned, although his country still remained independent. The situation changed dramatically when in March of the following year German divisions entered Czechoslovakia, out of which Hitler created a Bohemian and Moravian Protectorate, with a German governor, and an 'independent'

Slovakia.

This was in fact the end of independence, but the new President, Emil Hácha, who had taken over from Beneš, remained in Prague together with a Czech Government and the premier, General Alois Eliáš. A very complicated situation arose, since the Western Allies continued to recognize this state of affairs which had every appearance of legality. Therefore the French, although a Czechoslovak army was being formed on their soil, agreed only to the creation of a Czechoslovak National Committee with Štefan Osusky, the last ambasador, at its head. He was a Slovak and an opponent of Beneš. Another Slovak, the former premier Milan Hodza, formed a rival, solely Slovak, National Committee. Beneš himself was at the time in Chicago, where he was lecturing in sociology at the university, and when on 18 July 1939 he arrived in London, it was in a private capacity and he was something of an embarrassment to the British.[14]

The intervention of Poland, which took from Czechoslovakia the lands near Cieszyn, while Hitler was dismembering and occupying the rest of the country, caused great bitterness among the Czechs, but the Poles were still the only neighbours ready to give them any assistance. The Polish-Czech frontier came to life: despite German patrols, many people, especially Jews, crossed it fleeing persecution. Politicians and numerous officers and soldiers also slipped across. A transit camp was set up for them, but it was essential to make a decision and have some clear idea as to what to do with them. This had to be tackled carefully, so as not to provoke the Germans and give them an excuse to attack.

Despite his difficult personal position, Beneš continued to be recognized by the vast majority of Czechs and Slovaks as their natural leader and he himself, although the National Committee was working in France where the Czechoslovak army was re-forming, tackled this problem. A dozen or so senior officers, mainly from Intelligence, with its chief, Colonel František Moravec, at their head, gathered around him. They had managed to get out at the last minute and one of them, a former head of counter-intelligence, Major Bartik, was sent to Warsaw in April 1939. After discussion with the head of Polish Intelligence, Colonel Józef Smoleński, it was agreed that the Polish authorities would help to evacuate Czech military specialists, mainly airmen, gunners, tankmen and staff officers to the West, to France and Great Britain. This was immediately begun and about 600 airmen were sent out. Co-operation in intelligence also started, since the

Czechs, despite their loss of freedom, continued to have large resources in this area having moved their Intelligence headquarters to London. [15]

Beneš understood the need for maintaining contact with his occupied country which in June 1939, before the German attack on Poland, sent General Sergěj Ingr, a representative of the underground military organization, *Obrona Naroda* (Defence of the Nation), on a secret mission to him. Furthermore he received a signal from the Czech premier, Eliáš, who in great secrecy informed Beneš that he was putting himself at his disposal. Despite his official and very exposed position, Eliáš was one of the leaders of the Czech military underground. [16] The British were reluctant to accord Beneš any official status, but they did come to terms with reality. When Great Britain declared war on Germany on 3 September, Beneš immediately sent a telegram to the British Prime Minister expressing the Czech and Slovak people's total support for this decision. After some deliberation, the British Government came to the conclusion that he should be recognised *de facto* as the representative abroad of the Czechs and Slovaks. [17] Thus there arose a quite remarkable triangle linked internally by secret threads: the official government in Prague tolerated by the Germans and recognized by many countries, an underground organization and a free representation abroad. To some extent the French situation was similar, although at that time the French Vichy Government acted in a country not occupied by the Germans and its attitude towards General de Gaulle was very hostile.

Beneš' position was further strengthened after the attack in the West and the collapse of the Anglo-French front. The weak Czechoslovak National Committee lost the support of the defeated French and in practice ceased to exist, some Czech military units managed to escape and get over to Britain and the need arose for some political representation in exile. In July 1940 Beneš eventually managed to form a Czechoslovak government-in-exile in London. Its main aim was to erase the Munich settlement from the list of international agreements. The British did not recognize this government for almost a year, not wishing to create additional complications and difficulties for themselves, but they did agree to the formula that it existed to 'liberate Czechs from German domination'. This state of affairs continued until the outbreak of the Russo-German war. Russia then recognized Beneš' government and Great Britain followed suit. [18]

This sequence of events had its influence on the Czechoslovak state's diplomatic representation. The detachment of Sudetenland changed nothing, but the creation of a Bohemian and Moravian Protectorate and the birth of an 'independent' Slovakia had a great influence. This new little state wanted its own diplomatic representatives and managed to achieve this in some cases. The first country with which envoys were exchanged was Soviet Russia. Later Great Britain appointed a consul in Bratislava and had to agree to a reciprocal appointment. [19] Switzerland felt this immediately, since her central location and neutrality were an incentive to opening up a legation there. A further attraction were the large sums of money which the prudent Czechoslovak government had deposited in banks there before the war. The Germans knew about this money, wanted to lay their hands on it and rightly believed that the easiest way to achieve this would be through the Slovak envoy or consul. The Czech legation in Bern continued to exist, but did not have to defer to the Germans. The Swiss authorities found themselves in a very difficult position, for on the one hand they did not want to provoke the Germans, while on the other all their sympathies lay with the Czechs. They were spared great embarrassment by the previously mentioned Captain Sedlacek (see chapter 1, p. 9), who was in constant secret communication with London and who received orders from his chief there, Colonel Moravec. With the help of other Czechs in Switzerland he managed to transfer the money to a frontier town, thence to France and, after the collapse of the Western Front, to Great Britain and eventually to the United States. [20]

The chain of developments which strengthened Edward Beneš' position and led to his government's recognition by the Allies, also automatically strengthened Captain Sedlacek's position. In addition to helping Swiss Intelligence via *Büro Ha*, the Captain also ran his own Czechoslovak intelligence network, which maintained contact with London and his occupied homeland. It also had contacts with Polish Intelligence.

4

The situation of Poland developed quite differently. After the German attack on 1 September 1939 the capital, Warsaw, was threatened within the week and the Government together with the President of the Republic left, heading south-east. The strategic plan was to create a defensive position in that part of the country, which would manage to defend itself until the Allied divisions in the West took the offensive. This attack did not materialize; instead, on 17 September, fulfilling a secret clause in the Russo-German pact, units of the Red Army entered eastern Poland. The same day the Polish authorities, wishing to avoid falling into Soviet hands, crossed the Romanian frontier.

Poland and Romania were linked by a treaty of friendship, and thus it was reasonable to imagine that this neighbour would facilitate the passage through its territory of the Polish Government and Head of State on their way to their French ally. However, things turned out differently. Under pressure from the Germans and their allies, the Russians, Romania interned every Pole, although the Polish embassy continued to operate in Bucharest. The Government was joined by a great many Polish soldiers, and a semi-official exodus to Italy began at once by way of Yugoslavia. Italy, it was true, was allied to Hitler, but was sympathetic towards Poland, the Polish embassy in Rome was open and so the route to France had become almost a regular channel.

The Romanians guarded the Polish President, Government and Commander-in-Chief, who also turned up there, but closed their eyes to other important people who over the last few years had not held any official position in Poland. One of these was General Władysław Sikorski, an opponent of the ruling group in Poland and at the same time well-known and popular in France where he had lived for a number of years. He also arrived in Bucharest, but, with the help of the French, left within a few days and was in Paris by 24 September. He was in a strong position, for in addition to the sympathy of the French and their discreet support, he also attracted the attention of a great many Poles who were stunned by the rapid defeat and blamed their Government and President for it. Their recriminations were all the more strident since, just before the outbreak of war, the opposition parties had proposed setting up a government of national unity and had been rebuffed.[21]

By now thousands of Polish officers and soldiers had gathered in France, having escaped through Romania or directly from Poland by way of Slovakia and Hungary, and it was therefore necessary to set up some Polish military command. The interned Government was powerless, and the only person who had his hands free and the formal right to such action was the Polish Ambassador in Paris, Juliusz Łukasiewicz. For several days he assumed the sovereign power of his country and, after discussions with various Polish politicians who were also in France, on 28 September appointed General Sikorski commander of the Polish army on allied soil. This appointment pleased the French, who immediately accepted it, which was of considerable significance since the Polish units being formed on their territory required equipment and would come under French command. No sooner had this appointment been settled than another was made. Two days later President Ignacy Mościcki, interned in Romania, transferred his responsibilities to Władysław Raczkiewicz who was in Paris and who in turn on the same day entrusted General Sikorski with the task of forming a new Polish government. Within the space of a few days the General had become the leading figure in the Polish nation's continued struggle.[22]

At the same time, literally one day before General Sikorski was appointed commander of Polish forces in France and twelve hours before German units entered the capitulating Polish capital, the nucleus of an underground army was brought into being in Warsaw. With time it would encompass the whole of Poland under both occupations and, with the name of Home Army, would unite Poles in a further struggle. This army was subordinated to the Government in France as early as November 1939 and it became one of its trumps and instruments of action. Couriers began to travel between Paris and Warsaw bringing orders, reports and intelligence.[23]

General Sikorski's government was immediately recognized by the Western Allies as well as by all those countries which although neutral were in effect on their side. Therefore Polish legations and consulates continued to operate as if nothing had happened. At this stage of the war even those countries friendly to Germany, such as Italy and Japan, recognized this state of affairs.

This applied also to the Polish Legation in Bern headed by Wacław Komarnicki (in the spring of 1940 he was replaced by Aleksander Ladoś). The post of military attaché, by tradition connected with intelligence work, was filled at that time by Lieutenant Colonel Bronisław Noel, assisted by an intelligence officer, Captain Szczęsny Chojnacki.[24] The official cultural attaché, Stanisław Appenzeller, was also engaged in intelligence. He was responsible for the contact with the British agents of the secret service and later with the head of the American intelligence network in Europe, Allen Dulles. He was also put in charge of the secret radio transmitter which was first situated in the frontier fort of Saint Ursanne and later, after various incidents with the Swiss police, who discovered the transmitter and arrested the radio operator, in Locarno, in the mansion of the local mayor.[25]

The possession of a transmitter was important, for the Polish Legation, together with the consulate in the same building (a second consulate, almost inoperative, was in Zürich), as well as being in contact with the authorities in France, was also an outpost of liaison with the occupied homeland and with the bases of this liaison in Bucarest and Budapest. During the first months of the war, when the Western Front still existed and when it was comparatively easy to reach France from Poland through Yugoslavia and Italy, this outpost, bearing the code-name *Wera*, was just in the opening stages, but in a short time its importance was to become considerably greater. Almost immediately after the fall of France in August 1940, the Polish political authorities newly arrived in London sent instructions to Bern, changing the code-name to *Outpost S* and laying down a working order. In the meantime preliminary work was carried on; Lieutenant Colonel Noel took the code-name *Kobelin*, Captain Chojnacki *Lubiewa* and Appenzeller *Krucz*. The first courier routes were built up step by step and a listening post set up to catch any radio signal from occupied Warsaw. There the first radio transmitter was built in November 1939, but it was only in January of the following year, through a courier sent to the Polish Legation in Budapest, that the wave length and other details were agreed. Secret radio liaison between the occupied capital of Poland and the West began in February, but only took a stable form in April, via Budapest.[26]

The Polish Legation was also in active contact with other legations, chiefly the British, French and American, and also with the legations of some other countries which, as the result of war, were later under German occupation, namely the Belgian, Dutch and Yugoslav. The diplomatic representatives of the three great democracies were very helpful with currency manipulations and in obtaining passports from neutral countries for persons carrying out various tasks connected with military operations, which obliged them to make frequent journeys.[27]

Only one country could not benefit from all these facilities resulting from diplomatic privileges. This was the Soviet Union, which, after attacking Poland together with Hitler, had undertaken a new aggression, this time against Finland, and which had no diplomatic relations with Switzerland. She was extremely interested in espionage possibilities in the centrally located, neutral country and so had to look for ways of making the most of them.

3 Various Residents

1

For some years now a small, corpulent gentleman in glasses, and invariably wearing a black beret, has been coming to the department of maps of the British Library, which is located in the British Museum. He is not a frequent visitor since he comes from abroad, which can easily be recognized by his accent, although he speaks English well, using a large vocabulary. He often throws in foreign sentences, which shows a certain linguistic proficiency and the ability to express his thoughts freely in more than one foreign language. The object of his visits is to study maps, about which he is very well informed and about which he can talk with great gusto and knowledge. One also gets the impression that not only is he well acquainted with his subject, but that it absorbs him and is the focal point of his life. The Library staff know him as Dr Sándor Radó of the Hungarian Land and Map Department in Budapest.

Suddenly, in 1977, a sensation broke. A book called, *Codename Dora*, appeared in England. It was translated from a German edition, but the original had been published in Hungary and its author was none other than Sándor Radó. The book, in the form of memoirs, covered a great many years of his life and was a revelation. During the last war the quiet, inconspicious cartographer had been a very high ranking Russian intelligence agent, he directed a secret spy network in Switzerland and had sent to Moscow coded radio messages concerning the most important and most confidential German decisions. His work had had an enormous influence on the course of the second world war.

2

In November 1899 a son was born into the house of a small timber merchant in Budapest and was called Sándor. He was later followed by a girl and another boy, but only the firstborn showed any exceptional talents and a love of learning. He was interested in foreign countries, endlessly pored over maps and easily picked up different accents.

27

The Great War broke out and the young boy, barely seventeen, was called up, but before he went to the front, the Austro-Hungarian empire tottered. A little earlier a revolution had broken out in Russia and the news coming from that country began to affect youthful minds. It was then that Sándor encountered the writings of Marx and Engels and accepted their views. He obtained additional information from prisoners of war who began to return home after the Treaty of Brest Litovsk where, on 3 March 1918, revolutionary Russia signed a separate peace with the Central Powers. He was already a convinced communist when, in the spring of 1919, there was an uprising in Hungary and on 21 March a Republic was proclaimed with Béla Kun as its head. It was threatened on a number of sides and hurried attempts were made to raise a communist army for which Sándor volunteered. Despite his youth, he was made a political commissar and must in some way have taken part in the short-lived Red Terror, for when in August Béla Kun's government fell and Romanian troops entered Budapest and Admiral Miklós Horthy took power, he escaped from Hungary as fast as possible, crossing into Austria. He did not know that he was leaving his country for thirty-six long years.[1]

So began the communist activities in various countries of Sándor Radó, whose eyes were constantly fixed on the Soviet Union. Together with several other Hungarians he set up an émigré group in Vienna where he began to edit a monthly magazine called *Kommunismus*, which was the first communist journal outside Soviet Russia. He was not satisfied with this and, thanks to the indiscretion of a civil servant, hit on another idea. Viennese radio daily recorded communiqués broadcast from Moscow for the whole world (*Vsem, vsem, vsem*—for everyone) in order to pass them on to the Austrian government. For a small amount of dollars each month they could be purchased and sent to Western papers by a specially set up press agency. During these early years when inside Russia the civil war was slowly coming to an end and outside Russia was surrounded by a 'cordon sanitaire' (the words of the French premier Clemenceau), its communist government had no diplomatic representatives or propaganda outlets. Radó wanted to take the first steps in this field, but had no money, so he turned to Maxim Litvinov who, from his office in Stockholm, was trying to arrange trade links with various countries on behalf of the Soviet Union. Litvinov gave him some money and for several years the Russian Telegraph Agency, *Rosta Wien* for short, operated in Vienna.

Alongside it Radó set up another agency, called the International Telegraph Agency, *Intal*.

In 1922, having carried out his task in Austria, Radó moved to Germany, but first he spent quite a long time in Russia at the invitation of the government. There he met a number of leaders, including Lenin, took part in an international communist congress and made contact with Russian cartographers, since he was still very interested in this field. He was also introduced to the workings of the newly-constructed Soviet society and underwent initial espionage training.[2]

In Germany he married a local communist, Helene Jansen, and spent 1923–4 in Leipzig, where he was entrusted with the organization of armed workers' brigades which were preparing themselves for revolution. In his spare time he studied cartography and published his first map of the Soviet Union. The police began to show an interest in him and so once again he made for Moscow, where he extended his knowledge of espionage and sabotage.

A year later he again appeared in Germany, this time in Berlin, as correspondent of the newly-formed Soviet press agency Tass. Again he returned to Moscow and for the second time left for Berlin. There he started a daily magazine of two-tone, black and white maps illustrating various world events. This led to the cartographic press agency, *Pressgeographie*, or *Pressgeo* for short. During his Berlin years, in 1929 to be exact, Radó published his first serious cartographic work: An Atlas of Imperialism. There, in the German capital, he watched the arrival of Adolf Hitler as Chancellor. It was now time to leave immediately and so the Hungarian communist once again moved his base and arrived in Paris. Together with his wife and several other people, one of whom was Arthur Koestler, he started up the agency, *Inpress*. It supplied news of events in Nazi Germany and was widely distributed. This information rarely fell on fertile ground, since the comfortably well-off Western world was uninterested, but events were moving so rapidly in Germany that well-informed people had to anticipate a new war.[3]

3

Each Soviet outpost was always closely linked with Intelligence or was simply a cover for it and so this was also the case with Radó's agencies. With every visit to the Soviet Union he increased his knowledge of spying and his many years' activity in foreign countries, often working in secret, had helped him accumulate a great deal of experience in the field of illegal and undercover activities. His qualifications were enhanced by a good knowledge of several languages, international experience and his career as a cartographer, which justified frequent travel. For these very reasons in 1935 Soviet Intelligence Headquarters in Moscow entrusted him with a particularly secret and important task: he was to look for a suitable country in Central Europe and settle down there as a peaceful cartographer wishing to set up his own map-making business. This would be an excellent cover for an intelligence nerve-centre whose net would gather information about preparations for the approaching war.[4]

Radó had to consider those countries whose language he spoke, but Germany and France were no longer feasible, since he was already too well-known there, so he thought of Belgium. He went there and began to try for a residence permit, was refused and so turned his gaze towards Switzerland. In addition to its central location, it had also the advantage of being the home of the League of Nations, and Radó was fluent in all its three languages.

Switzerland was already over-populated and new candidates for permanent residence were continually arriving, but with enough money and proof of it, there was a good chance of a permit for a number of years. It was harder to get permission to set up a business, which could only be obtained when a limited liability company was formed with a majority of Swiss nationals on the board. Money was no problem for Radó and with it suitable partners could also be secured, so he received both permits and in the middle of 1936 settled in Geneva together with his wife, mother-in-law and two children.

His instructions clearly stated that he was first of all to become a peaceful and industrious Swiss citizen and only then was he to get down to his essential task, so Radó began to set up a cartographic agency, which he called *Geopress*. With the minimum of staff and working from his own flat he began producing political maps showing the most up-to-date changes. They were an immediate success, since the Spanish civil war had just broken out. The list of subscribers grew and included journals, libraries, universities, ministries, army staffs and various embassies as well as private individuals. Within a short time the agency was able to recoup its investment and begin to make a profit. The police were watching Geneva's new resident and knew that he was in touch with representatives of various countries in the League of Nations, but this was all connected with his work and aroused no suspicions. There must also however have been other reasons for the Swiss authorities being so accommodating towards a newcomer about whom they knew very little. It is possible that this was the work of the socialist majority in the council of the Geneva canton, or perhaps someone was intentionally not over-inquisitive. Radó himself writes that the only check on his past and political affiliations was a query whether the Budapest police had had any trouble with him.[5] What use was this when he had left his country in 1919? How could inquiries not have been made as to where he had been living and what he had been doing for twenty-seven years? The fact remains that the Swiss police, among the best informed in the world, did not discover that it was dealing with a married couple who had belonged to the communist party for many years, who had undergone espionage training in the Soviet Union and who had accumulated experience in a number of foreign postings. It is difficult not to assume that there was a mole inside the Swiss police, well camouflaged, who anticipated Radó's far reaching plans and wished to help him.

Feeling secure and benefiting from his reputation as a quiet and worthwhile inhabitant of Geneva, Radó slowly and carefully set about carrying out his main task. He as yet had no direct link with Moscow, but already had a new pseudonym prepared, *Dora*, formed by jumbling the letters of his own surname. For everyone else he was to be called *Albert*, while his wife adopted the name *Maria*. Experience over the years had taught him that in this work he could always rely on communists irrespective of their nationality, so he sought out some local contacts and formed in Geneva a small spy ring which included Swiss and foreign residents. Before he had managed to extend his contacts to other towns and even abroad, he was summoned in June 1937 to Paris where he secretly met a Russian who had the code-name *Kolya*. This was his first contact with Headquarters in Moscow, which ran Military Intelligence called *Glavnoye Razvedyvatelnoye Upravleniye*, for short *Razvedupr*. This one-way contact was nothing new and is always used in especially secret intelligence work, particularly with so-called 'residents', who stay for a long time in one country. Radó was already completely trusted by Moscow, but it was difficult to establish in advance whether his position in Switzerland would turn out to be adequate. That part of his mission had been accomplished to the

31

complete satisfaction of his superiors, so *Kolya* now gave him a number of explanations and repeated his instructions that he was to operate very carefully and prepare for the moment when Europe would erupt in flames. Meanwhile he was to tackle Italy where he could travel as a cartographer, and where he was to create suitable intelligence-gathering conditions for following the Italian units sent to Spain to support General Franco.[6]

Less than a year later, in April 1938, *Kolya*, contrary to all rules of conspiracy, suddenly appeared in Geneva and arrived at Radó's home. He was very upset at having been unexpectedly recalled to Moscow and told his host that he would give him all his contacts, since Headquarters had decided to entrust Radó with the whole spy ring in Switzerland. The next day in Bern he would put him in touch with a man who had great opportunities for spying.[7]

4

The Spanish Civil War lasting from 1936 to spring 1939 attracted a great number of volunteers from various countries to the side of the red international brigades. After their defeat some of them landed in camps in the south of France, but if they had nowhere to go since their countries had already been occupied by the Germans (Austria, Czechoslovakia and later Poland), or taken over by their political opponents (Spain), they found themselves in a very difficult situation. Some of them even ended in Dachau.[8]

Amongst those who returned safely home was a Swiss socialist, Otto Pünter, journalist by profession. During the fighting he had directed there his own intelligence network and had rendered the reds considerable service. He was not a Communist, but like many of his left-wing contemporaries, he had expected Russia, after her struggle with Fascism, to take the road to democracy. This was an error of judgement, but at that time, after his return to his native Bern, Pünter did not know this. He was convinced that the Germans, in alliance with Italy, would begin a war within the next few years and he wanted in some way to contribute to their defeat. He realized that if they were to win, no country in Europe, particularly a small one, would retain its independence. He again started to organize a new espionage network in the deep belief that he was working in Switzerland's best interests. Later, during the war, when Hitler attacked Russia and when the Western democracies started to send her colossal aid in the form of armaments and everything necessary for the waging of war, Pünter considered that his intelligence work on behalf of Russia was based on the same principles.[9]

This experienced leader of an espionage ring already had five towns in Switzerland which were clearing-houses for information coming from abroad: Pontresina, Arth, Kreuzlingen, Bern and Orselina, and from their first letters his code-name *Pakbo*, was formed.[10] He also had good contacts in his own country, in Bern, where foreign embassies were located, and in neighbouring countries.

Three Frenchmen resident in Switzerland and supporters of General de Gaulle worked for him. The first, code-name *Long*, was a journalist in Zürich who had worked for many years in Berlin as correspondent of a great Parisian daily and made good contacts there, mainly in the Ministry of Foreign Affairs. He had also good relations with German emigrants in Switzerland, namely with the very influential Baron Michel von Godin. His information was on the political, diplomatic and economic affairs of the Third Reich. The second contact, code-name *Nègre*, was a career diplomat with wide experience in consular work in Western Europe and now the French consul general in Bern. He obtained good information mainly on German heavy industry and was also a link with the Jewish resistance group in France, *Bir Hakeim*. The third man, code-name *Salter*, born in Alsace, was the press-attaché of the French Embassy in Bern and for this reason had good relations with Vichy. Previously he had also been a journalist in Berlin. He had good connections with the French resistance movement as well as with the Intelligence Service and later with the American Intelligence, whose representative on Swiss soil from November 1942 was Allen Dulles. *Salter's* clear and inquistive mind as well as his ability to select his information made him the *Pakbo* group's leading source. He obtained the exact date of the German attack on Russia, which reached Stalin, but which the latter ignored.[11]

The identity of these three men was a secret which Otto Pünter has preserved for many years. Now that all three are dead, he has decided to disclose them. *Long* was Georges Blun, *Nègre* Marquis Paul de Neyrac and *Salter* Louis Suss.[12]

All three Frenchmen were of the elite of their nation, they had frequently travelled abroad, and two of them had been in the diplomatic service for years, so they must have known well for whom they were working and where the information passed on by them through Pünter was going. Like him, they were not Communists, so they were not bound to Soviet Russia by the loyalty and discipline which forces people to betray even their own country when the red imperialists in Moscow require it. Their motives were similar to the motives of all those who considered that above all National Socialism must be brought down. In their eyes this appeared to be much more of a threat to Europe and the world than Soviet internationalism.

In addition to the Frenchmen, Pünter had three other informers in his own country. One of them was an Austrian émigré called *Lilly of the Vatican*, a journalist of Catholic views. He had excellent relations with influential church circles in Munich who received their information from *Wehrmacht* officers. It was of such great value that it must have come from the highest circles in *OKW*. German nuns brought it from Bavaria to Fribourg in Switzerland. *Lilly's* other contacts were as far away as Italy and Rome.

A further informant was Dr Bernhard Mayr von Baldegg (code-name *Luise*), in Lucerne, who was already in contact with Roessler (see chapter 1, p. 13) and who co-operated in both directions according to the tendency of Swiss Intelligence at that time. In the diplomatic circles of Bern was a Chinese press attaché, Pao Hsien Chu, known as *Polo*, who was acquainted with representatives of many countries and visited the German legation. Thanks to him it was possible to establish that a great many German consular officials belonged to the *SS* and *Gestapo* and to warn the appropriate authorities.

Pünter also extended his net to neighbouring countries, setting up important posts in them. In Austria in the province of Vorarlberg, not far from the Swiss frontier, there operated a resistance group whose leader, code-name *Feld*, sent important information. His main source was his nephew who was a radio technician in the elite *SS* panzer division *Leibstandarte Adolf Hitler*. Pünter claims that with the help of his parents who had a secret radio transmitter which operated well on the short-wave band, he sent short but important messages. If this was really so, these signals must have been brief and very far between, otherwise the *Gestapo* monitoring teams listening for partisan radio messages would have caught them.

A similar underground group, this time within Germany itself, operated in Stuttgart and was led by a civil servant, code-name *Rot*. He had his own informants in Berlin, Cologne, Frankfurt and other

German cities and sent military, political and economic reports. Thanks to his work the Allies received information on where to direct their air attacks. Pünter did not know him personally and maintained contact by means of a German émigré in Switzerland.[13]

Pakbo was also interested in Italy and had a good contact there in an underground anti-fascist group called *Rocco*, based in Milan, which assumed particular importance in July 1943, when Mussolini was removed from power and arrested and German divisions moved into Italy. It was also of great help later on when German parachutists under the command of *SS* Colonel Otto Skorzeny, freed the dictator from his exile on the Gran Sasso mountain and he set up a neo-fascist republic in Northern Italy supported by the Germans.

In addition to several other agents in Switzerland, such as *Diana*, *Leopard* and *Remo*, who worked in various government offices, Pünter had a further thirty people working as railwaymen, postmen, customs officers, businessmen and frontier guards in Basel, Schaffhausen, Kreuzlingen, Tessin and Geneva and a great many other towns. They carried out important work as contacts and couriers and provided a great deal of minor but valuable information.[14]

After the collapse of the Western Front and while Hitler was preparing to attack Great Britain and everything indicated that his fury would vent itself in that direction, an officer of Soviet Intelligence, code-named *Carlo*, whom Pünter had known from the Spanish Civil War approached him in great secrecy. He reported that notwithstanding present German operations and the pact with the USSR, war between Hitler and Stalin was approaching and that they should prepare for it. He had already earlier been in touch with Sándor Radó, who was his source of information on German plans and who had feelers all over Germany reaching to the very centres of decision-making. Such decisions were being considered in Hitler's most closely guarded inner group, while the dictator was ostensibly fully occupied with the destruction of England and was ostentatiously respecting every clause of the pact with Soviet Russia.

However it was not only *Carlo's* information which drew attention to the East and led to the supposition that, despite the attack on England, that was where the German divisions would strike. Hitler had announced that he had begun the construction of a great Germany which would last a thousand years and such a vast country could not exist without Romanian, or even eventually Caucasian oil, Ukrainian wheat and other natural resources found at that time within the Soviet empire. Certainly Stalin was scrupulously carrying out his obligations under his pact with the Germans, sending countless trains of raw materials to the West, but Hitler could not have been entirely satisfied with this, since they were not at his sole disposal.[15] Furthermore, he had a huge army of which only part would be involved in the event of a successful landing on the British Isles. The millions of soldiers, still filled with the euphoria of their victory in the West, would quickly become demoralized if no new theatre of war were created for them. Even a victory over the British Isles would not herald the end of the war, since there was still the British Empire which, with the help of the United States, would fight on, mobilizing half of the world against the Axis powers. Thus Hitler, after his victory over France, did not want further fighting, but an agreement with Great Britain. From this arose the decision to restrain the panzers at Dunkirk and also several conciliatory gestures on the part of the dictator. However, when Winston Churchill's great voice rejected all possibility of compromise, Hitler realized that the war would be a long one and that this was just the beginning. He knew that his country, even with its newly-conquered territories, would be unable to match the great reserves of raw materials in Anglo-Saxon hands. He could obtain them only by going East.

Otto Pünter, for many years involved in political and espionage matters, knew all these facts and arguments, agreed with them and realized that the war was not only about territorial gain, but also about the way of life which was so different in the West from what Hitler was offering. Being left-wing and not knowing the Soviet Union, he idealized it, likening it in his mind to the West, and was not aware that in fact there was little real difference between the methods of Nazism and communism. However, his judgement that the Soviet Union would have to play a great part in the overthrow of Hitler and his great power was correct. He therefore did not dither and needed little time to make up his mind. He accepted *Carlo's* suggestions and using him as an intermediary secretly met Sándor Radó.[16]

4 Two Orchestras

1

During the period when the young Soviet state, newly emerged from the revolution, was still surrounded by a *cordon sanitaire*, and when communist fifth columns were not densely distributed throughout the world, the penetration of Soviet agents into other countries was very difficult. The earliest diplomatic relations connected the Soviet state with Germany, thanks to a separate peace in Brest Litovsk in 1918, and so it was there that under various pretexts the first feelers of Soviet intelligence could be extended. It so happened that, following the exchange of diplomats, Germany was also the first country which stretched a helping hand towards Russia. After her defeat in the first world war and after the resolutions of the Treaty of Versailles, Germany had also found herself isolated; she was limited by various restrictions, largely in the area of military strength, and in revolutionary Russia she sought a partner who might benefit from mutual help. In April 1922 both countries signed an agreement in Rapallo, which, among other things, anticipated military co-operation. The Germans began to build factories producing poison gas, tanks and aircraft in Russia and to send their cadres there for joint exercises with Soviet officers. The idea was to evade the resolutions of Versailles and to prepare their cadres for a new war, which would be retaliatory in nature. In return the Germans invited Soviet officers to Germany and trained them in strategy and in dealing with technical weapons.

This co-operation did not at all rule out the necessity for the expansion of the Russian intelligence network inside Germany. It had been there in existence since the tsarist period, since an attack on Russia might well come from this region, as was confirmed by the events of 1914. Moreover the Germany of Kaiser Wilhelm II, bound by her alliance with the Austro-Hungarian empire, blocked Russian expansion in the Balkans, this being the more significant since the defeat by Japan in 1904–5 had blocked the Russian drive into the Far East. [1]

The revolution did not change the pattern of life in Russia, with lack of political freedom, secret police etc, but destroyed almost everything that had been built by the tsarist governments. Thus the intelligence network within Germany collapsed as well, but the Bolsheviks set it up again. They had to work quickly, as the first world war was still in progress and German divisions were still occupying large areas of Russia. The intelligence headquarters were set up in Moscow as part of the People's War Commissariat and became known for short as *Razvedupr* (see chapter 3, p. 31). headed at the time by General Jan Berzin and consisting of six sections, the second of which, the operational one, was divided into several units. The first of these covered Western Europe, and thus included Germany.[2]

The head of army intelligence operated in Berlin under the cover of some Soviet office or business and he had numerous agents who had been recruited from local communists. In this respect Soviet Russia never met with disappointment and could count on them at all times and in all places. This network did not have direct links with Moscow and all reports had to be directed to the military attaché at the embassy. Only in the case of war and the necessity of leaving his post did he transfer these links to the network, together with money, a radio and the code or cipher.[3]

Despite losing the war, Germany, situated in the very centre of Europe and still a large and industralized country, did not cease to be noticed by the wide world. At first it seemed that it would be seized by the flame of revolution which would bring about the same upheaval as in Russia; later there were great difficulties as a result of the resolutions of Versailles, and finally the great economic and social depression started which led to the rise of Hitler. The networks of various intelligence services crossed in Germany and vied with each other; again and again arrests took place and trials were held. Among the defendants were also Soviet agents, for the most part local communists who had tripped up. Many were caught, since Berlin was at that time the centre of Soviet intelligence not only in Germany, but also for France, Belgium and Holland. However during these years the attitude of the German authorities to Soviet Russia was so favourable and the inefficiency of the police so incredible that communist penetration allied to the Soviet intelligence service extended further and further and undermined the already feeble country. But this easy period was soon to come to an end, because the silhouette of Hitler which loomed on the horizon was already taking on a strong and determined outline, growing larger day by day, and the moment when the Brownshirts were to reach for power was drawing near.[4]

2

On 30 January 1933 Hitler became chancellor and straight away there began a purge of communists, whom the Nazis considered to be their most relentless enemies and therefore destined for destruction. The period of the Weimar republic had come to an end, as the police force consisted largely of kind-hearted officials who even when they demonstrated a willingness to tread on the heels of foreign agents and enemies of their country, were restrained by its authorities. During the course of several months the A1 section of the Berlin police was enlarged and a powerful organization was formed which history has come to know as the *Gestapo*. It was a weapon in the political struggle against the opponents of the new order, acting efficiently, decisively and brutally. Alongside it there operated another similar instrument, the security service of the *SS* (*Sicherheitsdienst—SD*). The criminal police force, called *Kripo* (*Kriminalpolizei*) was also of significance. In 1936 the *Gestapo* and the *Kripo* were united and became the *Sipo* (*Sicherheitspolizei*), which was joined in turn by the *SD* three years later to form the central state security office (*Reichssicherheitshauptamt—RSHA*).[5]

While this final structure of the security forces was taking shape the pursuit of communists persisted continuously, carried on simultaneously along several lines. Like the Nazis, they too were preparing to take over power, and because they were at the same time the most devoted agents of the Soviet intelligence service, they were to be found virtually everywhere. They had penetrated every office, every business and every factory, and Hitler's police formations had to use extremely precise methods in order to seek them out. Files with thousands of names were set up, certain addresses were kept under observation, networks of agents and *agents provocateurs* were detected and borders were watched; advantage was taken of the fanaticism of a large fraction of the population, which did not yet know where Hitlerism was to lead, and was fascinated by its initial successes. When the new government had been in power for three months, already over 20,000 communists found themselves behind the barbed wire of the concentration camps.

The destruction of the communist network was difficult as it reached very deep, but German methodology proved to be thoroughly effective and, after two years, the party of German adherents to the Soviet experiment (*KPD*) was forced to sound a general retreat. In October 1935 the leaders who had survived the pogrom gathered at a conference near Moscow and decided that it was necessary to disband the network of agents within Germany and to replace it by small groups controlled from adjacent countries. Berlin and the surrounding areas were to be controlled initially from Prague and later from Stockholm, the Baltic region and Silesia from Copenhagen, Southern Germany from Switzerland, the Saar basin from France, central Rhineland from Brussels and the western, industrialized part of Germany from Amsterdam.[6]

The leadership of the Soviet intelligence service, which had hitherto been operating so efficiently in Germany, had to come to acknowledge the new state of affairs and came to the conclusion that everything they possessed there had to be liquidated. Dr Gregor Rabinovich was specially dispatched from Moscow to liquidate all the *Razvedupr* positions in Germany.

This calamity coincided with another which took place in Russia itself. Stalin had begun a great purge: millions were being sent to countless concentration camps and hundreds of thousands were being liquidated. Among those who found themselves before the execution squads was the chief of *Razvedupr*, Jan Berzin, his deputy, Uricki, and hundreds of agents who had been recalled to Moscow. Germany, which had until a short while ago been completely infiltrated, became in the course of only a few years free from Soviet Intelligence.[7]

3

On the streets of Jerusalem one can come across an elderly man, tall and well built, with a tired-looking face, but still full of life and cordially disposed towards others. He is not too keen to enter into conversation on his life, but will not refuse if somebody else starts it. Many of his neighbours know that this is Leopold Trepper, that he came from Eastern Europe and that his life has been very eventful.[8]

Life began for Trepper in Nowy Targ, a small town in southern Poland, where he came into the world in 1904 into the family of a small shopkeeper. They were poor people, but they saw to it that their children had a good education. So young Trepper was sent to school, but when in 1917 his father died suddenly, he was forced to leave and went to work as an apprentice to a watchmaker. In a couple of years he had to try many other jobs to bring some money to his very poor family home.[9]

After the war, when the Austro-Hungarian empire collapsed and Poland became independent again, Trepper joined the Jewish youth organization, *Hashomer Hatzair*. It was inspired by Zionism and looked for the same solution for the Jewish people: to establish a national home in Palestine. This was after the Balfour Declaration of 2 November 1917 was proclaimed.* The organization was strongly influenced by Marxism and the currents which were filtering from the East, and Trepper became a Communist. After Jewish problems, the class struggle became his main interest and the object of his illegal activity. At that time he took the code-name *Domb* and later he kept it as his name for almost the whole of his life.[10]

In 1923 a general strike was called in southern Poland, it was political and Trepper was the organizer in Dąbrowa Górnicza, a small town in Silesia, where his family had settled some years earlier. He was arrested, had his first, not very pleasant experience with the police, and his life became even more difficult. He had two options: to go underground and begin an illegal life, or to emigrate to Palestine, hoping that a socialist state would be established there. In April 1924, with some other young people, he landed in Tel Aviv.[11]

The beginning was very difficult: he worked as an agricultural labourer in appalling conditions, then found employment as an electrician, but the palestinian climate did not agree with him. He married a girl named Luba Brojde, also from south Poland, and they both joined the Jewish underground forces fighting the British authorities. They very soon discovered that the political climate was also unsuitable for them. The country was too small for clandestine activity, they were arrested several times, he longed to return to Europe and to the underground revolutionary work on a much larger scale. Once again he decided to move.[12]

One of his friends, who had similar longings, went to France and, being also a Communist, entered the *Razvedupr* intelligence network there, gathering information about French industry. He was in touch

*The British Foreign Minister, Arthur James Balfour, accepting the Zionist aim, made a statement on Palestine that Britain favoured the establishment of a national home for the Jewish people.

with Trepper, helped him to get to Marseilles in 1929 and a couple of weeks later they met in Paris. The new immigrant directed his first steps to the local Communist party and started to take part in political demonstrations, but in a short time, on his friend's recommendation, Trepper also became an agent of Soviet intelligence. This gave him the opportunity of starting activity on a large scale.[13]

His initial steps in the communist underground were very primitive: only now did he begin to learn the essential technique of illegal activity. After only a few months he showed that he was coping admirably and that such activities suited him very well. In 1930 his wife Luba joined him in Paris.[14]

Now almost all his time was devoted to gathering information for his superiors in Moscow, but he also had to do something openly to satisfy the French police. In co-operation with the party he started to publish a four-page Communist weekly paper called, *Der Morgen*. His wife was also engaged in militant activity. In April 1931 a son was born to them and for a time they succeeded in combining their illegal activity with a normal life.[15]

Two years later, as a result of a tip-off, the French police eliminated the Soviet intelligence unit which had been set up by the Palestinians. Of the leaders only Trepper escaped, presumably thanks to his mastery of the illegal life-style, and he at once went to Germany to report at the hiding place belonging to the *GRU* in Berlin. It was mid 1932 and scarcely six months were to elapse before the moment when Hitler and his Brownshirts would come to power; great changes were on the way and they were already being felt by the highly sensitive threads of the underground intelligence networks. Trepper received the order to make his way immediately to Moscow, and he found himself for the first time in the 'motherland of the proletariat' which until now he had known only from other people's accounts and from the dreams of his youth. He became a member of the headquarters of the Soviet intelligence service in Moscow, but for four years no use was made of his services. He studied, he edited a Jewish journal, he worked a little and for a while he attended lectures on intelligence technique. At last in 1936 came the moment which was to decide the later course of his life. All the achievements hitherto made by the Soviet intelligence service in Germany lay in ruins, yet at this time in particular information from there was of the greatest importance, as the Nazis were very clearly pressing towards war.

Leopold Trepper was appointed chief of the Soviet spy network in Western Europe.[16]

4

The liquidation of the Soviet intelligence positions in Germany did not mean that the new chief of secret operations would have to begin everything from scratch. There had remained small well-camouflaged units, strictly isolated from other similar groups, which survived and were waiting for new instructions (see chapter 3, p. 40). They were controlled from countries surrounding the Third Reich, and one of them, which might in wartime be neutral, was to be selected for the Western headquarters of the new Soviet network. After some years in France his French was not too bad, so he chose Belgium and its capital, Brussels.

In the area there was already a German from Eastern Prussia, Johann Wenzel (code-name *Hermann*), a communist, who had worked underground in the Weimar republic and was in the service of Soviet intelligence. After its collapse in 1935 Wenzel was summoned to Moscow and sent to the political military school of the Red Army. He showed such marvelous skill in intelligence work and telecommunications that he was taken up by *Razvedupr* and a year later sent to Belgium. He formed a small intelligence unit there which consisted of several communists from various countries and he began to specialize in radio-communication and the forgery of personal documents. All radio messages from Germany and France to Moscow and the communist cells passed through him. He also had points of support and information in various towns in France, Holland and Denmark.

Three years passed after Trepper had received his appointment before he finally left Moscow and set out for Brussels. He had been to France, to Germany and to various other countries several times to settle some minor affairs and to sow the seeds of future intelligence outposts, but this time however his journey was different. The spring of 1939 had arrived, Hitler had swallowed up Austria and dismembered Czechoslovakia, Poland had received assurances from the West—there was no doubt that a new war was approaching and so the creation of an intelligence network in Europe became a burning issue. Trepper was issued with an excellently forged Canadian passport in the name of Adam Mikler, which had fallen into Soviet hands during the Spanish war, he learned the essential particulars pertaining to life in

Canada, and in spring he arrived in Brussels. He adopted the code-name *Gilbert* for Moscow, but among his own people he became known as *Grand Chef*.[17]

It was essential to create a legal set-up in Belgium as soon as possible, so Trepper entered into an agreement with his old acquaintance from Palestine and together they established a business exporting raincoats, with a well-known Belgian as one of the directors. The company set up branches in ports of Belgium, Denmark, France, Holland, Norway and Sweden, which constituted an excellent cover for the intelligence posts which were established alongside.

The new chief of the Western network was trusted by his Russian superiors, but experience told them that they could not be a hundred per cent certain about anybody in every situation and that the secret of success was strict control, mutual observation and something else, which in ordinary life would be called blackmail. At that time the Treppers had already two sons, but only the second, Edgar, was allowed to join him with his mother, Luba. Michael, the first, only seven years old, was kept in Moscow to be educated 'in the Soviet spirit'.[18]

Furthermore the superiors in Russia sent following in Trepper's footsteps to the West four intelligence officers who had been well trained and had been issued with reliable papers. Captain Victor Sukulov-Gurevich obtained the passport of a Uruguayan named Vincente Sierra, and a Uruguayan passport was similarly issued to an Air Force Lieutenant Mikchail Makarov, who was now called Carlos Alamo. The other two agents were to pass for Scandinavians: Engineer Konstantin Yefremov impersonated a Finnish student, Eric Jern-stroem, while Lieutenant Anton Danilov became the Norwegian, Albert Desmet. The latter was despatched not to Belgium but to France, in order to maintain liaison between the Soviet embassy in Paris and communist groups in Belgium and France. Sukulov-Gurevich, who used the code-name *Captain Kent*, and whose papers were particularly convincing, since he had for the sake of their authenticity gone to Montevideo in order to travel to Belgium from there, became Trepper's deputy. His close circle knew him as *Petit Chef*.[19]

Knowing these details today, it is difficult not to acknowledge that the reconstruction of the intelligence network in Western Europe by the Russians was begun in a highly logical manner. Despite the principle that they must always play the leading role in any show, they understood the exceptional nature of the situation which related to the new system in Germany in which the police, as in the Soviet Union, played a very important part and were extremely efficient. In adapting themselves to this situation, they entrusted the network not to a Russian but to Leopold Trepper. Born in Poland and with good contacts in Palestine, he spoke French reasonably well and had a good command of German. He had Western manners and habits, and he also had the qualities of a born conspirator. No Russian with a revolutionary upbringing had anything approaching similar qualifications and hence the decision came about to entrust this important position to a foreigner. He was of course a communist but this in itself was insufficient and so the Russian, Sukulov-Gurevich, who had been taken fully into his superiors' confidence, became Trepper's deputy and maintained continuous contact with him. He was an experienced and loyal officer who had fought with the international brigades in Spain. He had a great deal of experience of intelligence and of life in general and in his new role beside Trepper he became the eyes and ears of Moscow. The chief of the *Razvedupr* there was known by the code-name *Director*. Several people held this post in succession; one name which has survived is that of General Ivan Peresypkin, who took over in the summer of 1941, following the German assault on Russia, and remained there until the end of the war.[20]

5

The numerous Nazi police formations were crushing the political opposition and putting thousands of communists, social democrats, socialists and liberals behind bars, but they could not get rid of all their opponents. Some of them had long been against national socialism but had never revealed their views and so were able to survive, often in exposed positions, while others had developed an aversion to the new system during its period in government on seeing how it was treating the citizens of its own nation.

Among the opponents who did not conceal their views and hence found themselves behind bars very quickly was a young journalist, Harro Schulze-Boysen, a socialist, although his family belonged to the influential and fairly prosperous intelligentsia which held rather conservative opinions. A year before Hitler came into power he had become the editor of a radical newspaper, *Der Gegner* (The Opponent) which opposed both the existing order and also national socialism on account of its totalitarian principles. The Nazis closed down the paper straight away, arresting its editor and treating him with refined brutality.

Thanks to help from his mother who knew Hermann Göring personally, Schulze-Boysen was released and, being a reserve officer, was accepted by the Air Ministry, which had recently been created; however, he had not changed his beliefs. On the contrary, the belief that Nazism would become the terror of Europe and the world grew within him and led to his determination to challenge it to a fight for life or death. To this resolution was allied the decision that in the course of the fight he might have to co-operate with his country's enemies.[21]

Progressing along this line of thought, Schulze-Boysen (code-name *Choro*) began to seek contact with people in various exposed positions who might have similar ideas and could be useful in the gathering of intelligence-type information. He came across Horst Heilmann and Alfred Traxl who were in the secret communications department of the operations division of the Army General Staff (*OKH*), Lieutenant Herbert Gollnow of the sabotage and diversion section of the *Abwehr*, and Johann Graudenz, who was connected with aircraft manufacture. He also knew a radio operator, Hans Coppi, and had several other contacts in the Air Ministry. Some of his informers had no idea what Schulze-Boysen was clandestinely engaged in, and gave him information which they assumed he needed in the course of his job. Amongst them were Hans Henniger, a government inspector of *Luftwaffe* equipment manufacture, and Colonel Erwin Gehrs of the training division of the Air Ministry.

While this was going on, there was at work in Berlin another man who had decided to create an anti-Nazi intelligence unit working directly for Moscow for different reasons. This was Arvid Harnack (code-name *Arvid*), an official in the Economics Ministry, a communist and a Marxist, who had come into contact with the Soviet intelligence service as early as 1933, when the Nazis had come to power. No one knew about it, his superiors at the ministry held him in the highest regard. He received promotion, and in 1937 he went as far as joining the Nazi party in order to acquire the qualifications of the exemplary citizen. His secret contacts included the writer and journalist, Dr Adam Kuckoff and his wife Greta, and John Sieg, an

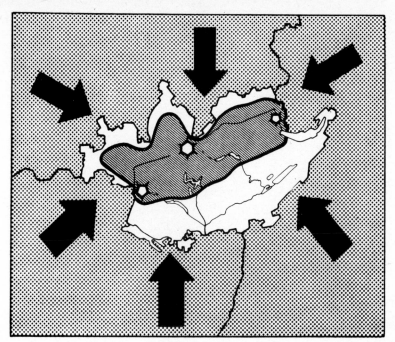

1 Map of Switzerland showing the defence area in the mountains called 'redoubt'

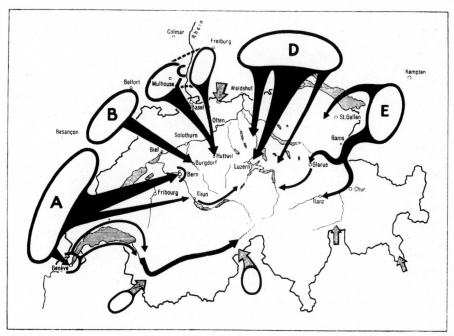

2 The German operation plan 'Tannenbaum'

3 'Dad's Army' (Civil Defence) in Switzerland in 1940

4 Henri Guisan

5 Roger Masson

6 Hans Hausamann   **7** Max Waibel

8 A lone Swiss soldier on duty in the mountains

9 Nazi rally in Zürich

10 Rudolf Roessler and Xaver Schnieper

American of German descent, who had returned to his country of origin from Detroit as a communist and was engaged in anti-state activities under an assumed name. He arranged Harnack's contacts with the communist underground which was gathering intelligence information. This was essentially related to economic affairs, in contrast to Schulze-Boysen's network which was concerned with military matters.

In the summer of 1939, just before the German attack on Poland, the headquarters of the Soviet intelligence service came to the conclusion that the two groups should be united. The military attaché at the Soviet embassy in Berlin, from whom Harnack received orders and to whom he passed his reports, acted as intermediary. The heads of the two intelligence units differed from each other greatly, and they took a dislike to each other from the very beginning. Schulze-Boysen was a theoretical idealist and basically an anarchist, and he carried out his highly dangerous clandestine work in his own way, mixing his personal and amorous affairs with the gathering of intelligence information. Harnack, a communist, was accustomed to discipline and could not stand amateurish improvisation. However, pressure from above prevailed, and the two who were so diverse began to collaborate.[23]

The feelers of Soviet intelligence thus began to extend throughout Western Europe: Trepper operated in Belgium, France and Holland, and the Schulze-Boysen/Harnack group in the very heart of Germany, but they had not yet been tied together to form a single unit. The German security, military, political and party forces already knew that something was happening and set out to search for traces of the new network. Moreover many radio signals were being intercepted which could not be deciphered at that time, but it was known that they were directed at Moscow. It has to be stressed at this point that all Soviet agents in the West always relayed their radio reports in German. In every service there develops a specific jargon, and so in the *Abwehr* the numerous signals of the hidden Soviet transmitters became known as 'playing' and taken as a whole they were given the name 'orchestra'. As these were the radio stations of Red Russia, the whole of the Western network of the Soviet intelligence service, using several stations in a number of countries, came to be called *Die Rote Kapelle* (The Red Orchestra).[24]

Before the integration of the Soviet intelligence outposts in

Western Europe which gave rise to the collective name given above, the German attack on Poland, which initiated the Second World War, took place. A situation arose which demanded action and so in the spring of 1940 Trepper's deputy, *Captain Kent*, arrived in Geneva to meet Sándor Radó, bringing with him certain instructions and the components for radio communication with Moscow, including the necessary codes. They supplemented the orders brought some time before by *Kolya* (see chapter 3, p. 31) and they changed the status of the Soviet intelligence network within Switzerland. It was to start being active with the setting up of several radio stations and was to begin direct collaboration with the *Director* in Moscow. Nevertheless this by no means meant that the group set up in Switzerland by Radó was to become part of the Red Orchestra. On the contrary: Moscow was anxious that this group shold act quite independently and remain in reserve in case the network directed by Trepper should break down. And yet, in spite of this logical principle, the Moscow Centre made a great mistake by sending *Captain Kent* to Geneva and directing him straight to Radó's apartment. In this way he learnt his name and address.[25] Some time later this mistake was to have dire consequences.

Yet the decision to keep the *Dora Group* on full alert was completely justified. The moment announced by *Kolya* had arrived: Europe went up in flames.[26]

6

When, towards the end of 1942, at a confidential meeting of conspirators Colonel Claus von Stauffenberg was asked what was to be done with Hitler, he gave a short answer: 'Kill him!'

Those two words which characteristically expressed the mood of the conspirators in the middle of the war, when it had already become obvious that Germany was not going to win, were nothing new however. From the initial moment of the Nazis' take-over of power, and even during the years before which heralded the social, moral and civil upheaval, the conservative German circles among the senior officers of the armed forces, the clergy and the intellectuals, sustained by *junker* traditions, were considering how to oppose Hitler. There were no conspiracies or underground associations in existence as yet and confidential discussions only were taking place, ideas were being exchanged and deliberations were being made in back rooms to decide what action should be taken. There was even an attempt to kill Hitler at the time when, as an almost unknown leader, he was forming his national socialist party, but his later serious opponents did not have anything to do with this.

Matters took on a different significance when the Nazis came to power and mass arrests of political opponents took place, closely followed by their imprisonment in the newly established concentration camps. The number of clandestine opponents of the new order grew, but the internal struggle for power, unable to continue for long, would have passed eventually with no great reverberations if it had not been for the preparations for a new war. This was opposed even by those who saw many positive aspects of the activities of the new rulers of the Reich, aware that they aimed at controlling unemployment, economic chaos and inflation.

At that time the chief of the General Staff was General Ludwig Beck, an officer with great authority, who was the main opponent of the German war preparations, and whom Hitler could not abide, but he had been forced to put up with him in the early years of his government. The general had many friends in the army whom he used to meet on a social level, he also attracted the attention of politicians who still reaped the benefits of freedom, and he gradually became leader of the opposition circles. In the army his beliefs were shared by the quartermaster of the General Staff, General Karl-Heinrich Stülpnagel, chief of the General Army Office, General Friedrich Olbricht, commander of the Berlin area, General Erwin von Witzleben, commander of the 23rd division in Potsdam, General von Brockdorf-Ahlefeld, commander of the 50th infantry regiment in Berlin, Colonel Paul von Hase, and chief of communications in the land army, Colonel (later General) Erich Fellgiebel. The last acted as a go-between with the other high ranking officers who joined the group after the beginning of the war. A special place was occupied by Admiral Canaris, the head of the *Abwehr*, who not only saw matters in the same way as General Beck, but after seeing the German atrocities in Poland, endeavoured to end the period of discussion and complaints and to begin to act. The brain behind this trend was his deputy, Colonel Hans Oster, a man of cool judgement, unswerving decision and prudence.[27]

Besides the military there was also a group of politicians, conservatives and liberals for the most part, together with industrialists and landowners. The leader of these was Carl Goerdeler, at one time mayor of Leipzig, who was secretly in touch with Karl Friedrich von Weizsäcker, chief secretary at the Foreign Office, with Erich Kordt, counsellor at the same ministry, with Ulrich von Hassell, the ambassador in Rome, who resigned in 1938, with Hans von Dohnanyi, a court counsel, and with a number of other people who had important positions in German society. A significant member of the opposition camp was Wolf Heinrich von Helldorf, the chief of the Berlin police, who was supported by his deputy, Count von Schulenburg, and by Arthur Nebe, the chief of criminal police. Goerdeler maintained contact with representatives of the Catholic and Protestant churches and with the group of the military.[28]

The conversion of the loose elements into an organization was brought about by Hitler himself, who was pressing for a military solution and was preparing plans which would lead to the acquisition of adequate *Lebensraum* (living-space) by the German nation. He scarcely confided in anyone and kept his plans a close secret, but he was forced to allow a few people access to them since he was unable to get everything ready on his own. Therefore towards the end of 1937 a conference was held in the Chancellery of the Reich to which were invited the war minister, Field-Marshal Werner von Blomberg, the commander-in-chief of the Land Army, General Werner von Fritsch, the commander-in-chief of the Navy, Grand-Admiral Erich Raeder, the commander-in-chief of the Air Force, General Hermann Göring, and only one civilian, the Foreign Minister, Konstantin von Neurath. There was characteristically no representative of industry, upon which the war effort would naturally be dependent. Also absent was General Beck, the highest ranking officer in the German armed forces.

Hitler anticipated that these experts, who were familiar with the state of the German army, would dissuade him from any war plans, but he hoped that they would bow to his authority. He met with disappointment, for the resistance put up against him exceeded his worst suppositions. Only Göring was on his side, but he was a party man and the closest associate of the new chancellor, gorged with ambition in the same way as Hitler and prepared for anything. Hitler did not give way and when a few days later General Beck, who had been told about the conference by von Fritsch and von Neurath, tried to intervene, he utterly refused to see him. The four participants of the conference who did not share the views of the *Führer* were under various pretexts deprived of their posts in the course of the following months or years—he never forgave them. This happened a while later; the immediate result of the revealed plans was the decision by the conspirators to unite and to start acting.[29]

It was easier to make the decision than to act upon it. The frail contacts of the conspirators encompassed only about fifty people, and further expansion of the conspiracy would be exceptionally difficult and dangerous, for the Nazi security forces were acting swiftly and with great efficiency. What way was there to threaten a system which had achieved a series of initial successes and had become fairly popular? The German officer corps was so inculcated with obedience, so bound by tradition, and so unequivocally conscious of the importance of the oath of loyalty that it was unlikely to condone any clandestine activity against the legal head of state. The large-scale crimes had not yet begun, and there was still some time to go before the decision would be taken for the mass liquidation of the Jews; the only serious accusation which could be levelled at Hitler was his progression towards another war. This could be opposed without the feeling that one was acting against the interests of one's country, so the resolution of the conspirators took this line. They came to the conclusion that if the Western powers were to be informed about Hitler's war intentions, it would not be an act of treason: on the contrary, it might save their country from another defeat. Despite all this, the internal resistance by the military was so great that the mission of making secret liaisons had to be taken on by the politicians, wealthy landlords and industrialists who had wide-reaching international contacts.

In the spring of 1938, after Hitler occupied Austria and incorporated it into the Reich, and when he was turning his attention towards Czechoslovakia, Carl Goerdeler went to France on two occasions in an attempt to persuade the French government to make a stand against Hitler. However, he did not find it willing to put up any kind of opposition, and when he arrived in London clandestinely on the same mission, he met with an even greater disappointment. The chief diplomatic adviser to the government, Sir Robert Vansittart, told him that his mission signified a betrayal of his own country.[30]

It was not an encouraging beginning, but it was nevertheless essential to continue activities, and so Admiral Canaris sent several of his close friends to the West, supplying them with excellently forged documents. The first to set out for London was Ewald von Kleist-Schwenzin, a conservative monarchist, who before his departure met

General Beck secretly and obtained his assurance that he would undertake to overthrow Hitler as soon as he could get a guarantee from the British that they would take up arms in the case of an attack on Czechoslovakia. Kleist even met Churchill, but the future great wartime leader was then but a member of parliament and his voice, warning against appeasement, was not at that time very popular. Two weeks later the industrialist, Hans Böhm-Tettlebach, set out for the British capital, but he had no success either. Von Weizsäcker also tried to intervene through an official at the German embassy in London and the High Commissioner of the League of Nations in Gdańsk, but London remained deaf to the warnings. It preferred not to believe in the German preparations and the readiness to start another war.[31]

General Beck, knowing Hitler's war plans, drew up a memorandum in which he indicated the possibility of bringing about another world war which Germany was bound to lose. He was counting on support from other generals, in particular General Walter von Brauchitsch, who had taken over the command of the land army from von Fritsch, and who had in confidential discussions shared General Beck's point of view. But von Brauchitsch did not keep his promise and did not lend his voice to the opinions of the other generals, so when in August Hitler announced at a secret conference that he would soon settle the affair of the Sudetenland by using force, General Beck resigned from his post.

There arose a situation which was even more advantageous to the conspirators, for fifty-four-year old General Franz Halder was appointed Chief of Staff. Colonel Oster, who had been his subordinate, now had very easy access to him and was trusted by him. Through this channel a confidential meeting between the general and Canaris came about, which resulted in the establishment of a consensus of opinion and a plan for further action. General Halder turned out to be considerably more radical than General Beck; he was a staunch opponent of Hitler's war preparations and he approved the plan for a coup d'état should the chancellor unleash war. At the commencement of operations Hitler would immediately be arrested by General von Witzleben and be swiftly brought to trial together with his chief associates. The wide-reaching conspiracy among the senior commanders and the police would ensure success. Everything was dependent, however, on the assumption that the Western democracies would stir into action should Czechoslovakia be attacked.

The British prime minister was then, alas, not Churchill but Neville Chamberlain, a conciliatory man who believed in promises and conventions. He was convinced that he would be able to change Hitler's mind and halt his dangerous plans. He had two meetings with him in Germany and through the intercession of Mussolini was able to convince him that an international conference was necessary. It was held in Munich on 29 September 1938 and the participants—Hitler, Mussolini, Chamberlain and Daladier—decided that Czechoslovakia should hand over the Sudetenland to Germany and that she would receive international guarantees concerning her remaining frontiers. The conspirators, who were already prepared for action, were taken aback, many of them were even impressed by Hitler, for he had again managed to achieve one of his difficult goals without the use of force.

The day on which the conspirators should have carried out their task arrived nevertheless, for on 15 March of the following year German tanks crossed the border of the already reduced Czechoslovakia, but it seemed as if their will-power had become paralyzed, for Hitler did not meet with any obstacles on the way to his new victory. It could be assumed that again the decisive moment to take action had not yet arrived, for the occupation of Czechoslovakia had come about without any shots having been fired, but a few months later, on 1 September, these shots were in fact fired, for the attack on Poland met with armed resistance. Moreover the other basic condition had also been fulfilled: on 3 September Britain and France delared war on Germany. Yet the conspirators remained silent and did not in any way reveal their opposition to Hitler's aggressive policy.

It would be naive to think that the Nazi security forces were unaware of the military and political conspiracy against Hitler. Many senior military men were under suspicion, politicians were being watched, proof of disloyalty among the clergy and the industrialists was being sought, and Canaris and his *Abwehr* were not trusted, but evidence of the plot had not yet been discovered. In the *Gestapo* headquarters the name *Die Rote Kapelle* had been in use for several years to describe the communist intelligence network, and so the conspirators of a different hue became known correspondingly by the name *Die Schwarze Kapelle* (the Black Orchestra).

The war had already begun, the German tanks were moving ahead through Poland towards the East where they would meet the allied

Soviet tanks, while underground among the most exposed and well-informed members of the *Black Orchestra* confidential consultations were taking place. They had to be active, they had to do something, but they needed to work out completely new methods, for Hitler went from one victory to another and a long and bloody war was on the way. The attention of the conspirators was increasingly turning towards the south, in the direction of Switzerland.

5 War and Action

The absence of a Soviet legation and of any Soviet consulates in Switzerland greatly impeded Sándor Radó, for it deprived him at critical moments of discreet assistance and protection. Since the outbreak of war he had often been short of money, for his cartographic business had lost many overseas clients, and he was obliged to turn to Moscow for aid, for which he had to wait since he did not himself have any means of communication. Sometimes even this form of aid failed, as happened in the case of *Kent*, who not only did not bring any money, but took from Radó as much as he could extract besides.[1].

In spite of his financial difficulties, the secret activities of the cartographer continued to flourish thanks to assistance from Communists on whom he was always able to count, regardless of their origin or nationality. This was all the more notable because in the early part of the war, when Stalin had bound himself to Hitler by means of an alliance and supported his war preparations, the Communists went through a period of great anxiety and confusion. They were disorientated and had no idea what to hold on to, but their loyalty and blind faith in the correctness of the ideas they believed in were so great that they accepted anything Soviet Russia did without a word of criticism.

One day in December 1939, a while before *Kent* had appeared with instructions and codes, Radó found a letter in his mail-box announcing that someone would come to him who would help him in his contact with headquarters. A young and good-looking woman duly arrived: they exchanged passwords and she gave her code-name as *Sonia*. She spoke German faultlessly, created a pleasant impression and moreover it was evident that she had a great deal of specialized training and experience. At that time Radó did not know that he was dealing with a top Soviet intelligence agent called Ursula Maria Hamburger, who sometimes went by the name of Maria Schulz; a German, known by headquarters in Moscow as *Wiera*. She had already reached the rank of major in the Red Army and had behind her the experience of being a Communist agent in Poland and in China. *Sonia* questioned Radó about his situation, promised help and told him that until he obtained his own means she would help him in his radio contact with Moscow. It was through her that he received the news of *Captain Kent*'s visit.[2]

The contact with *Pakbo* passed on by *Kolya* in the spring of 1938 (see chapter 3, p. 32) proved to be most valuable: important information began to flow in from several areas, and the need for personal and direct radio contact with headquarters became very urgent. The narrow communication channel provided by *Sonia* was by now insufficient and, moreover, contradicted the principles of conspiracy which demanded the greatest possible decentralization and the possession of several ways of dealing with the same matters. It was necessary to think about a personal transmitter.

A solution was first found in Geneva itself when Radó got to know an electrical engineer, Edmond Hamel, who had his own shop and who shared his political views. Hamel, a short, inconspicuous man, was married to a vigorous woman, considerably taller than himself, named Olga. Both husband and wife considered Soviet Russia to be the paradise of the working masses; they agreed to undertake the difficult and dangerous role of radio operators, adopting the code-names *Edouard* and *Maude*. *Sonia* supplied them with a transmitter and taught them Morse code. By the second half of 1940 Radó was able to communicate with Moscow directly.[3]

The progress of the war caused *Sonia* (who had two children from her first marriage and who was now married to an Englishman, *John*, who collaborated with her) to feel threatened in Switzerland, now surrounded on all sides by enemy troops. She decided to leave, but before she did so, in August 1940, she passed on to Radó one of her most valuable contacts.*

Sonia went, not to Russia, but to England. She was allowed to do so because she had married an Englishman. Some sources state that after the pact between Stalin and Hitler in August 1939 and the Soviet attack on Finland in November 1939, she had lost her uncritical faith in Communism and had broken her relationship with Soviet Russia. (Kurz, *Nachrichtenzentrum* ..., p. 116, fn 47).

Just recently an article by Antony Terry and Philip Knightley in *The Sunday Times* (27.1.1980) stated that *Sonia* was a Jewish refugee from Germany, the daughter of the well-known economist, Professor René Kuczynski. After her work as a Russian spy in China and Poland, she went to Switzerland in 1938, where she tried to recruit British veterans of the Spanish Civil War who had fought on the Communist side. She recruited two: Alexander Foote and Len Brewer, whom she finally married and with whom she

Alexander Foote (code-name *Jim*) was an Englishman, living in Lausanne, where he passed as a wealthy individual living comfortably off his capital. But Foote had taken part in the Spanish civil war on the side of the Red brigades, and on his return to England, towards the end of 1938, had been drawn into Soviet military intelligence. Ordered to go to Switzerland, he met *Sonia*, while initially living in Geneva; she included him in her network and began to teach him the craft of espionage. Foote was a clever man, at the height of his powers, physically well-built, cheerful and with a sense of humour. He had a middle-class background but little care had been taken over his education, and he had neither the desire nor the will-power to follow a regular profession. People of this kind often succumb to propositions which lead down the slippery path of intelligence work which from afar appears to be fascinating. At the time *Sonia* passed him on to Radó, *Jim* already had behind him a good deal of intelligence experience; he had a reasonable command of German and he spoke French with ease. The role of a comfortably-off individual living off the property he possessed suited him very well. It turned out that the occupation of secret radio operator tapping out coded messages during the night amused him, and he proved to be an excellent worker. He was responsible for the first radio contact with headquarters on 12 March 1941.[4]

Besides his contact with *Pakbo*, the possession of two radio transmitters and his own network consisting of fifty or sixty people, Radó extended his means by one further unit, which supplied him with essential information. It was controlled by Rachel Dübendorfer, who had been born in Poland and whose parents had emigrated to Germany. There she had joined the Communist Party, become an agent of the Comintern† and, in the Twenties, met Radó and his wife.

---

came to London on 18 December 1940. According to the authors of this article, she organized the British section of the *Red Orchestra*.

This information, which does not agree with other earlier sources, requires special research and evaluation, but will not be elaborated in this book, since it is outside its subject. One thing, however, must be stated here: if she was really active in Great Britain as a Soviet spy, in a different network from Philby, Burgess, Maclean and Blunt, her network did not form a British section of the *Red Orchestra*. This network, headed by Leopold Trepper, covered only Germany and some of the western countries, like France, Belgium and Holland, occupied by the Germans.

†Abbreviation for Communist International, an organization set up in 1919 to bring about world-wide revolution. Nominally dissolved in 1943 under pressure from the Western Allies.

At this time she already had Swiss nationality through her marriage, which had broken up because her husband had left her. She lived in Geneva and from here she controlled an intelligence network in Germany which provided information about the German war industry. She bore the code-name *Sissy* and was so highly regarded in Moscow that she had been decorated with the Order of Lenin. In her intelligence work she was aided by a friend, Paul Böttcher (code-name *Paul*), also a long-standing member of the German Communist Party and former Finance Minister of Saxony, who was staying with her illegally, since he had difficulty obtaining Swiss residence and work permits. Radó disliked Rachel and had various reservations about her, but in 1940 he had to carry out an instruction from Moscow which ordered him to make contact. According to him this order came about for two reasons: it meant reinforcing his own group and also reactivating *Sissy's* network, which had lost touch with Headquarters.[5] In fact, as became obvious later, there was also another reason: Moscow, conforming to custom, wanted to have beside Radó someone it trusted who could observe his activities and, if necessary, replace him.

2

On 17 September 1940 British monitoring stations caught a German radio message relaying an order from Hitler that all *Luftwaffe* air bases in occupied Holland were to abandon preparations for a decisive attack on Britain. This was decoded and read out the same evening at a meeting of the Chiefs of Staff in the presence of the Prime Minister. All felt a profound sense of relief; Churchill's expression was radiant. The message was proof that the Germans had abandoned plans for an invasion of Britain.[6]

The news of the change in the German plans reached Moscow just as quickly, for the *Red Orchestra* had agents everywhere, but the faces of the Soviet leaders must have assumed a totally different aspect. The Russians had been counting on the war in the West being a long one, but with the collapse of France they found their calculations had misfired, although they still expected that Hitler would undertake an attack on Britain and thereby become entangled in a long-term struggle. Suddenly, within a few weeks, all this ceased to be the case, and more than 200 German divisions were to be found on European territory with no obvious target of attack. The Ribbentrop-Molotov pact bound the two dictatorial powers very closely; goods and raw materials were being exchanged, and the division of spoils had brought the two aggressors even closer together. Stalin was carefully fulfilling his obligations concerning the supply of raw materials, but he realized that he had to abandon his expectation of a long and bloody war in the West and that a deadly threat was drawing near. He had to know at any cost what plans were being generated in Hitler's mind and he issued instructions along these lines to his Chief of Intelligence.

The *Red Orchestra* had a well-organized intelligence network within Germany, France, Belgium and Holland—Leopold Trepper held the whole of it firmly in his grasp—but these countries were already under Hitler's rule or, as in southern France, rigorously infiltrated by it. Swift communication with Headquarters was possible solely by radio, but such means were unreliable because the German security authorities were seeking and capturing the transmitters, and the link with Moscow was being broken incessantly. The Swiss network, called *Dora* after the code-name of its founder, Sándor Radó, was to have been kept in reserve, but already in the spring of 1940 Headquarters decided that it was necessary for it to be brought to life and prepared for immediate action, and *Captain Kent* came to Geneva with this aim (see chapter 4, p. 48). Now, since Radó had two radio transmitters in operation, the security of which seemed assured on account of the neutrality of the territory, the importance of the network became greatly increased, and Moscow demanded its full activation.[7]

Radó had links with the *Red Orchestra* group in Berlin which was controlled by Schulze-Boysen and Harnack, and on occasions he transmitted information obtained from thence to Moscow[8] although it was not essential for him to do so as his own network was distinguishing itself as it was. The most valuable information flowing in was from *Pakbo*, whose widely branching contacts reached various sources. The first news of new German plans began to come in in the latter half of 1940 from diplomatic circles in Bern, where indiscretions could sometimes be picked up. On one occasion the Japanese attaché mentioned to an acquaintance that following his victory in France Hitler together with Mussolini would attack Russia. On another occasion a Yugoslav diplomat who had good connections in Italy supplied information about the state of readiness of the Italian forces. Yet another time valuable information on the subject of German interests in the East was brought by an attaché at the Chinese mission who was within Pünter's network and bore the code-name *Polo*. Later, in the spring of the following year, when it was already known that Hitler would strike in the East and all that mattered was to determine the timing of the attack, information about the concentration of German divisions would prove to be of greater importance. At this time a valuable service was being provided by Mayr von Baldegg, a Swiss intelligence officer in *Pakbo's* network known by the code-name *Luise* and by two further contacts, *Feld* in Austria and *Rot* in Germany[9] (see chapter 3, pp. 34–5).

This is confirmed by two messages:

21 February 1941. To the Director.
According to information provided by a Swiss officer Germany currently has 150 divisions in the East. In his opinion the German will attack at the end of May.

Dora.

6 April 1941. To the Director.
All Germany's mobile divisions are in the East. The German troops formerly stationed on the Swiss frontier have been transferred to the South-West.

Dora.[10]

With every day that passed new information was flowing in, not only from *Pakbo's* network, but also from *Sissy*, although her agents were interested above all in the war industry. Now the most burning problem became finding out on which day the German attack might occur. A war between two powers, which had for almost two years been supporting each other and had unleashed a new fury of global proportions, offering only conquest and slavery, interested everyone, for it could give rise to an entirely new situation within the world order. For this reason information was flowing in to Moscow from various sources. It was being obtained by the intelligence service of the Polish Underground Army and sent to London from whence Churchill passed it on to Stalin, who was also being warned by President Roosevelt. Valuable information which was being obtained by the Czech intelligence service was communicated to Moscow by President Beneš who was then in Britain. Excellent intelligence was being gathered by a German journalist and long-standing Soviet agent, Richard Sorge, who was active in the Far East and who had close relations with the German ambassador in Tokyo, Eugene Ott. It was Sorge who obtained the information, priceless to Stalin, that the Japanese would not attack from the east, which enabled him to send the Siberian divisions over to the German front and to rescue Moscow.

All of these were endeavouring to establish the exact date of the German attack, and they were near to the truth. It happened however that it was ascertained by a French diplomat and journalist, Louis Suss, who was living in Switzerland, belonged to *Pakbo*'s network and was known by the code-name *Salter*. Indirectly therefore this was a contact of Sándor Radó's. At the end of May *Salter* passed on the information that the German divisions would attack in the East on 22 June 1941. Coincidentally another highly secret source gave the same date, so Radó immediately sent an urgent message to the *Director* in Moscow. He was most surprised when he not only received no praise, but sensed even a certain frostiness in the reply which acknowledged this information.[11] Not until later did there come any recognition, but by that time the German divisions were already in battle at Moscow and Leningrad.

3

At the beginning of the summer of 1939 there appeared in the *Neue Zürcher Zeitung* a small advertisement:

> Well-known important publishing house seeks energetic gentleman willing to put up share of 20,000 Fr. in order to expand the business. Permanent post, with prospects for progression. Knowledge of literature, good general education, also business sense. Offers in writing to Box No. J 7884, Advertisement Department, *Neue Zürcher Zeitung*.[12]

War could break out at any moment and all the more important departments and military headquarters were occupied with this. At the same time the holiday period was beginning and millions of Europeans were setting off for the mountains, the coast and quiet country retreats. So hardly anyone was interested in the business proposition, similar to thousands of others which appeared every day. Nor did anyone enquire which publishing house it was which was seeking a partner and capital—it was, actually, *Vita Nova Verlag*, directed by Rudolf Roessler. In fact he had already made contact with *Büro Ha* and had promised him intelligence co-operation (see chapter

1, p. 14), but during these latter pre-war months he was not giving this matter a great deal of attention, for his main concern was the financial situation of the business, which was not looking too good.

The advertisement did not however turn out to be completely wasted, for one letter did arrive at the number given in the newspaper. Roessler replied to it, and on 17 June he met the applicant in Lucerne. He was a German émigré, like himself, named Dr Christian Schneider, round about his own age and with similar interests. Inflation had dispossessed him of the property he had inherited in Germany; he had held several banking posts and contributed to a number of newspapers, and then finally became a translator for an international employment agency in Geneva. After a few years he got married and became a Swiss citizen. The two men took to each other, settled the conditions for their collaboration, and by autumn they had become friends and were managing the business jointly, although Schneider carried on living in Geneva. In addition they were united by their very similar political views and a rather pessimistic evaluation of the international situation in the early months of the war. [13]

In response to the current events Roessler gradually started to become active in the intelligence field and to send his reports to *Büro Ha*. They were of good quality from the very beginning, and with every day that passed Captain Hausamann's high opinion of them increased. Max Waibel, who controlled intelligence post no. 1 in Lucerne, and who often spoke about Roessler with his second-in-command, Mayr von Baldegg, thought the same about the work of the German journalist. They were amazed by the clarity of Roessler's analysis of complicated problems, and they were baffled as to where Roessler drew such precise and fast-travelling information. They observed his contacts and tried to find out with whom he corresponded, but all they could establish was that he was certainly not using a radio and that his numerous reports were reaching him by conventional means: by post, telephone and courier. He was also in constant touch with the German émigré community in Zürich. In the summer of 1940, when France fell, the value of his swift and detailed reports reached their peak. The information contained within them must have come from the highest and most confidential circles of the Third Reich. [14]

At this time Roessler was working exclusively for the Swiss intelligence service, but he was using two channels: one to the *Büro Ha* in compliance with the arranged agreement, and the other to the no. 1 post in Lucerne, for he had become friendly with Mayr von Baldegg and shared with him the information he possessed. He also did this because the co-operation with Baldegg was of mutual benefit: from him he obtained information of interest to himself of which he made some use. After the war Hausamann asserted that Roessler was also working for the British intelligence service, which was very probable, but for which there is no irrefutable proof.[15] However, there is no doubt that after the fall of France, when Hitler had lost the air battle and had given up the idea of invading Britain, and when the chance came up of a German attack in the East, Roessler became interested in Soviet Russia. In spite of the views held by some historians and witnesses of the events he was not a Communist and his liberalism dictated as strong a hatred of Stalin as of Hitler, but the clarity of his vision indicated to him the way the war would progress. If, after attacking Russia, Hitler would win this war, it would be very difficult, almost impossible, to defeat him. With all the colossal natural resources of the Soviet Empire, he would be stronger than ever. So everything had to be done to prevent the Germans winning in the East, and ideological differences should not obscure this obvious conclusion.

The professional collaboration between Roessler and Schneider was so intimate and the similarity of the views held by both so far-reaching that it would be difficult to imagine that the intelligence contacts of the firm's proprietor could have escaped the attention of his new partner. The inverse was also true: Roessler must have known that Schneider kept in touch with his friend at the international employment agency, Rachel Dübendorfer, and that her Communist opinions were connected very closely with Soviet Russia. Students of these affairs (Kurz, von Schramm, Lüönd) assert that during the first half of 1941 neither partner was yet thinking of working for Stalin's empire. Nevertheless Schneider's widow, during an interview she gave in 1966, stated that it was about that time that Roessler, writing to his colleague in Geneva, began to send him little notes containing information about Germany of great interest and of importance to Soviet Russia.[16] It would be hard to imagine that he would be doing this for no reason at all and that he was not expecting this information to go any further. The same applies to Schneider, who was passing the information on to Rachel, for he could not be so naive as to treat it all as a game at a time when the war had already gone on for two years and when Switzerland, sensitive about her neutrality, was clamping down on any illegal activity. Was Schneider aware that Rachel was connected with Radó, that she was passing everything relating to information about Germany on to him, and that these reports were being transmitted immediately by means of radio waves to Moscow? Again the answer seemed to be simply: why would he be doing this if he was not expecting any consequence? It is known for a fact that it was by this method that news obtained by Roessler in mid-June 1941 reached Moscow. This contained information about German preparations for an attack in the East and gave the precise date of the attack: the 22nd of the same month. [17].

4

On 22 June 1941 Radó switched on his wireless and heard a speech by Hitler: the leader of the German nation was announcing the attack on Russia which was to decide the thousand-year future of their great country. The following day a message was sent to Moscow from Switzerland:

23 June 1941. To the Director.
In this historic hour we vow solemnly and with unshaken loyalty that we will fight with redoubled energy at our forward outposts. [18]

Having made this declaration Radó started work full of enthusiasm. For many years, from the day on which he had become a Communist, his faith both in the rightfulness of the principles he professed and in the infallibility of the Soviet leaders did not waver for a single moment. Even at the time of the eruption of the volcano of German-Soviet understanding, when Communists all over the world were losing their heads, he considered the Ribbentrop-Molotov pact to be a triumph of Soviet diplomacy, which had managed to thwart the possibility of an alliance between the bourgeois states against Russia and had provided her with a powerful ally. Whenever any disturbing reflections arose in the depths of his soul there was always the answer: Russia had gained several invaluable years during which she could re-arm and modernize her forces. [19]. The fact that the alliance had united his idealized second motherland with an evil system did not cause him to lose any sleep. He considered that the purges, the countless

64

executions and the prison camps of Stalin were necessary, and he gave no thought to the methods used by Hitler, although he must have known about them from Soviet propaganda which had until recently been circulated widely. He was profoundly convinced that the Soviet Union was pursuing a praiseworthy policy, that her preparation for war was excellent, and that Germany had let herself become involved in something she would soon be regretting.

He did not give any credence to the first German reports of victories, taking them to be primitive propaganda, and for a few days he ignored them completely. But when the Swiss press and radio began to announce daily details of Hitler's great successes he felt a chill close to the heart. He listened to the German radio also, but above all else he took notice of the reports being supplied by his own network. There was no doubt: the German divisions were moving forward swiftly, while Soviet troops surrendered in their thousands, and with every day that passed, more towns fell and the likelihood of a Soviet defeat increased. Although surprised, disorientated and completely thrown off balance, he did not break down; being a man of action, he set to work feverishly.

He had to begin by taking stock of the means at his command and by sounding out the mood of the closest of his collaborators. He therefore went first to Bern, where he met *Pakbo*, and then to Lausanne to see *Jim*. In Geneva he had already met *Sissy* and her companion *Paul*, as well as *Edouard* and *Maude*. They had all been overwhelmed by the impact of the German attack and the German successes; these had not been expected, and they had fallen into a state of depression. They had to be shaken out of their stupor, and encouraged to become active.[20]

On 1 July an agitating message was received from Headquarters which demanded information about the German forces and the movements of their large units, and so the entire *Dora* network set itself to work in this direction. Under pressure from current events two of Püntner's agents, *Salter* and *Long*, had become most animated and, having acquired some excellent diplomatic contacts, began to supply information of interest about the German situation generally, while Rachel Dübendorfer's network sent in reports from the Reich concerning the German divisions. Information of a similar kind was coming in from France, where *Pakbo* had informers among the local underground activists. Thanks to these Radó was able to use his two radio sets to their maximum limits and to send many urgent reports to Moscow.

> 2 July 1941. To the Director.
> The Germans currently have Operational Plan no. 1 in force. The target is Moscow. The operations that have been started on the flanks are merely diversionary manoeuvres. The accent is on the central sector of the front.
>
> Dora.

> 7 August 1941. To the Director.
> The Japanese ambassador in Bern has said that there can be no question of a Japanese attack on the Soviet Union as long as Germany has secured no decisive victory at the front.
>
> Dora.

> 23 August 1941. To the Director.
> Twenty-eight new divisions are being organized in Germany. They are to be organized by September.
>
> Dora.[21]

Those were only minor examples only of some of the reports which were streaming in to Moscow every night. The Headquarters acknowledged them very quickly, demanding further details, and asking for more information. They were interested primarily in the distribution of the German units and in any changes in their positions; they wanted to know the production figures of the greatly expanded war industry, and they asked about the numbers of casualties at the front. There were questions also about the relations between the leaders of the National Socialist party and the marshals and generals in command at the front. One of the questions directly concerned Switzerland; the information had been spreading that Hitler was planning an attack on Switzerland, and Moscow wanted to know about the Swiss fortifications, the strength of the defending army and about mobilization. Both radio sets, which were working to the limits of their capacity, increased their transmissions further, and *Jim, Edouard* and *Maude* sat at their desks all night, endeavouring to put countless columns of Morse symbols into the ether so the *Director* could obtain the answers which were important to him. This was absolutely essential, for the German security forces were continuously tracking the secret radio stations of the *Red Orchestra* which were 'playing' in Berlin and Brussels. The *Abwehr* had a powerful monitoring station near Königsberg, in East Prussia, which caught signals passing to Moscow and back. It was in contact with the *Gestapo*, and several radio stations had already been discovered and liquidated.

Of course, if the German monitoring stations could pick up the signals of the *Red Orchestra* on the huge territory ruled by the Third Reich, it was impossible to believe that the Swiss security authorities did not know what was going on in their small country. Obviously they had decided to connive for the same reasons which had induced Roessler to co-operate with Soviet Intelligence.

At the moment when the pressure of messages in the air-waves on the Switzerland-Moscow line was at its height, in mid-October, Headquarters suddenly fell silent. This might have been expected, for the German divisions were by now at the outskirts of Moscow; nevertheless the sudden silence froze the hearts of the Swiss conspirators. Yet what could they do? The fall of the capital need not decide the result of the war; there remained nothing else to be done but to continue gathering information. A degree of optimism was introduced by the Swiss press, according to which Moscow was defending itself still, although the more important government offices had been transferred to Kuibyshev, 600 km further east. The setting up of a new radio station with a wider range and making contact both required some time. Radó and his agents, full of intense decisiveness, redoubled their efforts.[22]

Their optimism turned out to be substantiated, for at the beginning of December Moscow unexpectedly responded. It did so acting as if nothing had happened; it started to set questions, give instructions and knock out its messages without a trace of emotion. The secret radio contacts confirmed the news the press and intelligence reports were bringing: a turning-point had been reached at the front, and the German divisions had at the last moment been held back. A few days later there came another item of news, which completely transformed the entire international situation: on 7 December the Japanese, without declaring a state of war, attacked the United States fleet in Pearl Harbor, Hawaii. The following day the United States declared war on Japan, and three days later Hitler himself, reacting in a fury, joined in the duel with the great democratic power. There were German divisions at the edge of the English Channel, on the coasts of the Mediterranean, at Moscow and at Leningrad, but anyone with an understanding of the economic potential of the world knew already that Hitler was not going to win the war.

A great burden fell from the shoulders of Radó and his companions. They entered the year of 1942 in a completely different frame of mind: they had acquired a new willingness to work, while their difficulties hitherto seemed to them suddenly to have become trifling and unimportant. This mood was shared also by the agents in the field, since the number of incoming reports increased to such an extent that the setting up of a third radio station became essential. The greatest difficulty was finding someone able to take charge of it. Radó had a stroke of luck—he met a young and beautiful girl, Margrit Bolli, who lived in Basel with her parents. Her father, who was a civil servant, held extreme left wing views, and had interested his daughter in these. Full of youthful enthusiasm and wanting passionately to join in the struggle against Hitlerism, she agreed first to the role of radio operator, and then accepted the proposal to take charge of the radio station. She was introduced to the mysteries of the Morse code and the operation of the equipment by *Jim*, and her parents agreed to the installation of the radio in their home, so Margrit, who had taken the code-name *Rosa*, started her double role in radio operation and liaison. Her contacts were limited to Radó, his wife, *Jim* and *Pakbo* only. Transmissions from her parents' home did not continue for long however, for their nerves could not stand it, so the young girl moved to Geneva together with her radio set in the middle of 1942. She worked very well and, as did *Edouard*, *Maude* and *Jim*, mostly at night.[23]

All three radio stations, which were transmitting in German using a code which was extraordinarily difficult to crack, were detected fairly quickly by the German monitoring service. It had stations in Karlsruhe, Munich and in Stuttgart (see chapter 2, p. 17) and it established that signals were being sent eastwards from Switzerland, and that there were two stations 'playing' in Geneva, and one in Lausanne.[24] The *Gestapo* were unable to lay its hands on them because they were operating within the territory of a neutral country, but German agents did attempt to direct the attention of the Swiss to the problem. However, during this period the government of the small democracy showed a significant unwillingness to occupy itself with tracking Soviet agents. In the *Abwehr's* vocabulary the three radio stations of the *Dora* network were termed *Die Rote Drei* (The Red Trio).

In the middle of 1942, among the avalanche of messages which were flowing in to the three radio stations and which were being sent out by Radó to be transmitted as quickly as possible to Moscow, there began to appear, with ever increasing frequency, reports from an agent who bore the code-name *Taylor*.[25]

5

All chiefs of intelligence always abide by one basic principle which the nature of their work requires: they do not just demand information quickly, but they also want to know its origins. Insufficient knowledge about sources arouses suspicion and does not allow the information to be utilized fully, even when it is of great importance. Intelligence reports often provide the basis for capital political and military decisions; who would dare to supply a prime minister or commander-in-chief with information without being absolutely sure of its source?

No wonder Roessler was under constant pressure from the very time he began his intelligence work to name the sources from which he obtained his disclosures. It is true that at the outset, after he had been induced to collaborate and when he had made contact with the *Büro Ha*, he had reserved the right never to reveal the sources of his information. This condition had at that time been accepted, but the situation had since undergone some change. Then they had been expecting nothing special and had been counting rather on intelligent analyses; now it turned out that Roessler was supplying information of the greatest military and political importance. It was being passed on—to the Western Allies, in fact—and enormous use could be made of it, but it was essential to be certain that it had not been fabricated, that it was reliable, and, above all, that it was not carefully constructed false information.

Roessler stuck up for himself, resisted the attacks and evaded the pressures, and the situation dragged on in this way right up to 1942. It was then that his clandestine contact with Dr Schneider took on a more definite profile. He had hitherto been enclosing small scraps of paper containing information of interest with his correspondence only sporadically. It was thus that the important date 22 June had been conveyed—the day on which the Germans would, and indeed did, cross the borders of the Soviet empire (see chapter 5, p. 61). Amateurism was now finished with; the war in the East was no longer a German victory parade, Russia had withstood the initial onslaught and, supported with huge supplies from the United States and Britain, had brought about a stabilization of the wide front. There arose the possibility that the deciding drama of the war would be played out in the East. Roessler was aware of this and he decided that the occasional contacts would have to become co-operation on a regular basis. His entire network should now work almost exclusively for Soviet Russia. Political views did not have any part to play in this; the idea was the overthrow of Hitler.

The already existing disposition of personnel allowed this plan to be realized very easily because Dr Schneider had already been in touch for several months with Rachel Dübendorfer who, under the code-name *Sissy*, belonged to Radó's network (see chapter 5, pp. 57–8). In the autumn of 1942, when the Sixth Army of General von Paulus was approaching Stalingrad, Schneider, who bore the code-name *Taylor* in Rachel's set-up and had already performed several important intelligence services, told her about some new and far-reaching possibilities. He had come into contact with someone who was prepared to undertake the swift supply of important intelligence information concerning Germany of colossal significance for Soviet Russia. This person was setting only one condition: no-one would enquire who he was or whence he drew his information. He lived in Lucerne, and that was all. He was not demanding any payment for his work besides reimbursement for his actual expenses.

This offer was immediately relayed to Radó, who passed it on to Moscow with the additional information that it was from this very source that he had over a year ago obtained the precise date of the German attack in the East. Headquarters responded straight away, issuing a directive that the new contact should be taken up, and accepting its anonymity. Yet they did not wish to commit themselves without any conditions of their own, and they demanded that the secret informant should, in order to demonstrate and confirm his abilities, give answers to two questions: (a) which German formations were fighting on the southern section of the front, and (b) how many German prisoners-of-war had fallen into Soviet hands? Both questions were difficult but to Radó's astonishment *Sissy* supplied him with the answers within a few days. Headquarters replied very quickly, expressing satisfaction with the excellent report, and they announced that this new contact would be receiving many questions from them in the future. The code-name *Taylor* began to appear in Radó's despatches as being the source of information with increasing frequency. Radó himself never met *Taylor* nor did he know anything about him; all business was settled with *Sissy* acting as go-between. The new information network had to be given a specific code-name, so Radó, who knew only that its secret organizer lived in Lucerne, called it *Lucy Ring*.[26]

The territory hitherto covered by Roessler's intelligence commitments increased enormously by the great expanse of the eastern front and the information from Germany connected with it, but alongside this grew the pressure on him to name its sources. The Swiss intelligence service tolerated the hitherto awkward situation which necessitated the continual checking of important and urgent despatches, the Western Allies often made no use of them at all since their source was unknown, while Moscow although having agreed to the condition of anonymity at once began to wage war against it. The suspiciousness of the Russians, strengthened by a political system which trusted no-one and multiplied also by the habits of the intelligence profession, made it difficult for them to accept important and urgent despatches of great interest from a source completely unknown to them. Already after a few weeks Radó started receiving messages expressing dissatisfaction and demanding that *Taylor* should reveal with whom he was collaborating and whence this mysterious person was obtaining information. Moscow argued that it was true that what it had received so far had been valuable and genuine, but who could guarantee that it was not provocation by the *Abwehr* who was first lulling its vigilance by providing authentic information in order, at a moment of great importance, suddenly to feed it with false information which could bear decisively on contemporary events.[27]

This attitude was reasonable; Radó agreed with it, and he began to put pressure himself on *Taylor* via *Sissy* to supply details concerning the identity and the network of his informant. *Taylor*, like Roessler, put up a defence; he used the argument that he could not break his word of honour. Sometimes in conversations with *Sissy* he asserted that he did not know exactly who his source was, and at other times he promised that he would shortly be able to satisfy her adamant curiosity. Obviously he told Roessler about this at every meeting,

71

trying to persuade him to unveil his secret to some extent, else it might result in Moscow ceasing to show any interest in the despatches, whereas the idea was that they should contribute to the overthrow of Hitlerism as soon as possible. Pressing ever harder on his collaborator, *Taylor* was unaware that he was already under similar pressures from his Swiss contacts and that the revelation of information sources was being demanded by Captain Hausamann of the *Büro Ha* and by Mayr von Baldegg from the no. 1 post in Lucerne. Pressure also came from the British intelligence service, which was in receipt of Roessler's despatches, certainly from the Swiss, and perhaps also from him directly.

Under these circumstances, when further stretching of the string might bring about a loss of confidence and the rupture of the threads linking Roessler with those who were receiving the results of his work, he acknowledged that he would in fact have to cede the position he had fought for and lost. It cannot be denied that financial considerations might also have played a certain role here, for Roessler was receiving payment for his work. Without going further into the motivation it needs only to be stated that he made up his mind towards the end of 1942, and disclosed to his intelligence contacts the sources which were sending him information. They had been expecting a revelation and this did actually happen, but its scope was very limited. Roessler announced whence his information derived, but he provided his informants with code-names. The first of these was *Werther* who was in the command of the *Wehrmacht* (*OKW*), next there was *Teddy* who was sending reports from the land army command, (*OKH*), then there were *Stefan* and *Ferdinand* (or *Fernand*) of the *Luftwaffe* command, *Olga* of the reserve army command, *Anna* at the Foreign Office, and *Bill* at the armaments office of the land army.[28]

Roessler's reports contained information which must have originated from the highest circles of the Third Reich, and those who had been receiving it had surmised that this was so. Confirmation of this guess by the agent made a profound impression on them. His image grew even larger in their eyes, while at the same time their curiosity as to who was in fact concealed behind the informants' code-names also increased. The pressures exerted on Roessler were greatly multiplied, but this time he would not budge even an inch. No further word of explanation ever left his lips; no-one ever found out either the names or the positions of his informants.[29]

6

In 1966 a book entitled *La guerre a été Gagnée en Suisse, 1939–1945* (The war was won in Switzerland) was published in France. Subtitled *The Roessler affair*, it was written by two journalists, Pierre Accoce and Pierre Quet. During the course of their work they gathered much interesting information, and they elevated Roessler's intelligence achievements during the last war to great heights. In their documentation they advanced an entirely new assertion: the names, surnames and positions of Roessler's secret informants were known to them in full. They were not publishing them because the families might suffer repercussions in Germany; nevertheless they felt they had to at least give their ranks and the initial of the surname of each, and in some cases the first name also. They were allegedly: Generals Helmuth S., Hermann F., Rudolf G., Fritz T., Georg T., Colonel O., Major K., and Captains S., A., and O.[30]

This caused uproar amongst historians, amongst witnesses of the events, and above all in German society. The question of Roessler's secret contacts had been a subject of great interest for many years; many books, treatises and articles had been written about the matter; researchers had sought documents, interviewed witnesses and racked their brains as to how the mystery could be solved. So it was no wonder that the French revelations attracted great attention. The sensation proved to be short-lived however, because the authors, under great pressure from several quarters, were unluckily forced to admit that they had in fact made the whole thing up. None the less it proved once again that the problem was not only still current, but increasingly more fascinating. [31]

Throughout the duration of the war when strict secrecy was in force hardly anyone knew about the problem at all, but as soon as the fighting was over, when people set about writing up its history the mysterious man from Lucerne and his secret informants emerged to take up a prominent position. People began to examine his background, his life, his opinions and his politics, and they soon found satisfactory answers to all the questions, yet no-one succeeded in penetrating the mystery of his intelligence contacts. This was the more staggering because the individuals who were directly involved in these affairs were still living. Above all, Roessler himself was alive and so were Sándor Radó, Captain Hausamann, Dr Xaver Schnieper and also

Otto Pünter. Some of the concealed informants must have survived the war as well, yet no information could be found anywhere, nor did any authentic witness or document come to light which could explain the matter. Historians and writers who were interested in this puzzle— and there were those who were totally engrossed—were forced through sheer necessity into the realm of conjecture, speculation and supposition.

Other wartime mysteries were being examined and explained at the same time, and Roessler's achievements came to be linked with the *Red Orchestra* affair which had been revealed then. This association was further supported by the belief on the part of some researchers, incorrect as it happens, that Roessler was a Communist. If that were the case it would be easy to assume that he was in collusion with the group consisting of Trepper, Schulze-Boysen and Harnack, from which he used to receive his important information. It might in fact have been thus—all the more so, since Roessler had met Schulze-Boysen in Berlin once, when he could have discussed and determined collaboration procedures personally.[32]

There is no reason to reject the possibility of such a collaboration, but in considering it two factors must be taken into account. The first is the fact that the *Red Orchestra* was already in direct contact with Sàndor Radó (see chapter 4, p. 48). Why would an additional, difficult contact with Roessler have been maintained, when moreover he had no personal radio links with Moscow, which meant that he had to pass on all his reports destined for Russia to Radó. The second factor, considerably more important than the first, was the liquidation of the *Red Orchestra* by the Gestapo in the autumn of 1942, whereas Roessler's 'finest hour' in fact came just about that time. We also need to remember that Trepper's organization never penetrated the highest circles of the Third Reich, which was actually where Roessler obtained his most important information.[33] So even if Communist allies of Moscow were providing him with some information, this must have comprised only a fragment of what he obtained and it would have applied only to the early years of his operation.

The inquiries into Roessler's secret informants continued incessantly and the various researchers came to all manner of conclusions. Some thought that he obtained his information from deserters, industrialists and diverse enemies of Nazism scattered among various departments. Some were of the opinion that it was passed on to him simply by the Swiss secret service,[34] while others published revelations appropriate to sensational novels. One of these authors, Bernd Ruland, in his book *Die Augen Moskaus*, which was published in 1973, stated that Roessler's informants were in fact two women working in the communications headquarters of the *Wehrmacht*. They made copies of the most secret telegrams and, thanks to the exceptional carelessness of the security forces, they were able to smuggle these out to someone who rushed them to Lucerne. One of these women was said to have been the daughter of an officer who belonged to the anti-Hitler conspiracy, the other the daughter of a Communist who had been killed in the Spanish civil war. The author of these revelations had allegedly been their superior, aware of what they were doing, but keeping silent. To complete the picture of this classic tale of fiction there was supposed to be a document, drawn up by the two women and certified by a notary, deposited in a Swiss bank awaiting more favourable times.[35]

The former chief of German intelligence in the East, Reinhard Gehlen, went a long way in his fantastic conjectures concerning Martin Bormann, one of Hitler's closest aides, who shared the fate of the *Führer* in the underground bunker in Berlin in the final weeks of the war. According to Gehlen, Bormann was a Soviet spy.[36]

The German historian Wilhelm von Schramm was also concerned with Bormann, but he had specific reasons.[37] His intention was above all to attempt to draw attention away from the German officer corps which in his opinion was incapable of collaborating with the enemies of the Third Reich, regardless of the conduct of the Nazis. We now reach a very important point in our deliberations: could Roessler's informants possibly have been conspirators organized within the framework of a *Black Orchestra*?

In the course of my work on this subject I carried out interviews and corresponded with several senior German officers who had occupied highly placed positions in the war (General Leo Hepp; Colonel Karl Otto Hoffmann of the *Luftwaffe*; and Captain Johannes Möller and Captain Heinz Bonatz of the Navy), and all these expressed the opinion that the long-standing traditions of the officer corps, combined closely with a respect for the military oath, ruled out such a possibility. Even the most determined opponents of Hitler and National Socialism if they served in the armed forces, would never have taken such a step. This point of view is repeated in declarations by many other Germans and in many publications, as well as by von Schramm. But was this really the case? Had there not already arisen a disparity in opinion about the notion of treason?

Viewing the whole problem from a distance of many years and knowing many facts which had been cloaked in secrecy during the war, we are today able to determine what the nature of a political military conspiracy could have been and how it would have differed from other underground operations directed against the authorities at the time of the Third Reich. For the sake of contrast we should first take a look at the *Red Orchestra*. Leopold Trepper's activities were concerned only with intelligence; they had been initiated at the order of the chief of Soviet intelligence and the Germans who participated in such work were betraying their country, but nothing more. The motives of the Schulze-Boysen/Harnack group were different initially, but the final result was the same. All those who were working for the *Red Orchestra* were in the pay of a foreign power which was at war with their own country and represented a system which was not at all better than Hitler's. None from this group intended to take over power after the overthrow of National Socialism, nor did they have the support of any stratum of society.

In the case of the *Black Orchestra* the matter presented itself quite differently. The initially informal contact which linked about fifty or sixty people who had begun to collude shortly after Hitler had come to power evolved in the course of several years into a widely branching conspiracy of the nature of a secret internal opposition. It was not a foreign agency; it was not financed from outside; and it received support in conservative circles, among the clergy, from industry and from the officer corps. Its aim was the overthrow of Hitler's government and of National Socialism; its members were ready to take over power and had selected candidates for all the more important government and military posts, starting from the head of state.[38]

It has happened many times in the course of history that the political opposition in a given country unable to make a stand against the clique in power has sought support from its neighbours. This is what occurred in the case of the *Black Orchestra*. Its leadership, knowing that Hitler was preparing for another war, and expecting a further defeat and the destruction of Europe, decided on a step that was immensely far-reaching: it made contact with two countries which had been opponents of Germany in the First World War—Britain and

France—and warned their governments about the German intentions (see chapter 4, pp. 51–2). Was this treason? Was it acting against the interests of the state? Opinions on this subject have been very divided, but we can say today with hindsight and the knowledge that the Russians occupied Berlin, that perhaps it might not be.

The reasoning needs to be carried further however. The conspirators were counting on the intervention of the Western democracies; but they were disappointed. Austria came to be occupied, and the capitulation conference took place in Munich. This was followed by the dismemberment of Czechoslovakia, the pact with Stalin, and the attack on Poland. At last the Western powers shifted, and declared war on Germany, but they did not undertake any action, and Hitler carried off another victory. His popularity in Germany grew enormously, while the chances of a coup d'état with aid from outside decreased to nil. Yet action was essential; Hitler had to be removed even if it meant losing the war, as long as the price to be paid could be reduced to the minimum. Soviet Russia, the temporary ally at this juncture, was lurking in the East, waiting while the bloody war in the West continued as long as possible. In such a situation could not the conspirators of the *Black Orchestra* have turned their thoughts to Switzerland and the creation of a channel through which important information could be sent out to the West? After all Roessler was one of their own people; he belonged to the *Herrenklub* in Berlin, he had many friends in important positions in the armed forces, and he came from the same background as they. Could it not be possible that he might have gone to Switzerland in silent understanding with them in the first place, and that this might have been planned several years before the war?

This possibility certainly existed; it is confirmed by the fact that in the first months after Roessler came to live in Switzerland he was already active as a writer and demonstrating an astonishing amount of knowledge of the affairs of the Third Reich and great accuracy in predicting future events. There is significance also in the fact that he undertook intelligence work just before the war, entering into collaboration with *Büro Ha* and submitting excellent material straight away (see chapter 1, p. 14). At that time Stalin was still Hitler's ally and there was no question of sending reports out to the East, but these were needed badly by the western allies. Could intelligence cooperation between the *Black Orchestra* and Roessler have been justified

77

morally? Knowing the nature of the *Black Orchestra* and the reasons for its existence, we must give an affirmative answer.

Finally there remains one further aspect of such a co-operation: was it possible for the German conspirators to continue this collaboration when Hitler struck in the East and Roessler began sending his reports via Radó to Moscow?

The answer is very difficult, for the men who started the anti-Hitler underground movement, grouped together within the *Black Orchestra*, belonged to the conservative elements: the clergy, great landowners, rich industrialists and high ranking officers. They could not under any circumstances have wished Stalin to win, then wait for their country to be invaded by the Red Army. For them it would mean the end of the world they knew, the loss of everything they possessed and to which they were most devoted. The exchange of Hitlerism for Stalinism, combined with the defeat of their country, would have made no sense at all.

However, as the war went on, the situation began to change and younger people with less orthodox views began to join the ranks of the conspirators. To these belonged Colonel von Stauffenberg, who, although an aristocrat, saw the future of his country based on the lower classes. Moreover the unwillingness of the Western Allies to ally themselves with the men of the *Black Orchestra*, simply forced them to look to the East if they wanted to get rid of Hitler at any price. Could they have worked with Soviet intelligence?

For if not from them, where could Roessler have obtained his information, the value of which increased to unprecedented heights, reaching a peak just at the moment when the fortunes of war in the East were in the balance and when Russia needed all the help she could get?

7

General Franz Halder, the former chief of the German general staff, who had miraculously escaped the great purge which was carried out after the attempt on Hitler's life (although he had been arrested) expressed the following opinion in an interview he gave to the journal *Der Spiegel* in 1967: 'Almost every offensive operation of ours was betrayed to the enemy even before it appeared on my desk.'[39]

This statement must have contained a fair amount of exaggeration, for it is hard to imagine that the secret communications of a foreign

11 Sándor Radó

12 Helene Radó

13 Otto Pünter

14 Alexander Foote

15 Margrit Bolli

16 Edmond Hamel

17 Olga Hamel **18** Johann Wenzel

19 Victor Sukulov-Gurevich
(Captain Kent)

20 Leopold Trepper

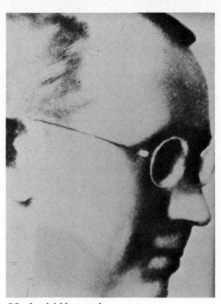

21 Harro Schulze-Boysen

22 Arvid Harnack

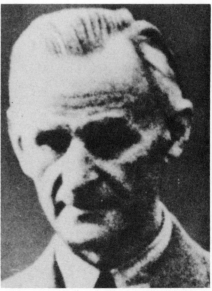

23 Ludwig Beck

24 Carl Geordeler

25 Claus Schenk von Stauffenberg

26 Wilhelm Canaris

27 Hans Oster

28 Heinrich Himmler

secret service could have been faster than German army communications, but it nevertheless contained a good deal of truth. Indeed the reports which passed from Roessler to Radó contained information which was not only highly important but also related to matters which had been decided at the last moment.[40] The speed with which information from the decision centre in Germany reached Switzerland was so great that conventional means of communication have to be ruled out. No courier route, even if such a route could possibly have existed, would have been able to deliver Hitler's most recent orders to Lucerne within twenty-four hours. It would have been theoretically possible for someone to have transmitted them by radio using a complex code; this hypothesis has been put forward, but it needs to be rejected. The security and monitoring services in Hitler's field headquarters and in the *Wehrmacht* command were too efficient to allow anyone to pursue such a risky game successfully for several years.

Having established the importance of Roessler's information and the high speed with which it travelled, we need, in seeking an explanation of how this was made possible, to turn our attention in the direction of the British intelligence service. It was operating very effectively at that time; it must have had informants deep within the German commands and it must have been capable of obtaining information of this calibre; but how could it have passed it on to Lucerne in such a short space of time? To answer this question we need to draw aside further the veil which until recently concealed one of the greatest secrets of the last war: *Enigma*.

It was only many years after the war that numerous researchers and historians who had been dealing with the Roessler affair for years learned for the first time of the story of the German cypher machine, the secret of which had been broken by the Poles and made use of extensively by the British at Bletchley Park.[41] They knew nothing about it before and so they could not consider it in the course of their conjectures. Yet the introduction of *Enigma* into the Roessler affair might help to explain this fascinating puzzle. Since the British were reading the most secret radio messages, and within twelve to fifteen hours at that, without the Germans being aware of it at all, there did exist a real possibility that this information could be sent on to Switzerland within the twenty-four hours. Was this happening, and what proof is there if it was? Until we have access to the archives of the British secret service and until all documents relating to *Enigma* are made available we cannot obtain the evidence, but the theory is no less worthy of consideration.

After the collapse of France Great Britain in effect stood alone, for those military formations of the nations occupied by Hitler which had managed to get to the British Isles were few in numbers and unarmed. Therefore the British Government looked constantly towards the east and followed closely every action of the Germans in relation to Soviet Russia, for it foresaw that the opportunist friendship between Hitler and Stalin would probably come to an end. The British Ambassador bore with Molotov's arrogance and kept in constant contact with him, for one of his tasks was to pass on to the Russians important information concerning the Germans. Sometimes it came from Bletchley Park and Churchill himself saw to it that it was sent on to Moscow, naturally with the strictest instructions that the Russians were never to be told in what way it had been obtained. The fact of this straightforward, diplomatic route has been confirmed by Peter Calvocoressi in his latest book, *Top Secret Ultra*, and although controversy has already arisen, in that Major Crankshaw has publicly denied that he was the go-between, it must be accepted that Peter Calvocoressi's statement is most convincing.[42] Through this channel Churchill sent Stalin a warning that Hitler was preparing an attack on him and that it would probably take place about the middle of June 1941.

The German invasion of Russia, which opened up a new, huge front, was for Great Britain a near miracle and therefore Churchill at once spoke over the radio, offering Russia every possible assistance. In a very short time, with the help of the United States and Canada, this reached colossal dimensions in the form of military equipment, food and every sort of supplies.

The existence of the eastern front and Russia's holding up the German attack was so important for the further course of the war that nothing could be neglected that might be of help to Stalin. Therefore the amount of intelligence material that reached Soviet hands via the British Embassy in Russia was stepped up, but it very soon turned out that Stalin was not making any use of it. His morbid suspicions made him reject anything suggested by the West. He completely ignored the warnings received of the German preparations for attack and almost paid for it by a crushing defeat. He saved himself at the very last moment, but the situation on the eastern front was critical, so another way had to be found by which important intelligence material could reach Russia. It had to be a way which would arouse no suspicions. Surely one of the oldest intelligence methods would have had to be used and a way found discreetly to pass on important information to the Soviet intelligence network. If this succeeded, Moscow would accept the information as authentic and make appropriate use of it.

It would have been possible to seek secret contacts with various prominent Soviet intelligence posts, but Switzerland presented itself as being the likliest of all possibilities, for Rudolf Roessler was operating there, in collaboration with Sándor Radó. The British intelligence service probably had direct links with *Lucy Ring*, but it could also have made use of the help of the Swiss intelligence service, which had continual liaison with Roessler via the *Büro Ha* and Dr Baldegg. Moreover the British embassy in Switzerland was functioning quite normally and its link between London and the Swiss intelligence service must have been discreet, fast and effective.

Enigma's connection with Roessler and the Soviet intelligence agency in Switzerland, was argued most cogently by Constantine Fitzgibbon,[43] and immediately gave rise to further speculations, which reached considerably greater depths than the early hypotheses. Since the *Lucy Ring* was capable of being such an efficient go-between in conveying information from the British secret service to Moscow, might we not assume that it had been set up by the British secret service in the first place? During the course of its long history British intelligence had already achieved a reputation for long-term operations, always looking ahead to the future and seeking new and unorthodox solutions. This theory remains suspended in mid air, as does the opinion that Roessler's post might have been created shortly before the war by the *Black Orchestra*.

Pursuing this line of thought further we could also place a question-mark beside the name of the English radio operator, Alexander Foote, who was working for Radó. The suggestion might be made that he was a double agent, working for the British intelligence service, but this theory does not seem to have any solid foundation. The fact that Foote fought in the Red Brigades during the Spanish Civil War, that he was later recruited into Soviet military intelligence and that he served it faithfully in Switzerland, does not rule out the possibility of his double role, on the contrary. What does definitely rule it out was his going to Moscow after the war. What double agent would behave like that? Even if he himself was so naïve, his British superior officers would never have allowed it. To put himself voluntarily into the hands of people suspicious of everyone, and whom he had deceived, to expose himself to the risk of cruel interrogation and to be forced to disclose all the secrets he knew, that would be madness.

Another possibility must be considered connected on the one hand with the secret of *Enigma* and on the other with another secret, also only uncovered after the war, but dating from much earlier: the matter of the Soviet spy network in Great Britain started up in the thirties at Cambridge University; of Burgess, Maclean, Blunt, but above all of 'Kim' Philby.

This member of the upper middle class, who, thanks to his background, education and connections, got into the intelligence service and during the war found himself in Section Five of MI6, had for several years before the war belonged to the Soviet spy network. He was led into it by a false philosophy of life, which permitted him to betray his own country for some illusory international ideas, which were nothing more than cunningly operated tinsel in the hands of Russian imperialism. Philby, by means of his high rank in the intelligence service, had access to the secret information sent from Bletchley Park through the Special Liaison Unit to a very few selected people.[44] One of them was his direct superior, the head of Section Five, Colonel Felix Cowgill, who had no secrets from him and when he was away on official journeys left Philby in full charge as his deputy. At such times this very intelligent and artful Soviet spy could study at will the despatches sent from Bletchley Park, de-ciphered by the cryptanalysts. They contained many of the most secret German orders and decisions, some of them concerning the eastern front and all those things which went to Moscow from Roessler via Radó.[45]

Is it not possible that Philby was this link which, without permission from his superiors, passed on to Switzerland and Roessler information important to the Soviets?[46] Of course, he would have had to be very careful and limit his activity in this respect to the most important information. He would have been only one of Roessler's informers. Naturally the question arises as to what kind of communication he would have used, but we face the same problem in connection with other people who co-operated with Roessler.

It might have happened thus, who knows? Witnesses are either dead or maintain silence and documents are not accessible. Any of the above solutions might have been used and the fact that today even the recognized authorities consider it to be impossible does not settle the question. Let us imagine that ten years ago someone had stated that *Enigma* had been broken and that British Intelligence had read the top-secret German dispatches. The most eminent authorities would have said at once: 'Nonsense, impossible!'—and yet today we know that this was so and we discuss the matter in the same way as many other authenticated, historical facts.

We are faced by a puzzle which probably will only be solved by time.

6 Canaris

1

Between the 9th and 16th of September 1939, near Kutno, between Poznań and Warsaw, about 100 kilometres to the west of the Polish capital, the first great battle of the Second World War took place. German columns plunged onto Polish soil from three sides: from the north, the west and the south, but the attack was most ferocious on the Berlin-Poznań-Warsaw axis where the Polish divisions put up the most vigorous resistance: they were defending their capital. The Polish infantry and cavalry, with poor artillery cover and a decimated air force, were unable to halt the German armoured columns, but courage and decision to fight to the last, with generals dying in the front line alongside their soldiers, evened the balance and managed for a few days to neutralize the Germans' technical superiority.

Nevertheless, within a few weeks Polish resistance was crushed everywhere, a task made easier by the advance of the Red Army as a consequence of the pact between Hitler and Stalin. Warsaw was forced to capitulate and the two invaders occupied the whole country. Thousands of families were left homeless while thousands more wandered around the country looking for shelter, having been evacuated during hostilities. Among them was Halina Szymańska, a handsome young women with three little daughters. She was the wife of the last Polish military attaché in Berlin, Colonel Antoni Szymański, and had left for Poland just before the war began. She had gone to some distant relations near Lublin, to the south-east of Warsaw. Her husband had remained in the German capital and she felt fear for his safety mingled with pain, humiliation and fear for the whole country and its people. At the end of the fighting she began to wonder how she could get to Warsaw where her parents lived and where perhaps she might learn something of her husband. The trains were not yet running, all private cars had been requisitioned and in any case there was no petrol; how was she to make this journey with three small children? Turning over various ideas, she was struck suddenly by a thought which at first seemed to her impractical and even dangerous: could she play on the fact that she was the wife of the last Polish military attaché in Berlin? Wavering between fear and hope and frantically looking for some way out, using her knowledge of German, she eventually took the dangerous step of approaching on the street a German major, who appeared to her to have an open and honest face. She told him who she was and expressed her desire to get to Warsaw to discover her husband's fate.

The officer at first looked at her as if she were mad, but stopped to collect his thoughts.[1] After a moment he asked if she remembered anyone in Berlin who could vouch for her. Then before her eyes appeared a short trim figure in admiral's uniform whom she had met several times and who had always aroused in her a feeling of friendship and trust. Yes, she knew Admiral Canaris.

The officer's indifferent face immediately came alive. He looked at her in quite a different way and began to ask questions. When she answered them all rapidly and without hesitation, he took her by the arm and led her into the doorway of the nearest house. In a few sentences he told the startled woman that she could rely on him, that her answers were all correct and that she was to go to a certain place the next day where a military car would be waiting for her. She would, however, go not to Warsaw, but to Poznań, where she would be able to find out about her husband much quicker.[2]

This one-day journey remained forever in her memory. They motored through countryside over which only a fortnight previously German armoured and motorized columns had driven, supported by dive-bombers in the air. Everywhere there were burnt-out villages, destroyed bridges and roads pitted with great bomb-craters. The fields were strewn with broken and motionless military equipment, scattered paper and the remains of horses; the bottoms of ditches were filled with the corpses of those who had fled from collapsing bildings only to be cut down by bullets from low-flying aircraft. They frequently had to leave the road to follow temporary diversions avoiding huge bomb-craters on which Polish soldiers, now prisoners of war were working, urged on by the shouts of the Germans in charge. The silent, expressionless people raised their heads and stared at the passing staff car. Their gaze carried so much unbridled hatred that the young woman hugged her children to her and made herself as inconspicuous as possible She could see that they took her for a

German and burning tears of humiliation rolled down her cheeks.

2

It was already mid-October, Hitler and Stalin had made up their minds and the defeated country was divided into two zones of occupation. The eastern part up to the river Bug was taken by the Russians, while the rest fell into the grip of the Germans, who divided it into two zones. Polish lands which before the First World War had belonged to Germany were incorporated into the Reich, together with more distant and important areas that at that time had belonged to Russia. Out of the small remainder, including Warsaw and Kraków, was formed the *General Gouvernement*, where Poles were allowed to live.[3]

Poznań was naturally on the territories incorporated into the Reich and the Germans forthwith began to germanize it and to move great numbers of Poles to the *General Gouvernement*. Within a few weeks the town completely changed its character; only German uniforms were in evidence, new street names were put up in gothic script and the Nazi flag hung over the castle. Simultaneously on the basis of previously prepared lists, Poles who were considered particularly dangerous for the new authorities were arrested and killed. Thus died Colonel Szymański's brother, a minor official, who was on the list for the sole reason that, after the First World War, he and his brother had hung the Polish flag on the town hall after Poznań returned to Poland. He was brutally murdered, without any trial or formal charge.[4]

Halina Szymańska, driven to Poznań by military car without any difficulties, took shelter with some distant relations of her husband, who by some miracle had managed to retain a large flat, and began to take stock of her situation. The German officer, who had helped her, had remained near Lublin, and for the time being there was no one to help her, so she waited for the moment when she could find out about her husband.

At the beginning of November she managed to discover that shortly military attachés of neutral countries would be coming from Berlin to Poznań to see the battlefield at Kutno, which the German army wished to show them. A faint hope stirred of meeting those officers whom she knew well. She especially hoped to meet the Swede, with whom she had been particularly close, since he had been studying Polish and was interested in Polish affairs. With the help of some friends she managed to get on the route that the passing cars would take. When they stopped, from one of them stepped a short, slim, greying man in the uniform of an admiral. It was Canaris. Mrs Szymańska took a few paces forward, the admiral spotted and immediately recognized her, and quickly came over. They exchanged a few brief sentences.[5]

The Admiral expressed the desire to have a longer talk with her, but if possible discreetly, out of everyone's sight, and he promised to send a car and that they would meet late one evening in the former German consulate. She was not to worry about the curfew, since the same staff car would return her home.

It was a strange conversation, which left her with much to think about. The Admiral turned out to be an easy and accessible person, but was not in the least pro-Polish. Despite his Italian ancestors, he felt German and he considered some German revisionist pretensions justified. He even said that Pomerania always had been and continued to be German and that it had rightly returned to the Reich. When, however, she asked him why he was helping her and whether it might not be embarrassing for him, he replied: 'humanity will not forget for a thousand years what Hitler is doing now'. She felt that the way the war was being prosecuted and above all the treatment of the defeated country's population aroused a certain feeling of revulsion in him.[6]

From their extensive conversation it turned out that Colonel Szymański was almost certainly not in Poland and that if he were, he would be in mortal danger as someone in possession of certain secrets of the Third Reich. If he were lucky, he might reach a neutral country and then get to the West.* She herself ought not to go to Warsaw, for it was already apparent that the occupation would be extremely severe and that her husband's recent appointment would also put her in great danger. She ought to leave for a neutral country as soon as possible and he could arrange this for her. He advised her to go to Switzerland, which would almost certainly not be drawn into the war and would provide a safe and adequate haven. Furthermore, she had three small children whom she had to support and bring up. Just before the war

---

*An exchange of diplomats took place in one of the Baltic states, but the Russians were already in control there and Colonel Szymański was sent to a Soviet prisoner-of-war camp in Starobielsk. He was rescued by a miracle as the result of British intervention. The prisoners of this camp were murdered by the Russians in the same fashion as Polish prisoners from two other camps whose bodies were later discovered in the mass graves at Katyn.

her husband had also been appointed military attaché to Bern and so Switzerland would certainly grant her an entry permit and she need not worry about the rest. It was good advice and to be followed.

The situation of the Poles who were still hanging on in Poznań became so difficult that Canaris billeted one of his officers in the flat where Halina Szymańska was staying. He was there to protect the residents and meanwhile preparations for departure were under way. Further conversations took place and they always left the same impression of being conducted by a cultured and decent man, who was nevertheless a German and had to have some ulterior motive. Merely helping a woman, who after all was a stranger, could not be adequate justification for such kindness which could even draw the attention of the *Gestapo*.

In the second half of December everything was ready, and Mrs Szymańska and her three daughters were driven to Berlin by car. She continued to have a Polish passport, which would undoubtedly have aroused the fury of every German official, had not an accompanying officer arranged everything, thus nobody checked any documents. In Berlin they stayed with a Spanish family with whom Canaris was friendly and, after a few days, this was followed by a lonely train journey to Düsseldorf. The family had its own compartment, and so the other passengers had no contact with them; all three girls spoke good German, but through the night-long journey there was always the fear that perhaps the conductor might turn difficult, or that the youngest girl might say something to him in Polish. Canaris's wife saw them off at the station in Berlin and gave them a small gift, and in Düsseldorf they were met by a specially detailed officer with a car. The journey to the Swiss frontier took place without problems and the frontier formalities also did not last very long. Another train ride followed and within a few hours Halina Szymańska was already in Bern talking to Captain Szczęsny Chojnacki at the Polish legation. It was one of the last days before the first Christmas of the war.[7]

3

It might seem strange, but it was true: Halina Szymańska, who had always been warned by her husband not to get involved in political discussions and not to ask questions, had no idea until she entered the Polish legation in Bern who Admiral Canaris really was. It was only when she mentioned his name as that of the strange German who had given her so much help, that Captain Chojnacki almost leapt from his chair. She was talking about the head of the *Abwehr*, the head of all German Military Intelligence.

This news was of such importance that it was immediately decided that straight after Christmas Mrs Szymańska would go to Paris where the new Polish political and military athorities were situated. She made the trip with Captain Chojnacki and they both explained the situation to the head of Polish Intelligence, Colonel Tadeusz Wasilewski. They were also received by General Kazimierz Sosnkowski who was directing from France an underground military organization in occupied Poland. It was recognized that this was a very important matter and that this friendship with Canaris should be continued at all costs and that in Bern secret contact should be made as soon as possible with the British Legation. The Polish military authorities, honouring their responsibilities as allies, advised Halina Szymańska to get in touch with the Intelligence Service in the greatest secrecy and offer them her services. On her return to Switzerland she took the necessary steps and had several conversations in Bern with the local head of British Intelligence, a Dutchman by descent, Count Frederick Van den Heuvel. The British envoy was at that time David Kelly, who in 1942 was succeeded by Clifford Norton. Van den Heuvel also recognized that this contact with Canaris could be of great significance and after discussion with his superiors in London suggested that she work for them on a regular basis. A monthly salary was agreed and it was also arranged that the children's education would be taken care of. These conversations took place in French and all further reports, which were always oral, were given in this language. All this was arranged in the strictest secrecy and ostensibly Halina Szymańska had become a clerical officer in the Polish legation's cipher department.[8]

After all these unexpected events, preceded by the shock of her country's defeat, all of which had taken place over a short period of time, and after finding accommodation in Bern and putting her children in school, she could at least collect her thoughts and consider everything. She continued to be under the great personal influence of Canaris to whom she was very grateful for all his help, which she could not have expected, but at the same time she could not help wondering what it was that he really wanted from her. Now that she knew that he was the head of German Military Intelligence, his intentions appeared in a quite different light. By helping her and facilitating her departure for Switzerland he had been acting nobly and trying, if only symbolically, to atone for the misery Hitler had brought to Poland, but this could not be an end to it. He was after all a German patriot and occupied a very high position which required the complete trust of the very highest state authorities. Halina Szymańska had never discussed with her husband his military duties and knew nothing about them, but she was well aware that in her present position, particularly after getting in touch with the Intelligence Service, she might have a quite different value in Canaris's eyes. He must probably have anticipated such a sequence of events and now that things had gone according to plan, although he could only guess this, he expected some benefits. He probably hoped that through her and her indiscretion and naivety he would be able to obtain information about the views and morale of the diplomatic circle in Switzerland. Perhaps his hopes were even more far reaching and he hoped that through her he might get a glimpse of the workings of British Intelligence and even of one or two secrets? As a young girl, like all her contemporaries, she had read a great many exciting adventure stories and now she suddenly realized that she herself was unexpectedly on the threshold of similar secret goings-on. She felt a great anxiety: would she be equal to her task, had she really picked the right path? After all this was espionage and only a step away from provocation, blackmail and treason. But then she thought about it. She had been instructed by her own military authorities, there was a war going on which had split her country between two brutal occupiers. Perhaps her doubts and reservations were unjust and perhaps it was quite the reverse and fate had been particularly kind to her and provided her with the opportunity to render the Allies and thus her own country great services? She felt relief, but at the same time she made a decision to be extremely careful.[9]

4

Barely several days had elapsed since her return from France when late one night Canaris appeared at her new flat. He was of course wearing civilian clothes and was incognito, but it was difficult to imagine that the Swiss authorities were unaware of his presence, although there is no proof of this in the Swiss archives.[10] In a long, friendly conversation he asked above all about her living conditions and about everyday and family matters. He promised to ease correspondence with her relatives and even sometimes to bring someone from Poland, but only if that person were not suspected by the *Gestapo* of political activities. Later he kept these promises a number of times.

Their further lengthy conversation dwelt on various matters and touched upon military and political problems. Canaris talked a great deal and freely, but he mentioned a number of questions in a very general sort of way. He did this in the form of opinions on the war's main protagonists, opinions which were both interesting and which ran into the future. He asked for nothing and made no suggestions, but he left the impression that he was eager for his remarks to be taken further, to the right hands. On the way out he promised that he would visit her again.[11]

The instructions from Polish Intelligence stated quite clearly that, in accordance with their agreement, all information would be given exclusively to the Intelligence Service, to which Halina Szymańska faithfully adhered. Poland indeed was also an ally of France and the Polish Government was on French soil as was the reforming Polish army, Poland and France also had many other ties, but the first rule of intelligence and secrecy is to have only a single channel of communication and this had to be followed at any price. This applied also to the Polish authorities and thus in Switzerland only Captain Chojnacki knew what Halina Szymańska was doing. For everyone else she was simply a typist in the cipher department and the wife of an absent military attaché. It had to be so, since Switzerland was penetrated on all sides by German security agents and Canaris's game was exceptionally dangerous and subtle and it was out of the question for the secret to fall into the wrong hands as the result of some carelessness or indiscretion.

Before the end of January a second and final meeting took place with the Admiral, this time in Italy. His adjutant arrived at Mrs Szymańska's and conveyed the information that Canaris would like to have a meeting in Milan, in a hotel. Italy was not yet in the war, the Polish embassy in Rome was still functioning and so a diplomatic passport was adequate. After a secret meeting they went out to dinner and, surrounded by complete strangers, where no one knew or watched them, they were able to have a long conversation. It was only then that the Admiral revealed the real reason for this whole affair, which had quite unexpectedly started near Lublin, taken shape in

Poznań, to assume its final form in Bern. There were various reasons of the greatest importance for which certain information on Germany ought to reach the West. It would take different forms: assessments, forecasts, dates and facts. He himself would no longer get in touch with her, since he was too well known and too exposed, but everything that they were talking about would have certain consequences and should be kept in the greatest secrecy. It was not just a question of people who could lose their lives as the result of some indiscretion, but of the eventual result, which could expedite the end of this dreadful war which threatened the existance of whole nations. He had complete trust in her, she was a Pole and belonged to the nation which had first learnt the real face of Nazism. The German vice-consul in Zürich, Hans Bernd Gisevius, would shortly get in touch with her in great secrecy. She should have complete trust in him and he would bring the information they had been discussing.

Halina Szymańska heard him out in silence, although she managed to control herself only with great difficulty. She had expected all sorts of surprises, had seen herself in the role of someone threatened by questions, entreaties and pressure, she had steeled herself for difficult talks for which she had no preparation, but what she did hear was a complete surprise. The short, slim man sitting before her and examining her carefully now suddenly appeared to her in a completely different light. She well remembered her husband's advice and just bowed her head and asked no questions.[12]

5

In 1933 a young man from a German middle-class family, which had already produced a number of civil servants, passed his final law examinations. He was Hans Bernd Gisevius, a giant of a man almost two metres tall with broad shoulders and weighing over 100 kilogrammes. This huge body was topped by a strange baby face, which made a very peculiar impression.[13]

The young lawyer was also planning a career in the Civil Service and tried to get in, but he was having difficulty. The Nazis had just come to power and there was a great expansion of the police services into which quite new people were drafted. Not only were people sought for simple tasks, but also others with higher education, particularly lawyers. Gisevius did not belong to the party, but he must have had good references, since he was accepted and was posted to the

Gestapo. He worked there for five years as an adviser, but this type of occupation did not suit him at all. This was the time of the merciless destruction of opponents of the new order, of concentration camps, mass arrests, the persecution of the Jews and lawlessness. The young man's family and cultural traditions clearly showed him that he was serving people who were bringing the country to ruin, and he had continual problems and conflicts with his superiors, so he decided to quit. He had already some experience and this time a transfer to the Civil Service, specifically to the Ministry of Internal Affairs, was not too difficult. There he found himself in the autumn of 1938[14]

Alongside the police forces Military Intelligence was also expanding and the deputy head of the *Abwehr*, Colonel Hans Oster, tried to swell and improve his numbers with suitable people. He was a resolute opponent of Nazism and thus sought candidates of similar views, in particular those who had at first been supporters of the new system or had co-operated with it, but who had later changed their minds and left. He had already had the opportunity of discovering Gisevius's views, since the latter had earlier been in touch with Canaris and had informed him of *SS* and *Gestapo* methods. The young lawyer's mind and professional training qualified him for the difficult work of intelligence, so Oster decided to bring him into his group. This was not easy, since employing in the *Abwehr* someone who had previously worked in the *Gestapo* required an appropriate document from this institution ('a clean bill of health'). Such a document, however, was out of the question, since Gisevius had left the ranks of the police after various difficulties, so Colonel Oster resorted to subterfuge. He had numerous opportunities in various directions and he had at his disposal an office specializing in forged documents, so he took advantage of this and through discreet and trusted people simply had the *Gestapo* reference forged.[15]

At this time relations between Canaris, the head of the *Abwehr*, and Reinhard Heydrich, head of the *Sicherheitsdienst (SD)* were already very strained, although ostensibly they met as friends. Gisevius had already had a number of brushes with the ambitious and brutal head of security and so he had to be careful. Canaris came to the conclusion that his new co-worker, of whom he expected a great deal, should be removed as soon as possible from prying eyes and he decided to send him to Switzerland. It was the beginning of 1939, the war was already appearing on the horizon, and having a trusted man inside a neutral country right in the heart of Europe could pay dividends. The *Abwehr* had the right to issue its own passports without any police or ministerial control, and so Gisevius received such a document and found himself in Zürich in the consulate-general as vice-consul.

Before his departure, the new *Abewhr* employee received some information concerning a number of extremely important matters of much greater secrecy than problems of Military Intelligence. Through Gisevius Canaris wanted to get in touch with the outside world and with people who could help in a conspiracy against Hitler. He had the highest hopes of contacts with the British and the Americans. Gisevius's official task was to examine the cases of various people who were at the time in the small republic and to provide Canaris and Oster with personal verbal reports. This required and justified frequent trips between Zürich and Berlin.

The new vice-consul began his difficult assignment and handled it well, having no trouble with the consulate staff and his diplomatic superior, when quite unexpectedly he began to have difficulty with the head of the *Abwehr* in Switzerland. The latter naturally was unaware of Gisevius' double role, had no knowledge of his connection with the *Schwarze Kapelle*, and so did not understand his behaviour and the frequent journeys. He began to ask subtle questions, became suspicious and eventually requested Berlin that Gisevius be recalled. In fact Gisevius remained, while his suspicious superior left, sent into retirement on the ground of a nervous illness. Such methods were already known forty years ago! The new head turned out to be even worse, but he had to remain. [16]

6

Halina Szymańska had indeed been warned by Canaris that Gisevius would make contact with her, he had been described to her and she had been told how he would identify himself, but she had expected that their first meeting would be preceded by a letter or at least a telephone call. She had no conspiratorial experience and the easy and uncomplicated daily life in Switzerland divorced her even more from any secret activities. She was thus taken by surprise when, at the beginning of February, under cover of evening and the compulsory, wartime blackout, a tall, large man appeared at her door. She invited him in and tried to be polite and natural, but this first conversation was not very successful. Gisevius made a strange impression on her which was difficult to describe. Perhaps it was his appearance, perhaps the contrast of his great bulk with his childish face, but it was enough to prevent her from trusting either the man or what he was saying.[17]

His subsequent visits, always under cover of darkness and always conducted with pedantic caution, showed that her initial impression had been unjustified and that he could be trusted and relied upon, nevertheless their conversations always had a certain element of artificiality. After every visit Mrs Szymańska remembered her meetings with Canaris which had been quite different and much more friendly and easy. Probably his Italian ancestry had something to do with it. He felt a German and wanted to be treated as one and yet in his manner there was a certain southern gentleness and directness. In his words there also rang a great sense of guilt for everything that the Nazis were doing in Poland. Gisevius was quite different: reliable, practical, trustworthy, once you got to know him, but heavy and very Prussian. Having been brought up in an atmosphere of mistrust and even enmity towards the former partitioning powers, reared on history and literature which warned of German militarism and duplicity, she was unable to break her instinctive mistrust. Moreover during his visit Gisevius gave no indication of his feelings for Poland and the other nations which had already suffered at the hands of the Germans. He was anti-Nazi and emphasized this very strongly, but he gave the impression that he was interested solely in overthrowing the system Hitler had created, not in righting wrongs or in blunting German revisionist policies.[18]

It was clear to both parties that they were links in a secret chain betwen Berlin and the West. Halina Szymańska had not the slightest idea of the existence in Germany of an anti-Nazi conspiracy or of its extent, but after her conversations with Canaris and the arrival of Gisevius, she realized that a certain element in German society did not accept Nazi methods and was opposing them. The mere fact that she had become an intermediary between Canaris and the West proved the existence of some internal forces with important people at their head, who were even prepared to co-operate in a German defeat, so long as it came about as speedily and cheaply as possible. They were prepared even to pay such a price for the removal of Hitler. Gisevius naturally had no doubts as to the nature of his contacts with the young Pole. He never inquired who her contacts were and officially did not know that everything they said reached the Intelligence Service, but he must have been well aware of this. In such matters the unsaid is very common.

The German's evening visits were quite frequent, but irregular. His information, always oral, dealt above all with political matters and was not very urgent. It revolved around internal German affairs, relations between the Army and the Party, the morale of the nation, general forecasts of future war aims and the Third Reich's political plans. This was the time of the few months of quiet when the Franco-British front crouched behind the Maginot Line, Allied aircraft appeared over Germany usually dropping leaflets and only at sea did the battle continue unabated.

Suddenly, in April 1940, came the surprise German attack on Denmark and Norway and then Gisevius' visits became more frequent, but he continued to bring information which had no direct connection with the military operations. It appeared that his superiors, thus above all Canaris, did not want to send the Allies details of actual military operations. This would have constituted a clear betrayal of German soldiers, bringing about the deaths of many of them. [19]

At the beginning of May Gisevius brought a warning that within several days a German attack would take place in the West, but he did not give the direction of its thrust. The results of this attack were so unexpected that further conversations with Gisevius assumed a special character. No one had expected such a lightning German victory; memories were still fresh of the years of murderous positional fighting of the First World War; the colossal success of the German war machine made a deep impression on everyone and it was clear that the Zürich vice-consul was inwardly torn. His Prussian heart was filled with the pride that must have overcome every German, and yet simultaneously this same heart contracted with fear at the thought of the future. The conspirators of the *Schwarze Kapelle* had expected that Hitler's victorious progress would be halted in the West and that then their hour would come. The rapid and quite unexpected fall of Paris followed by the Allies' complete rout, destroyed these hopes in a single blow. Hitler's disguised peace overtures towards Great Britain followed shortly and the situation became dangerous. If London were to start discussions with Berlin, not only would the conspirators' chances dwindle to naught, but their future and even personal security would appear in a quite different light.

Gisevius was, however, a resolute man and so, after a moment of indecision, he resumed his evening visits. The Battle of Britain was now being fought and the chances of a German landing on the south coast of England were in the balance, and he brought information on the political aspects of these plans. Then Hitler suffered his first defeat, the invasion of the British Isles was no longer feasible, Gisevius regained his composure and his information began to contain political hints on Soviet-German relations. The months passed and these hints began to increase and overshadow every other subject. At the beginning of 1941 the Russian problem decisively dominated and only the short campaigns in the Balkans against Greece and Yugoslavia, as well as the North Africa theatre, interrupted the regularity of the news coming out of Berlin.

In mid-June Gisevius again appeared at Mrs Szymańska's flat and this time, just as when France had fallen, he was, contrary to his normal behaviour, very excited. He brought the news that within the next week the German attack in the East would begin.[20]

Mrs Szymańska had no idea with whom Gisevius was in touch in Germany and did not know that one of his informants was Hitler's Minister of Finance, Hjalmar Schacht, who was also in secret touch with the secretary of the American Embassy in Berlin, Donald Heath, up to the last moments of American neutrality. It was Schacht who informed Gisevius about the date of the German attack on Russia. This secret collaboration saved his life at the Nuremberg trials, where he was acquitted.[21]

7 The Most Secret Contacts

1

On 16 June 1940, a few days before the surrender of France, one of the German armoured detachments which had reached the small locality of La Charité-sur-Loire, about 150 km west of Dijon, intercepted a train at the station full of refugees and documents being evacuated from Paris. Amongst these there were two boxes belonging to the French General Staff which contained reports, plans and notes concerning Franco-Swiss talks on co-operation between the armed forces of the two countries in the event of a German attack on Switzerland across the north-west border.

The Germans considered that these documents were of great importance, for they provided evidence of Switzerland's duplicity when she was attempting to demonstrate to them that she was completely neutral. The affair reached Hitler even, and since he was still thinking about uniting all Germans into one state and had a greedy eye on the Germanic cantons of Switzerland (see chapter 1, pp. 4–5) these documents could have spurred him into action. But as luck would have it the imminent danger to Switzerland passed, for France fell without any trouble and there was no need for an attack by way of Switzerland from the region of Geneva; Hitler directed his full attention towards the British Isles, although it was impossible to predict what might happen at a later stage in the war. The chief of Swiss Intelligence, Colonel Roger Masson, was aware that the Germans were in possession of these embarrassing documents, and he sought some means whereby they might be retrieved.

Although Switzerland was of course in sympathy with the nations of the West, related as she was to them by the same way of life, she nevertheless had to co-operate with Germany and to carry on an exchange of trade with her in order not to give any cause for offence. This was a self-evident necessity of life. There were many Swiss firms carrying out work for the German industry, supplying both components and finished products. Within the framework of such trade relations Switzerland received an order towards the end of 1940 for some prefabricated wooden barrack huts for the *SS*. The order came from a large firm in Berlin, *Warenvertrieb GMBH*; its representative was Hans W. Eggen, who had various interests in Lausanne and who held the rank of major in the cavalry reserve. Eggen had joined the *SS* after the Nazis had come to power, was made a *Sturmbannführer* (which corresponded to his substantive rank), and became secretary to Walter Schellenberg, a *Brigadeführer* in the *SS*. Schellenberg was among the closest associates of the chief of the *RSHA*, Reinhard Heydrich, being in charge of Section IV E, which was responsible for counter-intelligence in Germany and the occupied territories on behalf of the *Gestapo*.[1]

The order was accepted by the Timber Syndicate in Switzerland whose representatives were Paul Meyer-Schwertenbach, a captain in the reserve, and Paul Holzach. Meyer had at one time served under Colonel Masson when the latter had commanded an artillery unit, which had allowed him to become well known to him and to be trusted by him completely. Both Meyer and Holzach were working for Swiss Intelligence and rendering valuable services, although they had extensive commercial connections from which they derived substantial incomes. There was nothing unusual in this, for in a small country such as Switzerland not only the intelligence service but almost the entire army consisted of reservists who led ordinary lives following civilian occupations but were ready to be called up at any time (see chapter 1, p. 6). In time of war, and because of the vast expense of maintaining an army 400,000 strong, this method of operation, which drew individuals of independent means—and therefore working disinterestedly—into confidential national matters was fairly widespread. The *Büro Ha* of Captain Hausamann operated on just these principles (see chapter 1, pp. 8–9).

The way these things were done in Germany was different; being a large country and having extensive means, she had for many years boasted a professional army which had no duties other than preparation for war. Obviously there were also individuals there employed by big commercial companies who had international contacts and made use of these for intelligence purposes many a time in the service of the state, but it was not the custom for officers in uniform to carry on commercial business. There were many changes as a result of the Nazis coming to power because of the social upheaval that followed, and there emerged at the top a completely new set of people. Most of these had never had a chance of acquiring wealth and now that the party ruled the country unanimously, wonderful new opportunities opened up before them. The principles of National Socialism were opposed to the accumulation of personal wealth, yet the most highly placed officials of the party, with Göring at their head, ignored this completely. It was not unusual then that the *SS Sturmbannführer* Hans Eggen should conduct extensive business with Switzerland. It was justifiable in his situation to the extent that his frequent trips and numerous connections there enabled him to secure information which he then passed on to Schellenberg. In June 1941 this young general was transferred from the command of Section IV E to that of Section VI of the SS which was responsible for foreign intelligence, and so he urgently needed information of this kind, especially from a sensitive area such as Switzerland which was seething with various secret matters.[2]

Eggen's principal informants were of course Paul Meyer-Schwertenbach and Paul Holzach, the two representatives with whom he was conducting business. He made no attempt to conceal his real identity from them and the Swiss knew exactly with whom they were dealing. It has to be admitted that it must have been impossible for the German, working as he did for the foreign intelligence service *RSHA* and therefore a well informed and discerning individual, to be unaware of the secret connections of the two businessmen. Thus the co-operation must have been conscious on both sides and it must have been mutually advantageous to each. It cannot be denied that they might occasionally have tried to pass each other information which might have been misleading. Nevertheless the two Swiss were down in Schellenberg's records as established informants and they had even been given their own code-names: Meyer appeared as *Senner II* and Holzach as *Senner III*. At this period Colonel Masson had not yet come into contact with Major Eggen at all, yet in Schellenberg's records he bore the code-name *Senner I*.

The western allies, the British and the Americans, knew perfectly well that the Swiss were on their side at heart and that they wished them victory; besides which they gave actual evidence of these feelings. But they understood equally well that Switzerland was living under continual threat from the Germans and that she did not wish to aggravate them in any way. The Swiss-German contacts were a consequence of this; such contacts were kept under surveillance by the western intelligence services but they were to a large extent tolerated. General Guisan, the commander-in-chief of the Swiss army, found out by secret means that a telegram from the German Foreign Minister to his envoy in Bern had found its way into the hands of Allen Dulles, head of American Intelligence in Europe. It contained information taken to Germany by *Senner III* and obtained from *Senner I*, i.e. directly from the head of Swiss Intelligence. Guisan then invited Captain Hausamann from the *Büro Ha* to Interlaken for lunch and in a roundabout way informed him about the situation. Hausamann understood what was required without being given any clear order, and he warned Colonel Masson, his superior, about what was happening. These matters were difficult and delicate, for the danger of indiscretion and even provocation existed everywhere.[3]

Apart from the documents captured by the Germans at La Charité there was also another similar matter which worried Colonel Masson. In 1936 the chief of the Swiss General Staff, Jakob Labhart, had gone to Czechoslovakia to arrange co-operation over intelligence and other confidential matters relating to German armament and the imminent threat which resulted from it, in which both countries were interested. A document confirming the conditions and the details of the established contact was drawn up, and now that the Germans had seized Czechoslovakia this document could easily fall into their hands.[4] The main body of the German forces was at present engaged at the eastern front but the threat to Switzerland, although significantly reduced, had not ceased to be a real one. The German press was continually running attacks on Switzerland, and this was giving rise to anxiety. Some way needed to be found to determine the precise location of the embarassing documents and to create the opportunity of retrieving them; the sharpness of the incessant journalistic attacks needed to be blunted at the very least. Masson realized that his initial contact with the Germans could best be established via Major Eggen, and Paul Meyer arranged a meeting for them in December 1941. After a lengthy discussion the conclusion was reached by both that a meeting should take place next between the chief of Swiss Intelligence and Eggen's superior, Walter Schellenberg.[5]

2

There is a tendency for people who have certain ambitions and who are thwarted in their attempts to achieve prominence to attach themselves to the political group which has succeeded in taking power, and this certainly happened in Hitler's Germany. Walter Schellenberg was to some extent one of these. He did indeed join the National Socialist party in 1934 when it was already in power but the success of his career was due largely to his own abilities and capacity for hard work. While he was a student—he read law, having studied medicine for two years unsuccessfully—following a lecture which implied some criticism of the Church, he caught the attention of Reinhard Heydrich, who recruited him via two of his lecturers. Schellenberg had a brilliant intellect and soon assimilated all the principles of law. He worked unceasingly and in the course of a few years he had become chief assistant to the head of the *Sicherheitsdienst*. He was only 32 years of age when he was made a *Brigadeführer* of the *SS*, which was equivalent to the rank of general. The speed of his upward progression was restrained only by his poor health—he suffered from liver trouble.[6]

However, in a system such as the one Hitler had established even the greatest application and the sharpest intelligence were not sufficient in themselves to guarantee a good career; Schellenberg therefore adopted the path Heydrich had taken. The methods used by the head of the security service had proved effective—he had attained high position at a young age and within a short space of time—so he must have known the secret of success. Schellenberg began to keep indexed records of all his affairs and anyone he met who interested him. Each had a separate file containing personal information relating to his background, family relationships, contacts, inclinations and future aspirations. The cabinet in which these files were locked swelled with every day that passed. Schellenberg also took after Heydrich in employing complicated means to secure his office against unwanted visitors and his person against unexpected attacks. Although there was no friendship between them, nor even any degree of sympathy, both men were similar to the extent that both endeavoured to reach their goals by means of short cuts and both were capable of anything which might facilitate this, but while Heydrich embodied vitality and physical force, Schellenberg was, perhaps because of his health, superficially extremely mild, polite and even prepossessing. He was able to converse articulately about music, literature and art with an informed understanding of the subject. Beneath the facade however there was concealed a subtle calculating attitude towards the people he met and the matters he dealt with.[7]

From the middle of 1941 when Schellenberg took over *RSHA* foreign intelligence he must have had an interest in Switzerland, but the idea of a meeting between German and Swiss Intelligence issued not from him but from Colonel Masson.[8] For Switzerland the question of maintaining neutrality was of greater importance than anything else, but the threat from Germany was ever present and might now be even more serious than at the beginning of the war, for the situation at the eastern front was not progressing in accordance with Hitler's plans. It might have been assumed that his total engrossment with the area would have drawn his attention away from other matters, but this was not in fact the case. Switzerland, situated as she was on the way to Italy, wealthy, with highly developed industries and large reserves in her banks, an area of espionage intrigues, had always been an object of Hitler's interest. He could attack her purely for the reason that the chance of gaining a victory in Russia was becoming remote, and he needed an instant success combined with material advantages. This possibility had to be taken into account and it was therefore all the more necessary for Switzerland to make the greatest possible effort to extract from the Germans the compromising documents which might easily accelerate and give grounds for Hitler's decision.

In the middle of 1942, at the very time Colonel Masson was in a quandary as to how he should proceed, one of his intelligence contacts who was attached to the German embassy in Bern brought the news that the important documents were being held by the *Sicherheitsdienst*, in Berlin.[9] This finally tipped the balance; after a long discussion with General Guisan, the commander-in-chief of the Swiss army, the two officers came to the conclusion that a meeting with Schellenberg should not only be recommended but was in fact essential.

It was brought about on 8 September 1942 in the small locality of Waldshut in Germany, close to the Swiss border, to which Masson was taken by Major Eggen; the Swiss officer crossed the bridge on the Rhine below Laufenburg on foot and entirely unaccompanied. This initial meeting was a difficult one, for neither side really knew what to do or how to begin. Schellenberg felt more at ease, for he was on his own territory and was in no danger, whereas Masson, although representing a neutral country, could expect a trap. The main subject he had come to discuss was the documents which were threatening

Swiss neutrality, but he had first of all to sound out his opponent's intentions and attitudes. Since Schellenberg had accepted the proposal of a meeting, he must have had some purpose of his own in mind, and if this was the case, then he would be affable and compliant. This was confirmed straight away as soon as the two men shook hands, each measuring up the other wth a penetrating gaze. Schellenberg, knowing that he was dealing with the Head of Intelligence, who ought to suspect a trick at all times, immediately suggested they should leave the hotel and make for the bank of the Rhine where no one could overhear or disturb them.

Colonel Masson broached two subjects. The first was the arrest of an employee of the Swiss consulate in Stuttgart, Ernst Mörgeli, on a charge of espionage. Stuttgart was the place where units of the *Abwehr* and *Sicherheitsdienst* which were particularly interested in Switzerland were based, so there was little wonder that the young officer had fallen into a trap. He had been arrested and after standing trial had received the death sentence. Naturally this had not been carried out, because a foreign intelligence agent was as a rule exchanged for an agent of one's own who had tripped up on foreign ground; but the matter remained to be settled. To Masson's great surprise Schellenberg guaranteed his release without the slightest fuss. [10]

This prompted the conjecture that the meeting meant more to the German than was immediately apparent; Masson then raised another matter which was of consequence to his country. There was a press agency in operation since 1941 in Vienna, run by two Swiss, Nazi sympathizers Franz Burri and Ernest Leonhard, which was disloyally circulating attacks on Switzerland, undermining her neutrality and attempting to discredit the commander-in-chief of her army, General Henri Guisan. Masson was aware that there were grounds for these attacks, for Switzerland did sympathize with the Western allies; she controlled the black-out of her cities so that lights which were suddenly switched on could guide night flights, she tolerated enforced landings on her territory, and she collaborated closely with British and American Intelligence, although this was not officially made known. Again the Swiss officer was astonished when Schellenberg at once promised that he would curb the aggressiveness of the Austrian agency.

It looked as if the young *SS* general was prepared to make a number of friendly gestures and that it might be possible for Masson to raise the important matter for which he had risked the dangerous trip, but he hesitated. The documents which placed Switzerland and her neutrality in a disadvantageous position were allegedly within Schellenberg's reach, but it could hardly be assumed that a single meeting would bring about the intended result.

This first meeting was then concluded, but not before one further significant exchange had taken place. Schellenberg handed Masson a copy of a telegram which the American military attaché in Bern had sent to Washington in 1940, containing the information, derived from Masson, that 25 German divisions were preparing for an attack on Switzerland. After reading it Masson returned the piece of paper to Schellenberg; he explained that the telegram did not constitute evidence that Swiss Intelligence was collaborating with the West since the information in it had been communicated officially at a meeting at which all the military attachés, including the German, had been present. Masson realized immediately that the Germans must be deciphering the Americans' codes, and that Schellenberg was either boasting to him about this achievement or else warning him of its implications.[11]

3

Nearly five weeks later the two parties met once again, this time in Switzerland. On 16 October Schellenberg and Eggen, in civilian clothes, crossed the border at dawn, unseen by anyone. They were picked up by Colonel Masson's chauffeur and taken to Wolfsberg, Meyer-Schwertenbach's estate on the edge of Lake Constance. It was a very secluded place, far from the gaze of unbidden observers, where the discreet but most vigilant cloak of Swiss security would be able to fulfil its purpose with relative ease. This was extremely important, for the local population was at that time living in a state of great excitement, aroused by German-inspired Nazi demonstrations which were taking place in Switzerland. If Schellenberg were to be recognized a scandal might blow up which would wreck Colonel Masson's delicate ploy. Besides it was necessary to take into account the possibility of an act of provocation on the part of the Germans. Swiss Intelligence was well aware that the Nazis were not particular in their methods, and often engineered situations which allowed them to launch an assault on the pretext that provocation had been given. This stratagem had been employed prior to the attack on Poland, when they staged a raid on the radio transmitter at Gliwice in which prisoners from the Sachsenhausen concentration camp were made to take part, dressed in Polish uniforms. [12] Similarly, an attack had been launched on Holland using the pretext that she had permitted two British Intelligence agents, Major Payne Best and Captain Henry Stevens, to operate within her territory, in collaboration with the *Schwarze Kapelle*, with the purpose allegedly of preparing a revolution in Germany and the overthrow of Hitler. Actually Schellenberg himself had made contact with them, and he later lured them into a trap; on 9 November 1939, with the aid of a special unit of the *SS*, he seized them in the Dutch town of Venlo, close to the German border. [13] It was not the German but the Dutch frontier which had been violated, yet Goebbel's propaganda machine put a different interpretation on the incident. Now, if Hitler decided that this was the right moment for an attack on Switzerland, the murder of Schellenberg, a general of the *SS*, who had after all set out for the territory of a neutral country purely in her own interests, would have made an excellent pretext. This is why Masson's people, unseen and unheard, were observing each step taken by Schellenberg and his companion. Besides the two visitors, Colonel Masson and the host, also present was Paul Holzach, Eggen's close acquaintance, who had arranged the initial meeting between Schellenberg and Masson. [14]

The Swiss Intelligence chief anticipated his second meeting with the Nazi general with greater anxiety than the first. Both Schellenberg's promises had been fulfilled, in a short space of time moreover. Ernst Mörgeli had been released and put on a plane to Zürich, and the press agency in Austria (*International Press Agentur*) suddenly ceased its attacks. It was obvious that the contact which had been established was of consequence to Schellenberg, although he had not revealed so far what advantage there was in it for him. His repeated assurances that he was merely a friend to Switzerland were meaningless; he must have had some specific purpose in mind.

This time the *SS Brigadeführer*, in spite of being in a foreign country and dependent on his host's hospitality and protection, was even more at ease than on the occasion of the original meeting. He talked a great deal about himself: he recalled the beginnings of his career, he complained about the difficulties he encountered in the course of his work, and he spent a long time describing the joys of family life and the happiness the five children of his first marriage brought him. After a while he progressed to more weighty matters and entered into contemplation of the course of the war and the current political situation. It was only then that the reasons for which he had upheld the Swiss initiative of a meeting and decided to pursue the contact began to emerge. He maintained that the Third Reich was still powerful: her armies were now at Leningrad, at Moscow and at the Volga, but hopes for a swift victory in the East had vanished, while in North Africa matters looked frankly grim and it seemed to him that General Rommel's defeat was finally inevitable. Britain in his opinion did not have sufficient strength to open up another front in Europe, but the power of the United States, on whom Hitler had already declared war, would ultimately influence the outcome of the global conflict. He followed this account with a number of compliments directed towards Switzerland, her constitution and her place in Europe. [15]

Masson listened carefully, and one question ran through his mind again and again: was this in fact a veiled proposal of mediation in discussions with the West? If he had known the content of the confidential talks Schellenberg had for some time been having with Himmler he would have had a clear answer to the question he was putting to himself. In August 1942 at the Eastern front, in Jitomir, Schellenberg had had a decisive meeting with the SS *Reichsführer* and had managed to convince him that the war was now as good as lost, in military terms, since it was currently being waged against nearly the whole world, but that it might be possible to conclude it successfully by means of sensible diplomatic moves. Himmler accepted this point of view easily for, having himself created the might of the SS which could now hardly be contained within the boundaries of Germany, he saw himself taking Hitler's place, and was just waiting for an opportune moment. Now that the Eastern front had solidified, which ruled out the possibility of a swift victory, and the mighty United States had entered the ranks of the opponents, that moment was near. The first step was the removal of Hitler, by whatever means, and the second the assumption of power. There were no serious rivals; Hess was in England, Göring having grown morbidly obese and lethargic had by now lost his forcefulness, and Heydrich had just been murdered. Secret negotiations with Britain and with America for an end to the fighting as soon as possible should be initiated while Germany still had a good deal of strength. She would need to make some kind of payment for this conclusion and she could therefore return all her Western conquests, while in the East she could accept the principle that she would resume her 1939 boundaries. It might perhaps be possible for her to keep some Polish territory which had been hers before the First World War. Fighting with the Soviet Union would continue, and the Western allies would join in. Himmler considered this scheme to be entirely realistic, and he was expecting the German generals to offer him their support.[16]

While Schellenberg continued his account Colonel Masson listened and wavered in his opinion about what lay behind what he was saying. Surely this was an attempt to sound him out with the aim of discovering how Switzerland would be disposed towards mediation in establishing a separate peace, but perhaps purely personal factors were playing a major role here as well. The end of 1942 was now approaching, the war had gone on for more than three years, and anyone who was aware of the industrial potential of the adversaries knew that a victory for the Germans was out of the question. Schellenberg belonged to the group of Nazis which was called by those who surrounded Hitler, partly by way of a joke and to a certain extent contemptuously, as the *Märzveilchen* (spring violets). These were people who joined the party once it had come to power in January 1933; they were unlike the earlier fanatics and enthusiasts, and they were motivated by cold calculation. There were many naive individuals about who still had faith in miracles and in the *Führer's* promises that he would bring new weapons into combat and win the war, but the young *SS* general who was seated by the fire-place next to Masson and holding forth on the subject of the war at length was not one of these.[17] If the motive deduced by Masson indeed lay behind Schellenberg's overture then he would certainly continue to be co-operative and would render Switzerland further services in order to secure her favour when the Third Reich collapsed and when Hitler's closest collaborators found themselves at the mercy of the victorious allies.

It was necessary however to take into account another possibility, and this one was at the given moment the more probable. The Germans were well aware that agents of allied Western Intelligence were operating within Switzerland, that secret communication channels penetrated the country, and that confidential information was being sent out of Germany to reach her enemies by these means.[18]

Monitoring stations in the southern provinces of the Reich had caught a number of radio messages on their way to Moscow (see chapter 2, p. 17). On one occasion, on the night of 6 September 1941, they intercepted two messages from Radó, nos. 207 and 208. They were unable to decipher them, but there was no doubt as to their destination. A few months later, in December of the same year, they intercepted two more messages from Radó to the *Director*. This time they managed to crack the code.[19] Schellenberg was aware of this and he knew that someone in Germany who moved in the highest circles, within Hitler's entourage and in the *Wehrmacht* command, was betraying vital state secrets. These pertained for the most part to the Eastern front; the Russians were being supplied with information about German intentions, which prevented their being taken by surprise. Schellenberg had rejected out of hand the assumption that the Swiss security forces might be unaware of the Soviet and Western clandestine activities on their territory. If, in return for the favours granted by the Germans, Masson were to draw aside the blinds which concealed these matters even to a very slight extent, then they might be able, by following the communication channels, to catch those in Germany who were involved in the treason. In Schellenberg's estimation these must be people who had been conspiring against Hitler for several years and were in contact with the West, and now, bursting with hatred of everything connected with National Socialism, had despite their conservative principles begun to support Moscow; they had to be members of the *Schwarze Kapelle*. Schellenberg had not made a mistake in omitting the Communist *Rote Kapelle* from his deliberations, for he knew that nearly all its leaders and most important agents were behind bars in Germany[20] whereas the radio messages were still streaming to Moscow from Switzerland non-stop.

Colonel Masson grew almost certain that apart from securing his own safety should Germany suffer defeat, which now seemed inevitable, Schellenberg had in mind these matters above all. He had been expecting some clever question, but since none was forthcoming he decided at last to come to the fundamental issue. Bearing in mind Schellenberg's friendly gestures and the fulfilment of his promises Masson asked him outright what he intended to do with the unfortunate documents which had been captured by the Germans from the train at La Charité-sur-Loire. He was once again astonished at the reply he was given. Schellenberg promised that he would personally see to it that the papers were destroyed, so no one else would ever hear about them again.[21]

During the three days that passed the German visitors did not leave the house of the wealthy Swiss even for a moment. Then, again under cover of darkness, they crossed the border, this time in the opposite direction. The destiny of the war hung in the balance; so did the neutrality and security of Switzerland.

4

It has long been customary in Switzerland, whenever the possibility of war breaking out and the country being threatened has arisen, for the parliament to appoint a supreme commander of the army and to entrust to him all the duties pertaining to that position. The commander-in-chief becomes a general, a rank not normally in use in the Swiss army in time of peace. On 29 August 1939, two days before the German attack on Poland, Colonel Henri Guisan, farmer as well as officer by profession, was in accordance with this custom appointed to the post of commander-in-chief of the Swiss army and given the rank of general.[22]

He was then already sixty-five years of age but in excellent form; lean and tall, he was much liked by the soldiers and greatly respected by the officers who worked with him. At the beginning of the war after full mobilization had been carried out he commanded an army of nearly half a million, but with the course of events and a decrease in danger it dissolved little by little as industry and agriculture reclaimed their work-force. Towards the end of 1942 it consisted of not much more than 100,000 men, which was still quite considerable for such a small country. Guisan was a great advocate of continuous contact with the soldiers and his official car or his four-carriage train carried him almost non-stop from one edge of the country to the other. He carried out reviews, he examined the worthiness of fortifications, he inspected aerodromes, roads, tunnels and viaducts, and he delivered speeches to the troops.

On 30 January 1943 when the general was away on one of his routine inspection tours, the Intelligence headquarters in Lucerne, which was under the command of Max Waibel, who had by now attained the rank of major (see chapter 1, p. 7), received a disturbing report from its main Intelligence network in Germany, code-named the *Wiking Linie*. This network had been set up by Major Waibel

29 Walter Schellenberg

30 Hotel Bären in Biglen, the meeting place of Guisan and Schellenberg

31 Reinhard Heydrich

32 Harold 'Kim' Philby in 1933

33 Wolfsberg Estate, the meeting place of Masson and Schellenberg

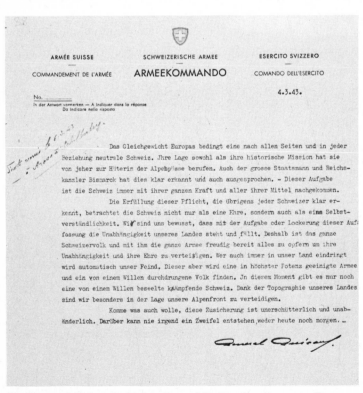

34 General Guisan's declaration of Switzerland's neutrality.
See p.115 for English translation

35 Allen Dulles **36** Halina Szymańska

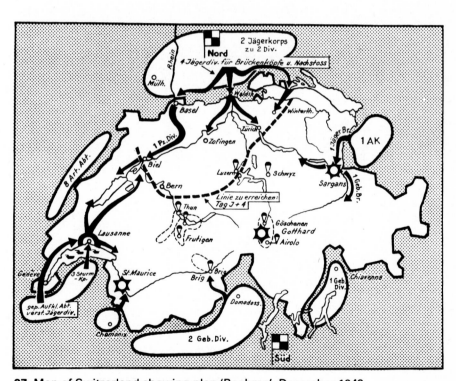

37 Map of Switzerland showing plan 'Boehme', December 1943

38 Roessler's grave

himself while he was stationed in Germany before the war as a young Swiss officer in the Staff College, and it gathered invaluable information with great efficiency. It was being supplied by senior officers in the German armed forces who were opposed to National Socialism and belonged to the *Schwarze Kapelle*. They were rendering Swiss Intelligence and the Western allies the same services in this sphere as were being provided to Soviet Intelligence by means of Rudolf Roessler.[23] The disturbing report concerned a meeting at Hitler's headquarters in October 1942 at which Göring, Himmler, Goebbels and Rosenberg had been present, when the matter under consideration had been the eventuality of an attack on Switzerland. It was necessary to treat this information with the utmost seriousness, for the *Wiking Linie* was one of the most important sources Swiss Intelligence had in Germany. From it they had obtained the date of the German attack on Denmark and Norway in the spring of 1940, and five weeks later it had announced the beginning of the great offensive in the West. It is essential to emphasize at this point that the *Wiking Linie* was completely independent of the secret links between the Third Reich and Rudolf Roessler, although the informants in both cases were members of the same anti-Nazi group.[24]

Swiss Intelligence was well aware that the German plans of operation were undergoing changes, for the battles in North Africa had taken a turn for the worse for the Third Reich and the possibility had arisen of an allied attack on the Italian peninsula, which would automatically induce the Germans to come to the aid of their southern partner. In this situation the communication routes running through Switzerland would take on an even greater significance. As it was, the Germans were making use of these without hindrance despite Switzerland's neutrality, but they might be persuaded that they would achieve greater control if they actually took them over.

The information the *Wiking Linie* provided was already a little late, for on 6 January Schellenberg had submitted to Hitler his report no. 52 which contained a number of details concerning Switzerland. According to Swiss sources the RAF was supposed to be preparing a large raid on the Brenner Pass in the Alps in order to block communications between the Reich and Italy. In consequence of this Switzerland was planning another general mobilization as she feared an attack from a new direction other than Germany. The purpose of the mobilization was defence: the Swiss would protect their country from

111

any invader.[25] Schellenberg's report was reinforced by the German ambassador in Bern, Köcher, who warned once again that the tunnels and viaducts had been mined and that Switzerland was prepared to blow them up and to destroy the results of many years' work to defend her freedom (see chapter 1, p. 6).

However at this time Swiss Intelligence, and thus the general staff, was not aware of Schellenberg's contribution; in any case there was no certainty that his action might bring about any result. Colonel Masson immediately set out to catch up with General Guisan; he described the whole matter to him, reminding him about the details of his two meetings with the SS general, and began to consider what needed to be done. They came to the conclusion that another meeting with Schellenberg was called for and that this time the commander-in-chief of the Swiss army should participate. Masson, alarmed and treating the German threat very seriously, wanted to go to Berlin incognito in order to arrange the meeting with the utmost efficiency, but General Guisan opposed this categorically.[26] When taking their decision, the Swiss officers did not know that Schellenberg was also thinking of another meeting and wanted it very badly.

5

Well nigh the whole of Europe was in the grip of war, yet air links between the Third Reich and the neutral countries were still in operation: Lufthansa connected Berlin with Portugal, Spain and Switzerland. So Schellenberg was able to catch a flight, and on 3 March 1943, accompanied by two sullen characters who were providing him with questionable protection, he arrived in Zürich. Major Eggen was already waiting for him at the airport, having flown in earlier, met Masson and finalized all the arrangements. The ostentation of the German visit was emphasized by the fact that rooms had been booked for Schellenberg and his party at the Hotel Bellevue, one of the largest and most exclusive hotels in the whole country. This was done at the behest of Colonel Masson, who had dropped the secrecy he had employed hitherto and decided that the meeting with Schellenberg should draw as much attention as possible. All the countries which were at war, with the exception of the Soviet Union, and many of the neutral states had diplomatic representation in Bern and it was obvious that news of the German-Swiss meeting, particularly in view of the participation of the supreme commander, would become common knowledge. Was this meant to be a warning that Switzerland would not yield to any pressures from the Western allies and that her relations with the other side were equally important to her? Perhaps, on the other hand, it was meant to emphasize the central position of the country, which might predetermine its intermediary role should early moves towards peace be undertaken? As it was however, Schellenberg objected to Masson's plans, and he decided he would stay at Schweizerhoff instead.[27]

The rendezvous selected for the meeting was the Hotel Bären in the village of Biglen, nearly twenty kilometres from Bern, on the road to Zürich; Schellenberg made his way there immediately by car, accompanied by Eggen and by Meyer-Schwertenbach and Holzach, who had also come to the airport. The bodyguard naturally came along too.

This time, since the talks were to be conducted on behalf of the Swiss by the most senior officer in position and rank in the army, the most important problem was tackled immediately—the country's neutrality. Schellenberg had been explicitly instructed by Himmler to discuss only this subject. Hitler himself doubted whether any contact with Switzerland was necessary; he was aware that meetings were taking place, but viewed them dispassionately. His agreement to any shadow of compromise in an attempt to bring the war to an end was entirely out of the question. He remembered the British reaction to the arrival in Britain of Rudolf Hess in 1941 and he did not trust the good intentions of the Western allies. He had taken their terms of 'unconditional surrender' to be final and he feared the reaction of the Italians and the break-up of the Berlin-Rome axis.[28] What he required was an unequivocal declaration by Switzerland to dispel all doubts that she would defend herself against an attack from any quarter, and not just from the German. The allies were already in North Africa and soon they might land on the southern shores of Europe. Would the Swiss allow them to march through their country freely, or would they put up armed resistance.[29]

This question was voiced by Schellenberg, and General Guisan felt it to be distinctly offensive. What grounds did he have to doubt Swiss neutrality? A few days previously in fact the general had been interviewed by a Swedish journalist and had stated very clearly that Switzerland would defend her neutrality against any agressor. It would be inconceivable that German Intelligence had failed to obtain the article, to translate it, and to pass it on to the country's leaders who were examining the Swiss problem. However, if that were the case, the general would be glad to supply a copy. He had left one at his headquarters in Interlaken, but he would have it translated and could hand it over within three days personally. He would be at Arosa, near Davos, observing the big ski-ing competition, which was an important event of a semi-military nature.[30]

The German accepted this proposal, and the remainder of the evening was spent in social conversation, during which a great variety of topics was touched upon and any difficult or sensitive subject avoided. Towards the end of the meeting as they were leaving the hotel a peculiar and almost comical incident occurred. The establishment's proprietor, who had recognized the commander-in-chief of the Swiss army, asked him whether he would like to sign the visitors' book. He complied with the request, and the others followed his example; perhaps the wine they had consumed influenced their behaviour. Anyhow, only Captain Meyer-Schwertenbach saw the gaffe, and despite the host's protests he tore out the unfortunate page. Masson noticed this, and left the hotel under the impression that the paper with the signatures had been destroyed, but he did not follow up the matter. It is quite likely that the Germans took it with them.[31]

The German visitors spent the next two days in Bern, not stepping out of their hotel once. Colonel Masson called on them and talked with Schellenberg on two further occasions, covering much the same ground. In the course of a discussion of the meeting with General Guisan the German stated that in fact a translation of the interview in the Swedish paper would not in itself be sufficient. Hitler set great store by Switzerland's conduct, and it was essential for him to obtain a signed statement from the general which confirmed in no uncertain terms that the country would maintain her neutrality and that she would defend herself against all agression.[32]

On Saturday 6 March General Guisan had a second meeting with Schellenberg at the Meyer-Schwertenbachs' home, after the ski-ing competition in Arosa had finished. Masson had already told the general that the German was demanding a statement. The document, drawn up on 4 March on the official notepaper of the army's main headquarters and bearing the general's signature, was duly delivered over to Schellenberg. The declaration was even more far-reaching than the Germans could have wished:

The equilibrium of Europe demands that Switzerland remain neutral from all sides and in every respect. Her geographical position as well as her place in history long ago appointed her to be the guardian of the Alpine passes. The great statesman Chancellor Bismarck appreciated this also and acknowledged it. Switzerland had always performed this duty to the best of her ability with all the means at her disposal.

Switzerland considers the fulfilment of this obligation, which is plainly acknowledged by every Swiss, to be not only a privilege but also the only possible natural state of affairs. We are conscious of the fact that the abandonment or disregard of this principle would bring about the collapse of our country. This is why the entire army and the whole of the Swiss nation along with it are gladly willing to sacrifice everything in order to defend their independence and their honour. Whoever invades our country is self-evidently our enemy. He will be confronted by a united army of the greatest strength and a nation imbued with a single accord. At such a time there exists only one militant Switzerland inspired by one will. Because of the topography of our country we are able to defend above all our Alpine front.

Whatever may come to pass this assurance is immovable and unalterable. No doubt can arise about that either now or in the future.[33]

General Guisan

The German visitor continued to remain in Switzerland still until 10 March and he had several meetings with Colonel Masson at Meyer-Schwertenbach's residence at Wolfsberg during which the Swiss Intelligence chief was able to settle another matter. Schellenberg gave his word that he would release the family of the French general Henri Giraud who had managed to escape out of German captivity, and have them sent to Switzerland; he was later to fulfil his promise.[34] In the course of one of these meetings the German finally came out with the matter that Masson had long been expecting. Schellenberg, anxious for the safety of the *Führer* who had bitter enemies within certain circles of the officers of the *Wehrmacht*, had been hoping to track down the traitors, not in order to place them under arrest, but merely to give them a warning before they were found out by the *Gestapo*. These

115

people had contacts in Switzerland and were sending information of great importance out of Germany; the Swiss Intelligence chief must be aware of this. Were he inclined to pass on a few names he would be rendering the Third Reich and his own country an enormous service. Masson declined to respond to this request because it would naturally have amounted to betrayal of a secret which had to be maintained at any cost. Should he have wished to divulge it to the German for any reason he would have been unable to do so because in fact he did not know the names at all.[35]

6

At the very time Schellenberg was on his way to Berlin General Guisan was having a most disagreeable conversation at his headquarters in Interlaken with the head of the department of military affairs in the *Bundesrat* (Swiss government), Dr Karl Kobelt. Military intelligence and counter-intelligence were strictly the responsibility of Colonel Masson, but the political authorities had their own confidential contacts, with the *Büro Ha* among others, and Dr Kobelt, being aware that the General had had two meetings with some fairly prominent German, demanded an explanation. General Guisan refused to give him any information, not even the name of the German visitor; he merely stated that he had accomplished a great deal towards the preservation of Switzerland's neutral status.

The head of the department of military affairs, otherwise the minister of war, to whom the commander-in-chief of the army was directly responsible within the framework of a democratic parliamentary system, had a different view of these matters. He was of the opinion that the contact was of a political rather than a military nature and, moreover, that the most senior officer of the Swiss army, both in rank and position, should never have become involved in a meeting with a German individual who was acting as a representative of the Nazi régime. The disagreement grew serious, and became the subject of a debate by the Swiss government. It passed a resolution which was communicated to General Guisan in writing by Dr Kobelt on 6 April. It consisted of a number of personal compliments, stressing the general's patriotism, while at the same time stating categorically that politics were the business of the *Bundesrat*, and not of the army, and that the meeting with Schellenberg could result in complications and difficulties from allied quarters.[36]

But before the despatch of this document came about, Switzerland was rocked by another wave of great apprehension. On 18 March the *Wiking Linie* sent a second disturbing message that the matter of an attack on Switzerland had yet again been discussed at Hitler's headquarters. Another source simultaneously reported that General Eduard Dietl, an expert in mountain warfare, had been recalled from Finland and that he had set up headquarters in Munich where he was preparing a plan of attack, having at his disposal choice parachute formations and several mountain combat divisions. Colonel Masson was shattered by this information and responded immediately, although very unwisely. Believing that Schellenberg was indeed sincerely favourably disposed towards Switzerland, he asked Meyer-Schwertenbach to get in touch with Berlin by telephone and to arrange for him himself to go there for talks with General Schellenberg and Major Eggen in order to find out whether there really was any danger. In doing this Masson gave away the fact that he was in receipt of information which was instantaneously being despatched from Germany by people who moved in the highest political and military circles. As a result, within a few weeks, one of the main informants of the *Wiking Linie* in Germany was placed under arrest.[37]

Luckily the state of anxiety continued for only ten days, for on 27 March the *Wiking Linie* carried another report which stated categorically that there was in fact no danger of an attack. From a different source came the information that within the operational section of the German land forces no-one was attending to 'Operation Switzerland' while the winter Soviet offensive continued. Also, General Dietl was not in Munich; he was directing the resistance to the Soviet attack from his headquarters in Lapland.[38]

The whole affair, which became known as the '1943 March alert', was interpreted in various ways, and the reasons which caused it are unknown to this day. It may have been an act of provocation, inspired by Schellenberg who, together with Himmler, was anxious to discover how quickly information 'revealed' in Berlin or at Hitler's headquarters reached Switzerland. This would have not only provided him with confirmation that Swiss Intelligence had informants in highly-placed positions in Germany, but also made the job of discovering their identities that much easier. One of them was indeed arrested, and although we do not know his name, that fact alone confirms that there might be some truth in the conjecture. Alternatively it is also possible that Schellenberg might simply have wanted to build up his image as Switzerland's 'benefactor' further; he may have fabricated the alert in order to be able to pass on the message to Masson later, via Eggen, that the danger had been averted, which would have given the impression that he had played a major part in the change of affairs.[39]

According to another theory the Germans, by raising a false alarm, wanted to provoke a Swiss reaction, which might have amounted to general mobilization, and this would have proved that the country indeed intended to defend herself against attack. If she were to defend herself against the Germans it had to be deduced that she would be obliged by the principle of total neutrality to defend herself against all other assailants, including the Western allied forces. For the Germans the lines of communication connecting the Reich with their southern ally, Italy, were also important. The Italians were hanging on tenuously and it was obvious that they would not last long. To encourage them to further resistance, they had to be shown that the Reich was in a position to assist them and was prepared to safeguard the shortest lines of communication. The attack on Switzerland, or merely the realistic threat of an attack, would prove to them that the Germans were still strong, that they were still willing to maintain the Berlin-Rome axis and that they were endeavouring to secure a route to the south via Swiss territory.

However, since the entire 'March alert' lasted scarcely ten days we have to accept that what lay behind it was an ordinary 'battle of nerves', waged by the Germans, with the intention of keeping the Swiss in a constant state of willingness to co-operate economically in full with the Third Reich.[40]

The 'March alert' was fabricated, but Switzerland was actually under continual threat from her northern neighbour; the Germans did not abandon their intention to conquer Switzerland, and drew up new plans for the attack every so often, until the very end of the war.

8 Allen Dulles

1

In July of 1940 Britain, fighting almost alone after the collapse of the Western Front, created a secret organization which was called The Special Operations Executive—SOE. It's task was to assist all underground movements in Nazi-occupied Europe, to drop parachutists and supplies, to set up secret routes for couriers, to sow unrest, to harass the occupying forces and to indulge in sabotage and diversion. Churchill defined its aims as follows: 'You are to set Europe ablaze.'[1]

Two years later, when the United States found themselves in the war, they set up in 1942 a similar organization and called it The Office of Strategic Services—OSS. It was modelled partly on SOE, partly on SIS and was given three main tasks: intelligence, operations and research, but it concentrated mainly on espionage, where it achieved its greatest success. Both organizations operated in Europe (SOE had a limited presence in the Far East) and they were meant to co-operate, but in practice this did not work out too well and co-operation turned often into rivalry.[2]

Colonel William J. Donovan was put in charge of OSS and, on assuming his new duties, he was promoted general. He was no longer a young man and had returned from the First World War as the most-decorated American soldier. After leaving the army he had gone into private legal practice, had shown some interest in politics and had made a number of interesting contacts. He had close relations with, amongst others, President Roosevelt and Winston Churchill. After the outbreak of war in Europe he went there several times as an emissary from the President on a number of secret matters. A year before assuming command of OSS he had been entrusted with the task of setting up a central agency to unite all espionage efforts in one organization, and he had begun seeking people suitable for his work. They were educated, usually highly intelligent lawyers, who worked with gusto and great dedication. They were soon all to find themselves in OSS.[3]

Among them was the fifty-year-old Allen Welsh Dulles, who was a well-known lawyer with wide diplomatic and espionage experience. Before setting up in private practice in New York, he had spent a number of years in various diplomatic posts. Earlier, just after the First World War, he had been a member of the American delegation to the peace conference at Versailles.

His good knowledge of Europe and its problems prompted Donovan to send him to Bern to set up in that central and neutral country, under the umbrella of OSS, an espionage and diversionary centre. Dulles flew to Lisbon and on 8 November 1942 he arrived in Barcelona at almost the exact time that the Western Allies were landing in Northern Africa. There was not much time to lose, for the news then came that German divisions had crossed the frontier of unoccupied France and were marching south swamping the whole country. Dulles caught the nearest train, crossed the still unoccupied part of the country and, after several difficult hours with French gendarmes near the Swiss frontier, reached Geneva and eventually Bern.[4]

Dulles officially joined his Embassy and received diplomatic status as an assistant to the Ambassador, but in reality he was engaged on something quite different and his main task was to follow events inside the Third Reich. He himself defined his task as follows:

I had been in Switzerland in charge of the work there of the Office of Strategic Services, organized and directed by the dynamic and resourceful General J. Donovan. My first and most important task was to find out what was going on in Germany. Among other things, Washington wanted to know who in Germany was really opposed to the Hitler regime and whether they were actively at work to overthrow it.[5]

Normally espionage, sabotage and diversion require great secrecy, yet Dulles's start in Switzerland was quite different, since one of the leading papers revealed that he had arrived as a special envoy of President Roosevelt to handle some secret matters. Contrary to what might have been expected, this announcement helped him, since, despite his official denials, the report was believed and his newly created espionage network began to be inundated with a flood of information. He was specialist enough to be able to handle this and distinguish valuable information from the usual run of nonsense and deliberate misinformation.[6]

2

After making his official visits and naturally making contact with the Intelligence Service, Dulles directed his steps to Swiss Intelligence, since without its indulgent neutrality and secret assistance, he would be unable to achieve a great deal. He had several meetings with Colonel Masson and they later became friends, Dulles showing great understanding for Switzerland's difficult position of trying to maintain neutrality while having sympathy for the Western cause. He thus was not surprised to find that, in addition to their contacts with Western Intelligence services, the Swiss also were in touch with the German and Italian Intelligence. On the contrary he felt that such a state of affairs could even be beneficial, since it might produce more information than might otherwise be possible. He promised assistance and co-operation.[7]

However these conversations with the head of Swiss Intelligence were of an official rather than a working nature, and so Dulles went further, establishing close contact with *Büro Ha* and its head, Captain Hausamann. It was agreed that their frequent meetings, which had to be secret, would take place on neutral territory in the private home in Zürich of Emil Oprecht, who ran a publishing firm there. The two men became friends quickly and in the interests of their countries began to exchange important intelligence. Dulles discovered a great deal of new information about Europe, which he knew well from his earlier diplomatic career. Much had changed since then. The Swiss did not tell him about his collaboration with Roessler, but, without divulging sources, he did give him information which might be of importance to the United States. It included German political decisions and plans on the Eastern Front, which were of great importance in global, political and strategic planning. For his part Dulles was able to disclose those American plans of which the Swiss authorities needed to be appraised. They dealt with the country's neutrality and a number of minor concessions, mainly in favour of Allied air units attacking targets in Germany and Italy.[8]

The American envoy contacted, in addition to Hausamann, Major Waibel, who was in charge of intelligence station no. 1 in Lucerne, with secret instructions to handle relations with the Western allies, as Masson did with the Axis powers. Here again, after several meetings and conversations, friendship and co-operation sprang up, which would play an especially important role during the last months of the war when the German army in Northern Italy was capitulating. Naturally, following Hausamann's lead, Waibel did not tell Dulles that he was in possession of the *Wiking Linie*, through which he received excellent reports from out of Germany. Nevertheless, the two did exchange information.[9]

Both contacts in Swiss intelligence were also valuable in further secret tasks; communications with Italian partisans in 1943 on the far side of the Alps, similar contacts with maquis in France and other sabotage and diversionary acts.[10]

3

Dulles arrived in Switzerland with an impressive amount of information on the German anti-Nazi movement, which he had received from prominent Germans who had taken refuge from the *Gestapo* in the United States. He knew its name, *Die Schwarze Kapelle* (The Black Orchestra) which had been coined by the Nazi security authorities, although he himself called the conspirators *The Breakers*, and he had enough espionage experience to realize that from genuine resistance work to provocation was only a short step. The British Foreign Office was especially conscious of this and through indirect channels warned the agents of the Secret Intelligence Service—SIS—to be particularly careful in their dealings with Germans who claimed to be members of the anti-Nazi organization (see chapter 7, pp. 105–6). Soon after his arrival in Switzerland Dulles received a warning from SIS.[11] However, fear of provocation was only a secondary motive for the Foreign Office's caution. At the heart of the British reluctance to deal with the German anti-Nazi movement lay a political assessment of its usefulness. British specialists on international relations felt that the Soviet Union would find out about any dealings with the German underground, would take this to be disloyalty and a plot to arrange things behind its back, and would itself arrange secret talks with the Germans with a view to making a separate peace. In fact Hitler rejected any thought of compromise, but the situation on the Eastern front looked bad, there was no question of a swift victory and eventual success looked less and less likely, so the dictator could indeed succumb to the pressure of those around him and accept a proposal to return to the 1939 frontiers, if it were suggested.

A considerable obstacle was the fact that, before Dulles had even managed to look around and make many contacts, in January 1943 the Casablanca conference took place at which Roosevelt and Churchill adopted a policy of 'unconditional surrender' towards the Germans. This greatly cooled the ardour of the anti-Nazi conspirators, who continued to hope that the Western democracies would make a distinction between Germans and would afford them secret assistance in their attempts to overthrow Hitler and bring the war to an early conclusion. The Western leaders' short-sighted and very harmful attitude, for which Roosevelt was primarily responsible,[12] differed greatly from the Soviet Union's actions and propaganda. At exactly the same time as this unfortunate decision was being taken in Casablanca, which direct and most unwelcome result was a hardening of the German nation in its insistence to fight to the last, the battle of Stalingrad was being decided. After Hitler's first great defeat, when almost 100,000 of his soldiers had to surrender, among them thousands of officers and several generals, the Russians increased their propaganda whose basic slogan was: 'we are fighting Nazism and not the German people'. Several weeks later a Free Germans Committee was set up in Moscow with General Walter von Seydlitz and Alexander Edler von Daniels at its head. Immediately after receiving the news of the Sixth Army's surrender at Stalingrad, Hitler in an unbridled rage ordered Field Marshal von Paulus and his generals to be deprived of all military honours, contending that they should have taken their own lives rather than show the white flag and condemned them as traitors who would soon be talking to the German people over Soviet radio.[13] Hitler's prophecy turned out to be completely accurate and Stalin's propaganda machine began to create cracks in the hitherto smooth front of German resistance.

Dulles had a very good knowledge of all these matters, since he held in his hand the threads of American espionage in Europe and understood that the Western Allies could, through their own mistakes, lose the battle for the soul of the German people. He was deeply concerned by this, since he knew that the *Black Orchestra* was composed for the most part of people with very right-wing, conservative views. It was, however, the only underground anti-Nazi organization in Germany which was seeking contacts with the West and so secret communications with it needed to be set up immediately. It was reasonable to expect that after some time it would be possible to exert some influence over it and to try to make it adopt a more centrist stance. This could happen if its ranks included representatives of a younger generation, who were more flexible and who understood that the post-war world would have to be different. Dulles was also well aware that the conservatism of the anti-Nazi military conspiracy was a great brake on its activities. The old Junker traditions required of a soldier total obedience and the upholding of his oath in all circumstances, especially since in its new form it named Adolf Hitler as the man who was to be obeyed at all times. [14]

4

For several years now Gero von Gaevernitz, a German, had been living in Switzerland. He already had American citizenship and was in close touch with the American embassy. At the same time he continued to have contact with the Third Reich through his father, a prominent German liberal, who had somehow managed to avoid the *Gestapo's* claws and taught at the universities of Freiburg and Breslau. It was precisely with this young German that Dulles got in touch and through him met Gisevius for the first time. He had heard about him earlier and knew that he was the vice-consul in Zürich and that in Switzerland he represented the most serious element in the German resistance movement. The first meeting took place in Zürich under the cover of darkness and the blackout, with every precaution taken. Gisevius also knew beforehand the American diplomat's role, so their initial conversation went smoothly and brought immediate results. Dulles was at once struck by the German conspirator's bulk, which must have greatly hampered him on secret assignments, but he recognized that his diplomatic status in Switzerland was a strong enough asset and thought no more about it. He was not troubled by any psychological worries, nor did he have any inhibitions, as had Halina Szymańska. He saw in the German a strong, resolute man who was in a fine position and could provide him with much important information. For his part Gisevius, having quite extensive political experience, from the first conversation appreciated that he was dealing with an espionage chief who did not limit himself to gathering information and transmitting it to his superiors, but who also could see the political ramifications of the war and was already thinking of the post-war years. [15] Gisevius was very much younger than the leaders of the *Black Orchestra* and thus, although a product of conservative circles, he realized that the defeat of national socialism did not mean turning back the clock.

In espionage work every new contact must have a code-name and so Dulles called Gisevius *Tiny*. Their subsequent meetings took place in Bern at Dulles's flat, and always late in the evening or even at night. Despite these precautions, their meeting-place was quite unsuitable and had to lead to the German's exposure. One evening, as they sat at dinner talking in German, the cook overheard them. She was of German extraction and, it transpired, an agent of German Intelligence. Intrigued by the conversation, she examined Gisevius's hat, found his initials in it and the following day passed this information on to her superiors. The German was summoned to his embassy and accused of having contact with the enemy. Thanks only to his presence of mind and the threat that he would immediately inform Berlin if anything was revealed, since he was thus engaged on gathering information for Admiral Canaris, did Gisevius manage to extricate himself from his difficult situation, but his secret contact was no longer secret.[16]

Despite their successful first meeting, these two men, representing countries at war with one another, and dealing with particularly sensitive questions, were unable immediately to trust one another completely. It was not simply a question of honesty and sincerity of intentions, there was also the need to consider preparation for the task in hand, discretion and espionage abilities. Gisevius observed his American counterpart, obtained additional information on him from some of his staff and every day gained a little more confidence in the methods he was using in his difficult mission. Dulles had an office on the Herrengasse where he operated in his official role of assistant to the American Ambassador and there he received as many visitors as possible. He was visited by representatives of German-occupied countries and also German satellites and everyone had something to say about the conduct of the war and the future of Europe. Dulles talked to German political refugees, to Austrians, to Hungarians, Italians, Romanians and Finns, he listened to their views, answered questions, accepted memoranda. His office was also a target for many 'professional' spies, who on the same day were able to talk to representatives of Swiss Intelligence, visit the *Abwehr* station, appear in person before an *SD* officer and finally reach Dulles to offer him some sensational report. The experienced American ostensibly treated them all in the same way, but he made very shrewd assessments and did not waste time reading worthless memoranda or conducting unnecessary conversations.[17]

For his part Dulles was similarly observing the huge German and collecting all available information on him. Within the first few months of their collaboration there took place an incident which highlighted a number of things. A constant stream of enciphered radio messages went from Bern to Washington, sent by the Embassy and by Dulles, and German monitoring stations in Stuttgart and the surrounding area tried to intercept them for the cryptanalysts. Gisevius gave the Americans a number of warnings and finally, in February 1943, on his return from Berlin, he brought a long list of signals intercepted by the Germans. One of them had been broken. Fortunately, it was not Dulles's cipher, but the Embassy was immediately informed and changed its ciphers. Several days later Gisevius brought another signal which gave details of an anti-German group in Italy (Badoglio, Grandi, Ciano). It had apparently been deciphered by Hungarian analysts and then turned over to German Intelligence.[18] This time it was one of Dulles's signals and he took two courses of action: he changed his ciphers for his correspondence with Washington and from time to time, in concert with his superiors, he used the broken cipher, but with the proviso that it now concealed information being used as classical disinformation.[19]

The incident with the signals raised Gisevius very high in Dulles's estimation and was furthermore proof that the German was loyal and honest and, moreover, that he had great possibilities open to him. He indeed started to provide excellent information about the German underground, about changes taking place in its ranks, about the *Black Orchestra* old guard's contacts with left-wing elements represented by the socialist Wilhelm Lenschner and about the entry into the conspiracy of many younger officers. The latter, above all General Friedrich Olbricht, General Henning von Tresckow and colonel Claus Schenk von Stauffenberg, also held slightly more left-wing views. Von Stauffenberg was even thinking about a social revolution of workers, peasants and soldiers.[20]

In the first phase of this co-operation Gisevius used to journey between Bern and Berlin himself, but when this caught the attention of Himmler, a deadly foe of the *Abwehr*, Edward Waetjan, a Berlin lawyer with an American mother, began to make the trips. He also became the object of the attention of the security services of the Third Reich and so his place was taken by Theodor Strünck, who survived in this capacity right up to the middle of 1944.[21] He was arrested and executed after the attempt on Hitler's life.

5

On the trail of the fullest details of the German pro-Western resistance movement, Dulles also met Halina Szymańska several times and invited her to receptions, but they never worked together. He once made some remark about Gisevius from which it transpired that he knew about her contact with the German agent. This was probably why he never brought up the subject with her. Moreover, since Szymańska was working in the Polish consulate, he was probably of the opinion that all the information she obtained was given to her superiors, who then turned it over to the British, for after all the Polish Government was in London.[22]

However, he was in close touch with the Polish legation, a contact which was maintained by both sides. This came about principally because the legation also had under its wing a secret communications outpost with occupied Poland (see chapter 2, pp. 24–5). It was run by the people who had official diplomatic functions, such as the military attaché, Lieutenant Colonel Bronisław Noel, then from May 1942 Major Szczęsny Chojnacki and finally, from September 1944, Major Bronisław Ludwik de Ville. This was the formal arrangement, but in fact this work was headed by General Bronisław Prugar-Ketling, the commander of the Second Polish infantry division, which during the fighting in France in 1940 had, under German pressure, retired over the Swiss frontier and had been interned there. The division had certain intelligence tasks and the General, who in this work had the code-names *Radlicz* and *Mars*, was in charge of the outpost and was in radio contact with the Sixth Bureau of the Polish Staff in London. Among other things, in 1942 he administered Halina Szymańska's oath. She assumed the code-name *Krzywda* and, in addition to her co-operation with the Intelligence Service and her duties as a cipher clerk at the consulate, also devoted her time to secret courier routes.[23]

After the initial collaboration with the Americans which dealt mainly in currency and passport matters, everything came to life when, after the fall of France, the Swiss outpost assumed a new meaning and acted in a new capacity until the end of the war. Through it travelled couriers from Poland carrying important information to the West, which was of great interest to Dulles. They afforded him an opportunity to understand better German methods and the German mentality, and they brought information from the rear areas of the Eastern front. He came into closer contact with Stanisław Appenzeller, who over the space of a few years had built up an espionage network in both occupied and unoccupied France and later extended it to Belgium and Italy, and received some interesting information. Furthermore, he was born in France, had an excellent knowledge of the West and had some first-class personal contacts which could come in useful. Dulles saw these possibilities, struck up a close relationship with Appenzeller and they met frequently and did favours for one another. The American was faced with the great problem of Italy, which was pressing, since the Allied attack on that country was drawing near and American Intelligence had very few sources there. Dulles was given the task of setting up his own network and sought suitable people. It happened that the Polish cultural attaché was able to give him some initial assistance. In a villa rented by Appenzeller at Vennes near Lausanne, in the spring of 1943, there was a preliminary meeting at which, in addition to the host, were Allen Dulles, Professor Edigio Reale, the French consul-general in Bern, Marquis de Nyerac, the Marquis Umberto de Nobile, and a Swiss federal councillor and mayor of Locarno, J.B. Rusca. Later the American came to benefit more than once from the help, advice and contacts of his Polish friend.[24]

6

Collaboration with Gisevius, however, was not the sum of Dulles's German contacts. He also benefited from the help of a senior official in the German Foreign Ministry, who was also an opponent of Nazism. He was Fritz Kolbe (code-name *George Wood*) and he supplied information on the Far East, Japan and the German missions operating in Tokyo and Shanghai. They sent signals to Berlin which, amongst other things, dealt with Japanese losses and their difficulties with the navy and air force, and copies of these messages came from *Wood*, by means of the diplomatic bag, to Switzerland and to Dulles. He met his informer several times, but this was a particularly difficult contact, which required the greatest caution.[25]

The American also had secret links with another official in the

German Foreign Ministry, Adam Von Trott zu Solz, whom however he never met personally, although he did come twice to Switzerland. It was he who in January 1943 submitted an important statement which preceded by several days the Casablanca declaration on 'unconditional surrender'. In his statement, sent personally to Dulles, he clearly stressed that the West was making a political error in not wishing to help the *Black Orchestra*, in aiming for the total defeat of Germany and wanting to avoid a compromise. In such circumstances the conspirators, although coming from right-wing circles, might turn to the East. After their short friendship, Hitler and Stalin would no longer be able to co-operate again, but the German and Russian peoples could come to some agreement among themselves.[26] Dulles shared the sentiments of this statement and so informed Washington, sending off a number of messages in the hope that they would get into the right hands. However, it was otherwise. In the United States capital the President's view that the Germans should be crushed without attempts at negotiations had been adopted as binding policy, and so the information on the *Black Orchestra* never saw the light of day. According to Cave Brown there is no trace of it in the archives of the Combined Chiefs of Staff, nor in the private correspondence between Roosevelt and Churchill.[27] British fears and American indifference resulted in no help or even promises going to the anti-Nazi German underground, all of which would have encouraged it to more decisive action. This was very much to the liking of the Soviet Union, which continually feared that a coup d'état in Germany and the removal of Hitler would produce an immediate agreement between the country's new leaders and the West and the creation of a joint, anti-Russian front. These fears had substance, since such were the plans of the *Black Orchestra*.[28] In the end the German people heard from the West only talk of 'unconditional surrender' and hid as best it could from the torrents of American and British bombs, while at the same time the German generals standing at the head of the Free Germans Committee in Moscow were speaking in friendly tones promising peace, work and freedom at the end of the war.

7

Contact with the German underground, which was seeking help from the West, was no obstacle to Dulles having secret talks with people whose duties required them to combat the same *Black Orchestra*. There thus developed in Germany a completely paradoxical situation: the members of the underground conspiracy were considered to be traitors and were being tracked by the German security authorities, who at the same time were themselves also turning to the West to come to some understanding. Such views were above all held by the head of the SS, Heinrich Himmler, to whom was also subordinated the RSHA and all its offshoots, and who thus was the most powerful figure in the Third Reich after Hitler. As early as the summer of 1942, during a visit to the Ukrainian sector of the Eastern front, he had come to the conclusion that the war could not be won militarily and that secret negotiations with the West should start (see chapter 7, p. 107). Thus the man whom Hitler blindly trusted and on whose loyalty he based his calculations was planning to take steps to which the *Führer* was categorically opposed and which he considered to be treachery of the highest order.

The idea of initiating secret talks with the Western Allies originated above all in Himmler's unbridled ambition, but he was not alone in his thinking. The same view was held by Field Marshal Fedor von Bock, although he sincerely disliked Himmler, and even by some members of the *Black Orchestra*, such as Dr Carl Langbehn and Johannes Popitz, who had come to the conclusion that the army would achieve nothing and that they would have to turn to the SS.[29] This logic appeared as extreme extravangance, since after all the SS was the bulwark of the Nazi system; yet that is what in fact happened.

Despite the influence of his position, Himmler had to be careful, since he had keen enemies in Hitler's closest circle, mainly Martin Borman, and so he could only set about realizing his plan by means of someone completely trustworthy, very discreet and versatile. Such a person was Walter Schellenberg and he was entrusted with this most secret and dangerous mission.[30]

The mere fact that the leadership of the German security authorities was secretly aiming at the same goal as the *Black Orchestra* created a situation of extreme paradox. What is there to say about these secret efforts when it transpires that in their negotiations with the West, conducted in the greatest secrecy, Himmler and *Die Schwarze Kapelle* used the same people?! It sounds quite incredible, but is indeed a fact that Schellenberg chose for an intermediary with Dulles in Switzerland a man who was to undertake a similar mission, but this on the instigation of Admiral Canaris. This man, from an old aristocratic family, was Prince Maximilian Egon Hohenlohe-Langenburg, who had great diplomatic and social experience and was splendidly suited to the task.[31]

The meeting took place in mid-February 1943, that is after Casablanca and its declaration, which was significant, since it demonstrates that the Germans looking to the West did not regard it as an insurmountable obstacle. All the requirements of secrecy were observed, the conversation took place at night and Dulles took great care not to be in the position of a man who, wanting to end the war as soon as possible, pleased no one. He must certainly have written a report of this meeting, but its whereabouts and availability are unknown. However a report produced by Prince Hohenlohe has survived and is in the *RSHA* archives.[32] In it the prince calls himself *Herr Pauls* and Dulles *Mr Bull*.

If this document is to be believed, Dulles, independently of his country's official policy, expressed opinions following the general line of reasoning of those Germans who were seeking some understanding with the West. Above all he did not see at the conclusion of the war a clear distinction between victors and vanquished and he did not foresee the dismemberment or division of the Third Reich. On the contrary, he wanted Austria to remain part of it and expected only a weakening of aggressive intentions on the part of Prussia. His attitude to Russia was almost identical with that of the *Black Orchestra* and the head of the *SS*, Himmler: the need to oppose her in her drive to the West and surround her again with a 'cordon sanitaire'. To this end Poland should emerge from the war with increased territories in the East. The German emissary gained the impression from the American's comments that, while Great Britain was aiming rather at a division of Europe into spheres of influence, the United States would prefer to see it as a single entity, thus creating a large and very extensive market. Germany would become a federation co-operating closely with a confederation of Danube states. This would guarantee the peace and development of central and eastern Europe. The meeting apparently ended with a promise by Dulles that he would get in touch with the American Embassy in Madrid, apprising it of the possible visit of *Herr Pauls* and would ensure him a good reception. There he was first of all to get in touch with a counsellor, William Walton Butterworth.[33]

It is hard to imagine that in this report, prepared for Intelligence internal consumption, Hohenlohe-Langenburg could have permitted

131

himself to indulge in wishful thinking and put false answers into Dulles's mouth which were far removed from the policies of the American President. Merely a few months later, in August 1943 in Quebec, Roosevelt was not only not contemplating halting the Soviet drive westward, but despite the resistance of Churchill, he opposed an invasion of the European continent from the Balkans, whereby the Allies could have forestalled the Soviet divisions. In fact he offered the Soviets more than Russia had ever possessed in Europe. Moreover Stalin was not even present at Quebec.

This account is probably more or less consistent with the truth and provides an example of how this experienced American diplomat manipulated people, spreading before them visions of the future that they themselves wanted most to see. It must also be accepted that Dulles, a cool and calculating man, himself saw the future of Europe in this light and would have acted accordingly if he had had a greater say over the decisions of the Western leaders.

Dulles had many similar conversations, and others were carried on in Stockholm, Madrid, Lisbon and Ankara, since there were many German attempts to make a separate peace, not only with the West, but also with Soviet Russia. They were carried on by emissaries of Canaris and Himmler and for this reason Schellenberg took part in them. None brought any result.[34]

9 A Year of Successes and Danger

1

On 22 December 1942 eleven people were executed at Plötzensee near Berlin: three women and eight men. They were the leading members of the *Rote Kapelle* in the German capital who, as a result of many months of observation, secret contact and radio monitoring, had finally fallen into the hands of the *Gestapo*. The leaders, Harro Schulze-Boysen and Arvid Harnack were hanged, together with Hans Coppi, Johann Graudenz, Horst Heilmann, Rudolf von Scheliha, Kurt Schulze and Kurt Schumacher. Elizabeth Schumacher, Ilse Stöbe and Libertas Schulze-Boysen went to the guillotine. The remainder of those arrested, 116 in all, awaited further interrogations, trial and execution. This great success for the *Gestapo* was a direct consequence of the confessions of Johann Wenzel who on 30 July 1942 had been arrested in Brussels, together with his radio equipment, and who had broken under the terrible pressure of torture. Unable to bear it, he divulged a number of secrets and the names of many of his friends. Many of these in their turn were unable to withstand the torture and revealed further names.[1]

The German security authorities took the activities of the *Rote Kapelle* so seriously that, immediately after these first arrests, they set up the 'Rote Kapelle Special Commission', whose task was to deal with the Soviet network in Berlin. The fact that this Soviet network was composed almost entirely of Germans, infuriated the *RSHA* authorities and spurred them on to action.[2]

The head of the whole *Rote Kapelle*, Leopold Trepper, survived the pogrom, since he was in France, furthermore, his networks in Belgium, France and Holland also survived, but not for long. Almost all those arrested made statements and told everything that they knew. The *Gestapo* thus had its task much simplified and day after day arrested further Soviet agents. The Germans were above all interested in catching Trepper and *Captain Kent*, together with other important leaders, so the *RSHA* formed yet another team, called the 'Special Rote

Kapelle Squad', which in October of the same year concentrated its energies on France. On 12 November it managed to seize *Kent*in Marseilles and two weeks later, on 24 November, German agents caught up with Trepper. He was staying in Paris, since he felt most secure in a great city, he changed his address, his appearance, kept doubling back on his tracks until eventually he fell into a trap at his dentist's waiting-room. The trap had been set by the *Gestapo* together with the *Abwehr*, which had agreed to co-operate in the battle with the *Rote Kapelle*.[3] According to the agreement between Canaris, head of the *Abwehr*, and Heydrich, head of *RSHA* (now dead), of which the *Gestapo* was a part, the *Abwehr* was supposed to confine itself to military intelligence.

Within a few weeks the *Grand Chef's* whole western network had to all intents and purposes ceased to exist. For reasons which are difficult to assess and explain, Trepper from the very start, even before his interrogation had begun, took the line of least resistance. He gave a whole list of addresses and many names, and he sent a number of personal letters inviting his co-conspirators to meetings where, in his place, German agents waited.[4]

The German security authorities' success was complete and there was cause for satisfaction on their part, but the whole story would be too simple if it were to end there. Not only had the leading Soviet agents fallen into German hands, but also their transmitters, ciphers and operating instructions. Moscow did in fact know that some arrests had been made in Berlin, since *Pakbo* had, through Radó, already transmitted this news towards the end of September 1942, but Moscow was uncertain who had been picked up and who was still free, and was impatiently awaiting some radio contact to be made.[5] The *Director* had a right to expect that the people working for the *Rote Kapelle* would be able to use their experience and not allow the ciphers to fall into enemy hands. Furthermore, he had the right to expect some resistance, at least on the part of his network's leading members.

Things turned out differently. Most of those arrested broke down, some decided at once to collaborate and the *Gestapo* began a game which is so popular in the field of espionage and all secret and covert activities. Using the same bases, transmitters and ciphers, the Germans began to send reports to Moscow, which were in no way different from the earlier ones, except in one vital respect: they were now being prepared by the *Gestapo*. Even the operators' touch and technique, as well as their actual morse transmissions, were identical, so that the Moscow receivers should not suspect anything. The Germans did not allow the captured telegraphists into the 'act', although they did have their co-operation, since they were afraid that, by means of some agreed signal, they might reveal their situation to the Russians. Instead the Germans copied them on records and taught their own operators to imitate them. This subtle and very difficult disinformation exercise did not last long, barely several months, but it did bring the Germans certain benefits.[6]

Meanwhile the more sophisticated members of the 'Special Rote Kapelle Squad', realizing that brutal physical and emotional pressure on prisoners does not always produce the required results, since people under torture often say anything, if only to get away from their interrorgators for a moment, adopted quite different methods. Several of the red network's main leaders, with Trepper, *Captain Kent*, Schumacher and Katz in first place, were accommodated in a magnificent old château near Paris where they could walk quite freely around the extensive grounds, talk and discuss with one another, receive books and enjoy an excellent cuisine. They were naturally guarded and their every step was monitored by discreetly concealed agents, but the illusion of liberty was very strong and this relaxed nerves and weakened resistance. Additional interrogation took place in the form of friendly conversations in the course of which highly proficient German experts extracted further information from the prisoners, without the need to apply any pressure. Other members of the *Rote Kapelle* found themselves in similar, if less luxurious, surroundings in private flats in Paris and Brussels.[7]

The illusion of apparent freedom was increased by having group outings to the local cinema, to the doctor and to the shops, which all had an effect on the prisoners, but also lessened control over them. During one such trip on 13 September 1943 Trepper asked to be driven to the chemist and, profiting from his good knowledge of the local geography and his escort's carelessness, he managed to give them the slip. He had regained his freedom, but was 'blown' and unable to return to his work and the *Rote Kapelle* ceased definitely to exist.[8] A direct reason for this had been the collapse of its first members once caught by the *Gestapo* and the efficiency of the German security authorities, but at the heart lay a fundamental error on the part of Moscow. If, instead of trying to achieve its beloved centralization, the

Soviet capital had permitted quite separate and independent networks to be formed in Germany, Belgium, France and Holland, the German success would never have been so complete and effective.

2

Nevertheless the purge of the red network in Germany and Western Europe had not been complete. Radó remained in Switzerland with his ring and three transmitters. At one time he had been foreseen as a reserve net for the Soviet organization in the hands of Leopold Trepper, but now the gaze of an exceptionally troubled Moscow could turn only to him. His position was a very important one for at the same time as the *Red Orchestra* was being liquidated, in November 1942 the Western Allies landed in North Africa and the German divisions moved forward in France, occupying the whole country. The Soviet legation in Vichy was very quickly closed down as was the secret radio communication with Moscow, carried out by the military attaché.

The end of the *Rote Kapelle*, particularly in Berlin itself, should have brought Rudolf Roessler's successes to a halt, for according to a number of people who were involved at that time, and several later historians, his main sources in the German capital were Soviet agents.[9] Quite the reverse happened. Precisely during the time, from the end of 1942 and throughout almost the whole of 1943, when these agents were in the hands of the *Gestapo*, Roessler had the most success. With the aid of Radó and his three transmitters, night after night messages went out to Moscow bearing in the headings over and over again the code-names of his most important agents in Germany: *Werther, Olga, Anna, Teddy,* and again *Werther, Werther, Werther.* From time to time some of them were transmitted without any sign of authorship and then only Roessler himself was mentioned under his code-name *Lucy*, but each one was of the utmost importance. For example:

> Autumn 1942 from *Lucy*.
> The German army high command sees no possibility of the Soviets' assembling troops in the uninhabited semi-desert known as the 'Black Fields' south-east of Stalingrad. The flank of the German army is consequently unprotected here.[10]

This was information of the highest significance and must have been acted upon by Moscow, since it was from that very flank that the

Soviet offensive finally came, which eventually led to the first great German defeat on the Eastern front. After the loss of North Africa this greatly weakened the German overall position and German prestige, but the Russians were well aware of the character of their opponent and expected him to show himself soon. In addition to tactical plans, they were also interested in German production and the possibilities of introducing new improved weapons. This was expressed in the questions which Moscow headquarters sent Radó.

22 February 1943.
Please ask Lucy to discover in Germany with the utmost urgency:
a) What new types of tank T-3 or T-4 are being built at present in Germany. Technical, tactical information about these tanks.
b) The monthly production figures for these tanks.
c) Have T-3 and T-4 tanks been modified and of what do these modifications consist.
d) Are there any plans for the summer of 1943 to re-equip armoured divisions with new tanks and new artillery or with old, modified tanks with thick armour and possibly new armament.

Director.[11]

28 March 1943. To *Dora*
1. Request you fill out Teddy's information about armoured vehicle types with tactical and technical particulars: thickness of armour-plating, armament, speed. We very much want details of the monthly output of armoured vehicles.
2. It would also be useful if Teddy could give us the monthly figures for aircraft production in Germany and Italy and details of German military-aircraft types.

Director.[12]

By May *Teddy* was able to send Roessler a partial reply to these questions, which was contained in a message sent by Radó.

... Under pressure of the transition to defensive warfare, since December 1942 the German High Command has been stepping up production of fighter planes and close-combat aircraft, concentrating particularly on the following types:

137

Messerschmitt 109, Focke-Wulf 190, Ju-87 and Ju-88.

In March the German armoured-vehicle industry produced 320 units of type T-3, between 400 and 410 units of type T-4 and 90 units of type B-1 [*Tiger*]. [13]

Naturally the German High Command's strategic intentions, based on new equipment, were also of the greatest value and Moscow inquired about them on several occasions. On 20 January 1943 the *Director* sent a message:

Find out what plans and concrete intentions the Wehrmacht High Command has to counter Red Army's offensive and above all how they mean to ward off or neutralize the Red Army's assaults. What differences of opinion are there in the Wehrmacht high command as regards the measures to be taken and the plans that have been adopted? Pass this order on to all members of Lucy group . . .

A month later, on 22 February, a second, similar, message was received.

We have to know the Wehrmacht High Command's plans as regards the Kluge army group in the middle sector. Everything you can tell us about the middle sector of the front is of the first importance. [14]

This last question was especially characteristic, since it proved that the Russians felt where the German attack would fall.

It is generally held that the German defeat at Stalingrad was a turning-point in the Eastern struggle, and this is a justifiable view with the one proviso that it was not a decisive battle. The German onslaught was finally broken at Kursk on that very central sector of the front. The German High Command anticipated that after assembling great forces, it would fall on the unprepared Russians, defeat them in a short battle, head for Moscow, capture it and turn the tide. This, plan called 'Operation Citadel', would have succeeded, had there been surprise, but this was never achieved, since Roessler's contacts, located at sensitive points in the German High Command, passed on to him the most secret decisions.

On 20 April 1943 information arrived from *Werther* concerning preparations for this very offensive: 'The new deadline for the German attack is 12 June.' [15] Two weeks passed and again *Werther* sent another message:

> 6 May 1943. To the Director.
> From Werther, 2 May.
> The re-formation on the mobile and armoured divisions is
> subject to delays. The deadlines for re-formation and readiness
> to move for the 60th mobile and the 16th armoured divisions
> have been postponed by four weeks because these units are
> insufficiently equipped with vehicles and tanks as a result of
> delayed deliveries.
>
> Dora.[16]

A month passed and a very important message went on its way to
Moscow:

> 11 June 1942. To the Director. Urgent.
> ... The German High Command wanted first to launch a
> thrust against Voronezh and the lower Don with the 1st tank
> army and part of the 6th army.
> Then around mid-May they were considering first throwing
> the 4th tank army and the 11th army corps against Kursk.
>
> Dora[17]

As a result of such information the Russians not only knew how
much time they had, but were able to estimate fairly accurately what
strength the enemy had to attack them with. *Werther* was not far out:
on 5 July the Germans threw into the Kursk salient 2,700 tanks and a
million men, but waiting for them were two fronts commanded by
Rokossowski and Vatutin, with a third front, Konev's, in reserve. The
Russians had somewhat fewer tanks, but for the first time were able to
muster more aircraft than the *Luftwaffe*.[18] Their intelligence, mainly
due to *Lucy*, was magnificent.

By 12 July the battle was over and had brought the Russians
complete victory. Hitler had lost half a million men, most of his
tanks, and his ability to wage an offensive was finally destroyed. All
that remained was defence and retreat.

3

From the very beginning of the war Switzerland had been under
observation by the *Abwehr* and the German security authorities, which
in the south of their own country, in Munich and Karlsruhe, but above

all in Stuttgart, had their stations and very strong radio monitoring equipment (see chapter 2, p. 17). During the war's first months and the fall of Poland this was of lesser significance, but the situation changed when hostilities spread to the West. Switzerland could become a battlefield and the Germans were aware that her sympathies lay with France and Great Britain. They thus intercepted everything that was sent from the small republic over the radio waves.

This period, however, passed quickly, for the Western front collapsed within a few weeks and, after Hitler's first defeat in the Battle of Britain, there was throughout Europe a period of several months' apparent peace and anticipation. It was only in the spring of 1941, when the Nazis stretched out for new conquests in Greece and Yugoslavia, that the courier and radio trails came to life, spurred on by the fact that many signs pointed to an approaching German-Soviet conflict. The Monitoring station in Stuttgart began to intercept more and more signals which were directed to the East from Switzerland. Every day their number rose.

June came and with it the massive German onslaught in the East, and then the night-time signals calling Moscow from Switzerland became even more strident and irritating. German radio monitoring doubled its efforts, and the cryptanalysts, under great pressure from their superiors, laboured ceaselessly over the difficult cipher. Finally in December of the same year they had their first success: they managed to decipher the text of two signals sent by Radó to Moscow which contained information on the Eastern front and whose accuracy greatly alarmed the Germans.[19]

The cipher used by Radó was very difficult to break, but the Russians had anticipated that their signals would be intercepted and read so, like the Germans, they tried constantly to complicate the system.[20] Radó changed his message keys daily and the German analysts, despite their initial success, were unable to achieve a great deal. Their work kept coming to a halt, sometimes they were able to read only a few sentences, but their doggedness enabled them to read, during the course of the first half of 1942, a certain number of signals going to Moscow as well as questions and instructions sent from there to Switzerland.[21] It transpired all too clearly from these that the Soviet network in the small republic knew a very great deal about German plans and decisions and that it had sources inside Germany and then not just anywhere, but in important centres of planning and command. The war in the East, contrary to initial surmise, was dragging on and it was apparent that the deciding battle of the whole German aggressive adventure could take place there. It was essential to use all means and methods to choke this Swiss arm of Soviet Intelligence as soon as possible.

4

German Intelligence, which was the concern not only of the *Abwehr* but also of the *RSHA*, was already in possession of a great deal of fragmentary information about the *Dora* group and its contacts which had been accumulated by the *Büro F* and also by a great many agents who, in the guise of businessmen, travelling salesmen, engineers, directors of firms trading with Switzerland and others, crossed over the frontier. It was more difficult for them to operate in French-speaking Switzerland where Radó and his three radio transmitters were located, since there were no local Nazis there openly parading in uniforms down the streets, but they did achieve certain successes. New agents appeared in the place of those whom the police caught. There were apparently altogether about a thousand of them throughout the whole country.[22]

Just at the very time when German agents succeeded in obtaining their first details about the *Dora* network in mid-1941, Walter Schellenberg was appointed to take charge of the international intelligence side of the *RSHA* and turned his gaze towards Switzerland (see chapter 7, p. 100). Several months passed before he found out a little more about the Red espionage net there and then his interest grew. This interest heightened even more when in December he was given two radio signals destined for Moscow, which had been deciphered. He reached the conclusion that the reversal of these achievements of Soviet Intelligence on Swiss soil required a much greater effort and he decided to have recourse to the infiltration method.

The Geopress firm, which had been developing very well in the last few years before the war, had had to limit its activities considerably, having lost its international clientele. Nevertheless it was still in existence and Radó, who together with his wife was now fully occupied with espionage matters, was looking around for some assistance. The firm had to continue, since it was a cover for their secret activities and, furthermore, it also brought a profit, which could not be ignored. The supply of money from Moscow was always most erratic.

Towards the end of 1941 Radó was sought out through Communist contacts by a married couple, George and Joanna Wilmer, whom he had known even in Russia when they had studied espionage together (see chapter 3, p. 29). The identity of George and Joanna, who used the code-names *Lorenz* and *Laura* in their undercover work, has never been fully established, although they were supposed to have been born in Russia, and they spoke Russian, German and French equally well. They were in Switzerland as political refugees, had no financial problems, but wanted to return to their work and get in touch with Moscow headquarters with whom they had lost contact some time before.[23]

Radó was extremely careful, weighed each step and although he was dealing with people whom he had met many years before as Communists and Soviet agents, rejected the idea of taking them into his firm. This would have required him to reveal his address, since as a cartographer he worked at home. He had first to satisfy himself as to their current situation, the more so since what they said about their last few years was scanty and imprecise. First of all, using Foote, he sent a request for information to headquarters, and when he received a satisfactory reply, which furthermore encouraged him to bring the couple into his work, he put them in touch with the Englishman and recommended close co-operation. George and Joanna were specialists at microfilm photography and could be useful.[24]

Foote, like Radó, was very careful and so he first of all had several conversations with them on neutral ground in local restaurants. These preliminary meetings made a bad impression on him, the Wilmers were spendthrift, bragged about having rented a magnificent house in Lausanne and at the same time were asking him rather too pointedly about his secret work. They talked a great deal about themselves, but only about the pre-war period, and it was impossible to find out anything from them about their life and activities since 1939. The Englishman decided to weigh his every step and after each meeting he concealed his tracks and doubled back before going home. The Wilmers invited him round several times to their house and he then discovered that the pockets of both his coat and jacket, which he had had to take off because of the heat, had been searched.[25]

The experienced agent's suspicions were correct, the couple had been sent to Switzerland by German Intelligence and had been given instructions by Schellenberg himself. This had come about as a result of the widespread arrests in Germany in 1939, just before the attack on Poland. The Wilmers, who had arrived in the Reich from Russia in 1936, had shared the fate of a great many other Soviet agents, despite the official friendship between Hitler and Stalin, and found themselves in prison at Plötzensee. Saving their lives and demonstrating great aptitude in reducing photographs to fractions of a millimetre, they changed sides and, as many members of the *Rote Kapelle* were later to do, revealed the names of a great number of agents. After several years' work in the *SD* archives they won the confidence of their new superiors and Schellenberg, who was becoming even more interested in Switzerland, decided to use them. They arrived in Geneva liberally supplied with money and with the task of penetrating the *Dora* network. They met Radó and Foote, and although they were unable to establish their addresses, they managed to confirm that the nerve-centre of Soviet espionage in Switzerland was in Geneva and that the secret radio stations should be sought there and in Lausanne.[26]

Foote was not aware of all this, but he had become very suspicious, warned Radó, set a signal to headquarters and took great care to ensure that the suspicious couple discovered neither his address nor the name under which he was living in Switzerland.

This was not an isolated attempt at infiltrating the *Dora* network. Not long after the appearance of the Wilmers in the spring of 1942, a French journalist, Yves Rameau, contacted a friend of Alexander Foote, with a remarkable tale. He purported to be at the head of a French underground organization which had a great deal of important military information and he wanted to find a way of delivering it to Moscow since he had lost contact himself. Moscow headquarters apparently knew him under the code-name *Aspirant*. After a few days Rameau was put in touch with Foote, but he was suspicious, and answered shortly that he had nothing to do with such matters and immediately informed Radó. The warning came in very useful, since Rameau also turned up in Geneva and contacted some White Russians living there as well as the local Communists. He got no further, since he was just too noisy, too anti-fascist, and he too strongly emphasized that he was a supporter of General de Gaulle and that his views were very left-wing. Radó's people in Geneva easily picked up these details and he was able to get in touch with headquarters and ask if *Aspirant* was known there. Moscow sent a negative reply, cautioning care and Radó was additionally able to establish that the 'French journalist' came from Germany, that he almost certainly was called Ewald Zweig, from which originated his pseudonym: *rameau* in French and *Zweig* in German mean the same thing—branch. He spoke French perfectly, since he had worked for French Intelligence before the war, but after the country's occupation by the Germans he offered them his services. Radó had met him many years previously in France and so he had to be doubly careful not to be spotted by him.[27]

German infiltrators were seeking various ways of getting at the people and things they wanted to find and so the whole Soviet network in Switzerland was threatened from different sides. The youngest and most inexperienced were the most vulnerable and so it was Margrit Bolli, a pretty twenty-three-year-old girl who at the beginning of 1942 had been drawn into the work, who faced the next challenge. She had taken the code-name *Rosa* and had assumed operation of the third radio station hidden in Geneva (see chapter 5, p. 68). Her recruitment had greatly complicated the life of the overall chief. Radó, contrary to every principle of espionage, had become emotionally involved with her and she returned his affections. This caused further mistakes in their undercover work, since at first, under the pretext of official business, he had visited her almost every day, although he was meant to share this task with his wife, and then he rented a flat for his family in Bern and himself remained in Geneva, justifying this on the grounds of security and personal safety.[28]

His daily visits to the young girl's flat could not fail to draw attention to themselves, but they did have the advantage that he could observe all her reactions with greater sensitivity than anyone else, since he was personally involved. In the autumn certain signs began to worry him and he felt also that his visits were no longer awaited. His anxiety rose when closer observation allowed him to establish the reasons for this sudden coolness: Margrit was very interested in someone, perhaps even in love.

The head of the network had no trouble in ordering surveillance, which in this case had a double significance for him. Within a few days he knew what was the matter: Margrit had met a handsome young hairdresser, Hans Peters, in the local shop and had fallen in love with him. There would have been nothing strange or dangerous for her espionage work in this, except that the young man was a German and

144

that he called himself an opponent of Hitler. Radó found himself in a very difficult situation. His instinct as an experienced agent told him that this friendship could turn out to be very dangerous, yet at the same time he could hardly use this argument without putting himself in a hypocritical position, especially since he was dealing with a girl in love. He had to remain silent and limit himself to observation, particularly as he had no proof of any foul play on the part of the German. He suffered greatly that *Rosa* now only had time for official business with him and that she met her boyfriend frequently. He was jealous, but did not lose his self-control and was really anxious when he heard that Margrit was inviting her German round to her own flat. It was after all in that same flat that she kept the undercover radio station and from there that the most secret, enciphered messages were sent to Moscow.[29]

5

The scattering of the *Rote Kapelle* and the results of the interrogations provided the Germans with the opportunity to gain further information about Radó's activities and about those who were working with him in Switzerland. *Captain Kent* revealed everything that he knew about him; in other words his name, code-name, address, profession, marital status, qualifications and many other personal details. Worse than that he also gave his code, wave lengths, transmission times and method of operating his radio stations. All this could be changed, but only with great difficulty and only after full knowledge of *Kent's* forced confession, moreover German cryptanalysts had thus obtained some more information which was of great value to them in their difficult task.[30]

In addition to Radó, Rachel Dübendorfer had also become vulnerable. She had the code-name *Sissy*, which was known to a Swiss citizen belonging to the *Rote Kapelle* with the code-name *Niggi* who was arrested in Brussels in November 1942. This was a very serious threat, since all information from Roessler went through her. All attempts to change this state of affairs came up against his stubborness which could not be broken. Several months passed and in April 1943 *Sissy* was even more gravely threatened. In its continuing hunt for the red network the *Gestapo* arrested in Paris a man who had the code-name *Maurice* and who was a courier between the French capital and Switzerland, where his contact happened to be *Sissy*. Neglecting the rules of conspiracy she had brought him into her own home and had introduced him to her friend, Paul Böttcher, as well as to her daughter and the daughter's fiancé. She now began to reap the fruits of her carelessness, since very soon afterwards she started to receive mysterious telephone calls, which were a German attempt at provocation. Radó increased pressure on her to drop her work for some time and move to another place, hoping that he would somehow manage to arrange his contact with Roessler, but both from him and from her he received a negative reply.[31]

Unfortunately the suspicions about *Rosa's* boyfriend turned out to be justified. Hans Peters, who had settled in Geneva even before the war, was a member of the local semi-legal national socialist organization and had been recruited by the *Abwehr* as its agent under the code-name *Romeo*. His superior was an official at the German cosulate in Geneva and also an *Abwehr* agent called Hermann Hensler who had the code-name *Rhenanus*. At the time that all this was taking place, no one in Radó's network knew these details and although he himself was against this liaison, *Rosa* continued it and met her German every day. The latter was able to follow her without any difficulty and since she was a courier between Radó and Foote and Pünter, he recognized them all, at least by sight.[32]

The Hamels (*Edouard* and *Maude*) who maintained the radio station in Geneva were also endangered and to such an extent that the Swiss police arrested them on 27 October 1942 and searched their flat. They managed at the last minute to destroy some already enciphered and ready-to-transmit signals and hide the transmitter in a prepared spot in the cellar. A thorough search of the whole flat produced in toto just some pieces from a back-up set, but Hamel managed to defend himself by claiming that they belonged to a vibrator which he had for medical reasons. *Edouard* was in police custody for three days, but after several interrogations was released. It transpired that this whole case had been brough about by Hamel's brother who had been stopped while distributing communist leaflets to illegal addresses, and that it had nothing whatsoever to do with German infiltration. Nevertheless, the fact remained that another priceless radio station was in danger.[33]

The penetration of the *Dora* network proceeded apace with the increase of surveillance and further German progress in the area of breaking difficult ciphers. In 1942 a whole series of messages was read, but this was the time when Roessler was just making contact with

Radó and so the code-names of the informers who fell into German hands were mainly from Otto Pünter's group: *Long*, *Polo*, *Luise* and *Feld*. However, by the end of the year, during the battle of Stalingrad, the messages began to include code-names from the *Lucy Ring*. First of all appeared *Taylor*, and then starting with the first months of 1943 there were: *Anna*, *Olga*, *Teddy*, *Bill*, *Stefan*, but above all *Werther*. What the cryptanalysts managed to read demonstrated these agents' great efficiency and their excellent sources of information. It was just at the time when the Germans were licking their wounds after the defeat at Stalingrad and were plaintively trying to find out what the Russians knew of their future plans, that on 16 March 1943, Margrit Bolli's boy friend managed to get from her a signal which she had just delivered to *Jim* for sending to Moscow and the contents of which she knew before it was enciphered. German monitors managed to intercept this same signal when it was already enciphered and on its way to Moscow. This was a breakthrough.[34] A comparison of the message in clear and its enciphered version greatly facilitated the German cryptanalysts' task. Henceforth the number of signals sent from Switzerland to Moscow and which were read, increased dramatically. Their content left no room for doubt: this was intelligence material of the highest class, revealing to the Russians almost all the secrets of German army decisions.

Radó was aware of the danger in which his group was, he recognized the signals which pointed to a far-reaching German penetration, but he knew nothing of the cryptanalysts' success caused by his own girl's dreadful mistake. Meanwhile German Intelligence, the *Abwehr* and *RSHA* Department VI, concentrated all its efforts to discover the names of Roessler's informers who were concealed under different code-names. Walter Schellenberg attempted to do so, when in the spring of 1943 he was once again in Switzerland for further discussions with the head of Swiss Intelligence, but he achieved nothing (see chapter 7, pp. 115–16). Likewise countless agents surrounded the *Dora* group and its numerous offshoots and the *Büro F* in Bern worked on nothing else. The German embassy frequently requested the Swiss authorities to arrest Sándor Radó, but equally without success. Profiting from the nearness of the frontier, the Germans even tried to establish the location of the three radio stations using special radio direction finder vehicles on the Italian and French sides. Then came an opportunity which promised success. On 23 April

1943 the cryptoanalysts deciphered a signal from the *Director* to Radó containing a number of questions concerning the *Lucy Ring's* contacts in Berlin. It needed only an answer for the Germans, once they had intercepted and read it, to have in their hands information allowing them to arrest people concealed at the heart of their political and military decision-making.[35]

But once again their hopes were dashed. Rudolf Roessler, the gentle, quiet, grey man, yet again demonstrated that he was a master of secret espionage work. He again refused and Moscow headquarters received no answer; but neither did the German operators in their monitoring stations nor the German analysts.

10 Pursuit

1

During the course of the war there were several warnings that Switzerland was under threat from Germany; each was treated very seriously, for the Germans had motives for attacking the small neutral country. Therefore, although it turned out that the alarm which had been raised in March 1943 had only been a battle of nerves (see chapter 7, p. 111–12), the second alarm, which was sounded towards the end of the same year, again brought about the full mobilization of those responsible for the country's defence.

This one, however was not a mere figment spread by people who were concerned with keeping the Swiss perpetually in a state of anxiety. On 3 September Italy had capitulated, and this had been announced officially five days later, on the same day that the Western Allies had landed in Italy at Salerno. On 12 September Mussolini was freed by SS paratroops from Gran Sasso, the mountain on which he had been imprisoned by the new Italian government of Marshal Pietro Badoglio, and the former dictator, aided by Hitler, set up a provisional Fascist republic in the northern part of the country. However the only forces in Italy able and willing to put up any resistance to the Allies were the Germans, and now they were surrounding Switzerland on all sides. Hitler directed that Italy should be defended to the last and, since Air Chief Marshal Albert Kesselring was in command, a lengthy and difficult campaign was forecast. The shortest route of transporting supplies to the battle divisions lay through Switzerland, and so yet another plan to seize the country was contemplated.

The preparation of this plan, named *Operation Boehme*, was undertaken by an SS staff colonel of the same name. It was based on a thorough knowledge of the principles upon which the Swiss army had been operating since 1940 and were to continue doing so until 1944. Switzerland was determined to defend her freedom from any aggressor, even the most powerful, but her General Staff were aware that the means of defence they had at their disposal were very limited. They had decided therefore to take advantage of the mountainous nature of the country and to set up a defensive redoubt in the Alps capable of withstanding attack for a considerable length of time. This followed a line running from the eastern end of Lake Leman north-eastwards to the south of Bern, then from Lucerne northwards to St. Gallen, following on south-eastwards to the region of Davos, and finally along the southern slopes of the Alps back to Lake Leman, completely enclosing the area within (see map, p. 5). This plan did not find favour among the Swiss, because it envisaged that, in the event of an attack from all sides, half the country would have to be given up, and the most economically valuable region at that, including the most productive agricultural land; however, they had no alternative. It was only in the summer of 1944, long after Italy had capitulated and when the strength of the German forces had been severely impaired, that the General Staff changed their minds, and acknowledged that it would now be possible to set up the country's defences along her frontiers. [1]

The attack on Switzerland would only have some point if it were possible to capture the whole country within a short space of time, and the Alps, the redoubt in particular, for that was where the viaducts and tunnels leading to the south were. In view of this Colonel Boehme planned an attack in two phases, one following the other almost immediately. The first would be carried out by the powerful armoured detachments, and its aim would be to capture the low-lying regions, seize all the airports, and destroy the Swiss army before it was able to secure the mountain fortifications. The second would be carried out by choice paratroop units, dropped on St. Gotthard, Lucerne, Schwyz, Thun and Frutigen, and its aim would be to capture the mountains and all the important road and rail links. [2]

There was a certain element of risk in this plan of attack, for it was difficult to predict the strength of the resistance of the Swiss army, the resolve of the population or the courage of the political leadership, but the Germans believed that the fighting would not be heavier than it had been in Norway in 1940. Another factor which dictated great caution was the lack of certainty that they could succeed in capturing the mountain region before the Swiss blew up the tunnels and viaducts they had mined long before. This would be an act of tremendous national heroism, but the possibility could not be discounted (see chapter 1, p. 6). On the other hand, following their recent defeats, the

Germans were in need of an instant and impressive success, and Hitler might indeed decide to channel a part of his forces into action against Switzerland. This would be no simple matter, however, for the assault would have to take the form of a very precise and sudden surprise, which demanded the use of first-class units with considerable experience, whereas these were needed at the Eastern front.

2

Swiss Intelligence managed to secure the details of the German plan, but they were unable to establish when the *Wehrmacht* were going to set it in motion or when they might abandon it. For this reason the Swiss, having learned over the years to be both patient and cautious, did all they possibly could to avoid provoking their dangerous neighbour and to grant her every wish, without calling too much attention to their neutral status.

Schellenberg knew this and he increased the pressure he was putting on Colonel Masson to set about the business of the Soviet spy network in Switzerland. It was inconceivable that the Swiss security authorities could be unaware, even without receiving any information from outside, that foreign intelligence agents were operating within their territory. After all Roessler was in contact with both the *Büro Ha* and with Mayr von Baldegg of the no. 1 Swiss Intelligence post in Lucerne. Since Roessler had established links with Radó, who was himself in control of an extensive intelligence network and was also in continuous contact with Moscow by means of his three radio transmitters, the circle was complete. This must have been known to Swiss military counter-intelligence. Moreover the *Büro Ha* was in touch with Allen Dulles via its chief, Captain Hausamann, and so operations in this area were also within the sphere of knowledge of the security authorities; besides, Dulles had approached them himself. The Swiss police knew about other foreign intelligence networks in addition to these.

The disruption of the *Red Orchestra* and the confessions of many of its members enabled Schellenberg to gather additional information about the activities of Radó and his collaborators. He learned a great deal about them, and he got to know the names of some of them and their addresses, while the German monitors operating on the French and Italian sides of the borders established that there were three radio transmitters 'playing' in Geneva and Lausanne. Schellenberg passed all this information on to Masson, and demanded that Switzerland demonstrate her neutrality in practical terms and put a stop to the whole business. His persistence increased to the point that, in addition to putting all his agents in Switzerland on the alert, he was contemplating the possibility of an independent move against the Soviet agents in order to capture some of the more important spies, in the same way as had happened with the English in Venlo in 1939 (see chapter 7, p. 106).[3]

The pressure Schellenberg was bringing to bear certainly had some effect, all the more so since Switzerland, by keeping her eyes closed to Soviet spying activities directed against the Third Reich from within her territory, was infringing the regulations governing neutrality. This could not however have been the sole cause of the ensuing events, or else the Swiss security authorities would have become involved in the affair at an earlier stage; a significant role was played here by a shift in the overall pattern of the war. As long as Russia had been retreating along the entire front and it seemed she would collapse under Hitler's blows, aiding her was a logical necessity. Now that the situation had changed and the Red Army was pressing forwards, anyone whose sympathies leaned towards the West and who pursued a Western style of life reasoned that its progress should not be allowed to proceed too quickly. Switzerland was capable of influencing this state of affairs since important intelligence information was being dispatched from there to Russia; if she were to put a stop to this, it would be possible to affect the course of events at the Eastern front to a certain extent. The armies of the Western allies were marching onwards along the southern borders of the German front and they had already landed in Italy; the outcome of the main attack, which had ultimately been directed towards northern France, but which could equally well emerge at the Balkans, hung in the balance. The race towards the heart of Europe was on and if the right political decisions were made, the Western divisions could outstrip Stalin's, and thereby liberate countries like Poland, Czechoslovakia and Hungary; as it was these countries experienced only the exchange of one occupation for another.

The Swiss authorities were probably thinking along these lines when they decided that they ought to become involved in the affair of the Soviet spies. The German historian Wilhelm von Schramm is of the opinion that Allen Dulles, who was observing the speed of the westward march of the Red Army also with some disquiet, may have influenced this decision. This is quite likely, although it is hard to imagine that the American could have acted in a way which was violently inconsistent with the policy of his country. The same historian also draws attention to the fact that towards the end of 1943 Soviet Russia no longer required her intelligence operations in Switzerland, as she was winning the war, and was moreover obtaining information via new networks which had been set up after the *Red Orchestra* had been disbanded. The Russians were also receiving messages from more than a hundred radio transmitters which were sending reports from their supporters behind the German front-line; the Red Army was winning, and the victor always attracts friends. Besides, Moscow had by then cracked the Germans' codes and, although it took some effort, they were able to obtain a great deal of information about German decisions and plans. According to Schramm the Moscow headquarters stopped sending Radó money towards the end of 1943, and lost all further interest in the individuals who had been sending them information of such importance out of Switzerland during those difficult years.[4]

3

On 8 September 1943, the very same day on which the capitulation of Italy was announced and on which the allies landed at Salerno, Swiss military counter-intelligence moved into the attack with the assistance of the police. They knew that two of the radio transmitters were in Geneva; Lieutenant Maurice Treyer attempted to track them down using three mobile short-range monitoring devices. He picked up signals from Swiss military transmitters as well but he was able to distinguish the various sounds from each other; soon he established the areas in which the foreign transmitters were 'playing', and the net began to tighten. We do not know if he was slow because of lack of experience, or because he was under instructions, but it was 11 of September, three days later, when he finally managed to determine the whereabouts of the first transmitter, and it was given the identification symbol LA. Locating it proved to be a relatively simple task, for the monitoring device had indicated that the signals were emanating from a secluded private villa, no. 192 Route de Florissant. The search for the second transmitter took a little longer: it was two weeks before its exact location could be established. It was situated in an apartment house, no. 8 rue Henri Mussard, and it became identified by the symbol LB; the apartment was rented by Margrit Bolli. At the beginning of October she received a visit from someone who claimed to be from the electricity board and, suspicious of the manner in which he appeared to search the premises, she alerted Radó. He advised her to leave immediately and return to her parents in Basel, while he despatched Edmond Hamel to collect the radio set, which had to be hidden straight away. The girl was deeply involved with her German boyfriend and, not wishing to leave him, she decided to ignore the advice and to remain in Geneva.[5]

During the early hours of 14 October the federal police under their chief, Inspector Charles Knecht, executed two fast and accurate operations. Several dozen armed men with dogs surrounded the villa from which every night Olga and Edmond Hamel transmitted to Moscow the messages Radó supplied. The police entered the villa silently and made their way upstairs; Olga, in her nightdress and seated at the transmitter, looked up suddenly to see armed men all around her. A search of the premises was scarcely necessary, for everything lay exposed. The transmitter, a number of messages, a great many other documents and several pages from code-books were seized, and the Hamels were placed under arrest.

Simultaneously another police detachment, considerably smaller in number, carried out a raid on *Rosa's* apartment in the centre of town, but the girl was not there. She had been kept under surveillance for some time, and consequently she was soon traced to her boyfriend's home; both were placed under arrest. Margrit was made to return to her apartment since the police were not permitted to search the premises in her absence. To their surprise the transmitter which the monitoring device had detected in the apartment was missing, although they did find various radio components and several pages from a code-book, which they took away with them. Margrit was taken to the cells of the police station together with her boyfriend; she was unaware that her plight was due to his betrayal.[6]

Radó experienced a narrow escape from the police, and he would certainly have been arrested had the Swiss been using the method of operation of the *Gestapo* or *NKWD* whereby every house or apartment which had been raided became a trap for anyone who called in the course of the next few days to fall into. In the afternoon following the Hamels' arrest the network chief paid a visit to the house and after knocking on the door several times and receiving no reply he attempted to contact the Hamels by telephone. Fortunately for him the police were not lying in wait for unsuspecting callers, and several hours later he found out what had taken place, for the evening edition of *Tribune de Genève* mentioned that some foreign agents had been arrested in the town the previous night. That same evening his local Intelligence network was able to provide him with a number of details concerning the two arrests.[7]

The operation was successful, and it showed that the police knew a great deal and that they were taking steps in the right direction. Two transmitting stations had been lost along with their operators and only one remained, in Alexander Foote's apartment in Lausanne. Radó had to warn him immediately about the potential danger and, abandoning conspiratorial precautions out of sheer necessity, he telephoned *Jim*, and told him that 'Edouard had been taken ill suddenly and was in hospital'. The timeless primitive verbal code used by conspirators all over the world had been in existence for as long as the telephone. Foote naturally took this to mean that Hamel had suddenly been arrested and was in prison; the information was of some importace to him because he was about to meet Hamel in order to collect a number of messages in need of transmission urgently. After Margrit Bolli's deactivation Hamel had taken over her courier's duties.[8]

Immediately after the telephone call Radó made for the station and took the next train to Lausanne. Cautiously he ascertained that the house where Foote lived was not being watched before he called at the apartment and had a short talk with him. Foote had already suspected that something was up since he had received a message from Moscow demanding to know why the two transmitters in Geneva had gone dead. They decided that *Jim* should send an urgent reply to the headquarters straight away with the information that the Hamels and Bolli had been arrested, using his own code since Radó's might already be known to the police. Next they needed to set about finding another location to which they could transfer the last remaining radio set, but this was no easy task; they would have to leave things as they were for a while. Radó agreed to this reluctantly, having guessed that the next police operation, which was about to be launched shortly, would be directed against the only transmitting station he had left.

From Lausanne he went straight to Bern in order to see Pünter. He told him about the imminent danger and gave him the address of some friends of his in Geneva who lived in the university quarter, where he would go with his wife if he was in trouble, and where Pünter could find him if he needed to. These moves were in contradiction to the rules of conspiracy; however people may not always be aware of all the implications of their actions following a sudden shock until long after the event. Moreover this was all happening within the confines of a neutral state, where the concept of danger seemed considerably less serious than in a country at war, and the consequences of arrest were less drastic; Radó would be able to go into hiding quite easily and could construct a new life for himself somehow, for the local Communists were ready to provide immediate assistance. During the course of these hectic few days he managed to find out, with the help of Pünter and his contact in Swiss Intelligence, Mayr von Baldegg (*Luise*), that no further arrests had been made.[9]

At the time, the first occasion during the period he was involved in espionage in Switzerland when he was actually in danger, Radó could not be aware that Walter Schellenberg, the man who was ultimately responsible for the threats and the arrests, was paying another visit to the country. From 16 to 18 October he again had talks with Colonel Masson at the Wolfsberg estate; their meeting was concerned above all with the Soviet spy network in Switzerland, and the *SS* general was putting great pressure on the Swiss over this matter.[10]

4

Three people had been arrested, two transmitters had fallen silent and the third was in danger: the entire Intelligence network was in a critical situation. Radó had sufficient experience of espionage to realize that his next steps would have to depend on finding out as accurately as possible how much the Swiss police actually knew about them. The best source for this information would be those who had been arrested, since their interrogation had already begun, so Radó cautiously started looking for a way to reach them by way of his Communist contacts. He was able to find out fairly quickly that all three were in Geneva's Saint-Antoine prison; Hans Peters, Margrit Bolli's boyfriend, was soon released, which was a mistake on the part of the Swiss police, for it revealed that he had played a specific role in the whole affair.

Several people in the local *Dora Group* network who were connected with the Communist party began to examine carefully the chances of reaching those arrested. All were being detained in separate cells, and they established that contact could be made fairly easily with

Edmund Hamel. The warder responsible for his cell, like many warders in various prisons all over the world, consented to smuggle correspondence across secretly. The motive for undertaking such a task, in flagrant breach of prison regulations, and especially so in the case of prisoners undergoing interrogation, is nearly always financial and sometimes ideological. The motive on this occasion was never actually determined; suffice it to say that as a result of corresponding with Hamel, Radó was able to grasp the situation, and from his point of view it looked most unsatisfactory. The police had in their possession all the papers which the Hamels had hidden in their house, and they also knew a great deal about the whole network and its operation. During questioning the Hamels were shown a photograph of Radó; the examining officer knew that his code-name was *Dora* and that he was in charge of the network. He had also found out that Radó had entered into secret correspondence with Hamel, and he removed the warder who had been in collusion with them. In fact the prisoners denied ever having met the man whose picture they were being shown, but this did not make Radó's position any less dangerous. The questioning might become prolonged, in which case a great deal could be found out from the accused by means of confrontation or shock tactics. *Rosa* had been providing liaison between Radó and Pünter as well as Foote, and it was quite conceivable that she may have been followed for some time; the police might already be on the track of the two men, and could place them under arrest, even if the girl was capable of remaining silent. In one of his letters Hamel said that the matter of the third transmitter had come up during the interrogation; the police were already busy in Lausanne in an attempt to establish the location of the 'playing' by means of a short-range monitoring device. [11]

Directing a large-scale espionage operation is an extremely difficult task, particularly in a country such as Switzerland where every citizen is willing to co-operate with the police, when one does not have an apparently regular and generally accepted occupation of one's own, and this was the prospect Sándor Radó was now faced with. Until now he had been a well-known and highly esteemed cartographer, he had managed his own firm, and he had never been in any kind of trouble with the police; but now that his cover had been blown he had no alternative other than to leave home immediately and to begin living underground. It was essential that he should go into hiding, since he had ascertained beyond any shadow of a doubt that his movements were being watched, and so he knew that his arrest was possible any day now.

He could have gone straight to the friends who had previously promised to hide him, but Radó, after discussing the matter with Foote, came to the conclusion that he should consider the British diplomatic mission in Bern first; they were after all allies and their war aims were the same. Besides, Foote, being British, would then be able to ensure the possibility of continuing his activities without interruption and operating his transmitting station. Although he was known to be a wealthy Englishman living in Switzerland off his capital, fragmentary information was already reaching him that the police believed him to be an agent of British Intelligence; they had not touched him because Britain was held in great respect in Switzerland, independently of the general pro-Western sympathies in the country. One of Pünter's agents, *Salter*, the press attaché at the French embassy, who had good relations with the British, could act as intermediary and discover whether there were any chance of being able to shelter at the diplomatic mission, at least for a short while. [12]

It is hard to imagine how this could have come about and why Radó, having collaborated with the Russians for so many years, could have remained unaware of the way his superiors in Moscow thought and acted; suffice it to say that after sounding out the British and receiving a generous invitation from them, Radó sent a message to Moscow via *Jim* about the matter, towards the end of October. The response, which came on 2 November, contained the terse statement that any association with the British was completely out of the question, and the order that they should go into hiding immediately. Moscow preferred Radó's network to terminate its existence rather than become connected in any way with the Western allies. [13]

Radó was to pay a heavy price before long for his naivety; for the moment it was essential that he should vanish from the attention of the Swiss police. For several months, ever since Margrit Bolli's secret and her liaison with the young hairdresser had come to light, the entire Radó family had been together and was again living in Geneva. Now Helena's mother would stay at home along with her two grandchildren, while the husband and wife moved out. Helena left first, and was taken quite openly to the local clinic under the pretext of ill health. It was more difficult for her husband who was the main subject of the surveillance; after cleverly evading the agents watching his house under cover of darkness he managed to reach the home of Doctor Pierre Nicole, a friend who shared his sympathies. His wife joined him there a few days later, after a roundabout journey during which she doubled back and forth, changing taxis several times.[14]

The hiding place was excellent and the people who were providing it were completely trustworthy, but the chances of continuing operations had shrunk almost to nil. Geneva is not a large city by any standards and the inhabitants of a given area are usually familiar with each other by sight at least; any new face is noticed, particularly in the university quarter where by and large members of a single social class are concentrated. Besides, war was being waged all round, and Radó's identity was known to the police. He might even already have been put under arrest while still living at home; presumably this had not happened only because the police were hoping that by following him and keeping his home under observation they might obtain some information about his contacts and thereby extend the list of people in whom they should be taking an interest. There could also be another reason for the lack of activity on the part of the police. If we were to go back as far as 1936 we would recall the ease with which the Swiss police and the Socialist authorities of the canton of Geneva granted Radó residence and work permits which enabled him to set up home and a business in Switzerland (see chapter 3, p. 31). It is conceivable that someone in an appropriate position who held the same political views as Radó might have been watching over him and shielding him against any trouble from the security authorities.[15]

Whatever happened did happen, but the initial arrests proved that peaceful times were over and that the situation had now become dangerous. But operations still had to continue regardless, so Radó once again got in touch with *Jim* by telephone and arranged a meeting for 8 November in the Eaux-Vives Park. However, the assignation turned out to be a complete failure when Foote perceived that the taxi driver who had dropped his chief off at the park immediately disappeared into the nearest public telephone box. Radó had in fact altered his appearance somewhat, and the driver need not have been calling the police: he might well have been making a personal telephone call. Nevertheless both men panicked. They ran across the park until they reached a restaurant on the other side. They charged through the kitchens, startling the cooks, and emerged into the street, where they separated immediately. Radó barely had time to give Foote his secret address. The whole escapade was probably the result of an overactive imagination, but people who fear for their safety and are terrified of being hunted down often react in this manner. After a lengthy detour Radó finally returned to his hiding place; he did not step outside again for six weeks.[16]

5

The logic on which conspiratorial operations were based dictated that Alexander Foote, whose radio transmitter represented the last communication link between the *Dora Group* and the Moscow headquarters, should go into hiding as quickly as possible. This demanded a change of address and the finding of a place in which the radio transmitter could be quietly installed, but the problem proved to be insoluble, particularly in view of the time factor. During the war moving house in Switzerland was very difficult for foreigners as the police had to be given a reasonable explanation as to why this was necessary. One good reason was a transfer to a different place of work, but Foote could not use such an excuse since he was playing the part of a well-off individual with private means. Besides it was better not to attract the attention of the police who were already in pursuit of those associated with the spy network as it was. A sudden desire to move house might arouse their suspicions and could provoke a search of the premises. Another alternative was to follow Radó's example in finding shelter in a private house, although in this case the possibility of installing the transmitter and operating it regularly would have to be abandoned completely. *Jim*, although fully aware of the danger he was in, remained at his post.

But in the meantime Lieutenant Treyer, following his success in Geneva, had moved to Lausanne with his truck-mounted short-range monitoring devices, and started to surround the third radio transmitter, to which he had assigned the symbol LC. The problem in this case was considerably more difficult than in Geneva, since Foote was living in the centre of town, in a densely populated area and in a large block consisting of a great many apartments. Also, in contrast to the first police operation which was a surprise attack, Foote was aware that he was the subject of police investigations and that monitors were attempting to establish the location of his transmitter. He guarded himself against detection and thwarted the interception by continually altering the wavelength of the signals and the call-signs he was using. For this reason Lieutenant Treyer kept losing track of him every so often; he had to make amendments to the data he had collected so far, and this meant that the day of the final coup was being postponed. He intended to catch the operator while in the act of transmitting or receiving radio signals. He was being aided in his endeavours by military cryptographers, who had in their possession the tables of codes which had been seized during the raid on the Hamels, and could thereby decipher the intercepted messages. The cryptanalyst responsible for this was Marc Payot.[17]

Radó was immobile, so on 16 November Foote called on him at his hiding place and picked up a number of coded messages for transmission; he promised to return in four days' time. He had not touched the transmitter for four nights running in order to fool the monitors, but late on the night of the 19 he decided to call Moscow in case there were any orders for his chief. It turned out that the headquarters indeed had a lengthy message ready which he needed to receive.

Shortly after midnight he set to work and soon he was completely engrossed. Suddenly there was a pounding at the door; he heard the thuds of heavy blows, followed by the crash of splintering wood, and moments later a dozen or so policemen appeared in his apartment, their guns drawn. During the few seconds it had taken them to batter down the door he had managed to burn the messages over a candle and to shatter the transmitter with one blow of a hammer, but the fact that he had been caught illegally operating a radio transmitter was none the less indisputable.[18]

Foote did not turn up for the arranged meeting and since he had always been very punctual Radó, alarmed, launched an investigation into what had happened, using the highly inadequate path of his contacts with the outside world. It was a week later that he found out that his last radio transmitter had been lost and that in the hands of the police was a man who knew his present whereabouts.

His initial instinctive reaction as a conspirator was to set about changing his address as quickly as possible, but this was no easy matter. He pushed the idea to one side for the time being, hoping that *Jim* would be able to stand up to questioning, for a short while at least, and he turned his attention to a more important problem: the contact with Moscow. All three radio transmitters were lost and their operators under arrest, yet the Intelligence network was still operating and yielding information of great interest. Roessler continued to be active, Rachel Dübendorfer was still at liberty, and so was Otto Pünter. For several days Radó wondered whether he might be able to construct a replacement transmitter, find or else train an operator, discover a place where the secret station could be set up, and return, albeit on a smaller scale, to the old routine. But, reluctantly, he rejected this idea: all the electronics experts he had were in prison, the police were on the alert and perceptive, and it was impossible to find anyone willing to let premises for such a purpose. There could be no return to the past; yet Moscow needed to be told of the situation that had arisen.[19]

At the beginning of December Otto Pünter visited him on business. He brought with him the news that the British diplomatic mission had renewed the offer of refuge, but Radó felt unable to accept it all the same, on account of Moscow's instructions. However, having considered the various ways of contacting the headquarters he proposed a plan which *Pakbo* acknowledged to be a sensible one and which he undertook to carry out. Radó composed a lengthy message describing the situation in which his group was currently placed, which Pünter encoded the same way he had done many times before and then passed on to the press attaché at the Chinese embassy, Pao Hsien Chu, who was an agent of his, known in his network by the code-name *Polo*. He in turn encoded the message using his own key and transmitted it to Tshunking, where the Chinese government was at that time, engaged in a war of several years' duration against Japan, who had invaded the country. Along with the message he enclosed a request that it should be passed on to Moscow immediately.[20]

There is no evidence to prove that the message actually reached the headquarters; however it is certain that it represented the last attempt by Radó to contact his superiors in Moscow, and it marked the end of his espionage activities in Switzerland.

6

The fact that *Jim* had been arrested compelled Radó to go on the move again; Foote might begin to talk during interrogation and moreover he had after all been to see Radó on 16 November, three days before the arrest: it was extremely likely that he was already being followed at the time and he could easily have led agents of the federal police or military counter-intelligence to Radó's hide-out.

As long as life treats one well one has many friends, but it takes only the first stroke of bad luck for their number to decrease significantly. This is what immediately happened to Radó. But the local Communist community once again showed international solidarity, and he, a foreigner and an agent of a foreign power, hunted by the police, was able to find refuge notwithstanding. It took the shape of a secluded apartment on the topmost floor of a large town house, with no neighbours on either side, but extremely small in size. The Radós moved there towards the end of 1944, under cover of darkness, heaving even the mattress up themselves; they were given a tiny room, whose only furniture was a single collapsible bed. On this they had to sit in silence all day long, for the family had a daily help, and they had to stay quiet after she had gone home as well, since their hosts played bridge every evening. At night they only just had enough room to lie down, and any movement caused the springs of the ancient bed to squeak unbearably.[21]

Now that he was completely immobilized, in every sense of the word, in a room the size of a prison cell, and totally dependent on his hosts, who were providing them with food, newspapers and a smattering of local information, Radó was able to gather his thoughts together, take a look backwards, and consider the future. Secret reports about his network were also reaching him, via his party contacts; he therefore knew what was happening to those who were still at liberty, and he also knew that the Hamels, Margrit Bolli and Foote had been transferred to the Bois-Mermet prison in Lausanne and that they were being held in separate cells. He was able to look back with the feeling that his duty towards Moscow had been accomplished well, without a doubt, but it seemed to him that this was all in the past now and could never be reconstructed. It was true that Roessler, Pünter and Rachel Dübendorfer were still gathering information of great importance, but what was the use? The construction of a transmitter, the training of an operator and the finding of safe premises were all beyond the reach of his current capabilities.

Meanwhile the progressive encirclement of the remaining members of his intelligence network advanced further. This was not a particularly difficult task, for the conspiracy movement in Switzerland had few of the skills which the same individuals would have shown had they been operating in a country under German or Soviet rule, where they would have had to deal with the *Gestapo* or *NKVD*. Only real danger and continued repression by the security authorities, along with severe consequences of arrest, and inhumane interrogation, could induce such a sharpening of the instinct of self-defence that a conspiracy movement would act efficiently and reduce the risks it took to an unavoidable minimum. There were no such menaces in Switzerland, a traditionally neutral and liberal country, and even now that the police had finally gone into action it was still not a matter of life and death. Clandestine meetings in their own house, knowledge of names and addresses of individuals who were supposed to be in hiding, and telephone conversations from one private flat to another between close associates—all this created a web of mistakes, which made the work of the security forces that much easier.

Further arrests could have followed very soon afterwards, but military counter-intelligence wanted to try first of all to make use of the information which had fallen into their hands with the arrest of Alexander Foote: the radio frequencies, the call-signs and the code used by Radó. They tried a subterfuge similar to one in which the Germans had succeeded after the *Red Orchestra* had been disbanded and the secrets of its radio links with the headquarters in Moscow had been captured (see chapter 9, p. 134–5). If the Swiss authorities could manage to make secret radio contact with Moscow and to maintain the impression that it was *Jim* who was responsible for this activity, it might provide much further information of importance which could help them to catch all the members of the Soviet spy network in Switzerland more easily. The attempt failed however because Foote had been able to inform the *Director* that the Hamels and Bolli had been arrested shortly before he himself had been apprehended, so Moscow was prepared for surprises, and sensed that the operator was an impostor because of the awkwardness of the touch to which it was accustomed. The Swiss subterfuge was not forgotten in a hurry in the Soviet capital, and it was to play a certain role after the war, when various difficulties arose as the two countries were about to enter into diplomatic relations.[22]

The period of respite was over, and the Swiss counter-intelligence service informed the police that the remaining suspects under observation were to be arrested. On 19 April 1944 the activities of Rachel Dübendorfer (*Sissy*) and her companion Paul Böttcher (*Paul*) came to an end. At their home the police found in a large envelope a total of ninety-eight reports concerning German political and military affairs. Some of them bore proof that the information contained therein had been supplied by deserters who had taken refuge in Switzerland and had subsequently been made available by someone within the Swiss Intelligence service.[23] A number of coded messages from Radó were also found. *Sissy* had been storing all this information in the hope that the means of transmitting it to Moscow would arise again.[24]

These arrests inevitably led to others, for *Sissy* was the link which, via Dr Schneider (*Taylor*), connected Radó's network with Rudolf Roessler (see chapter 5, p. 70–1). Exactly one month after Dübendorfer and Böttcher's arrest, on 19 May, the local police simultaneously arrested Roessler in Lucerne and Dr Schneider in Geneva; on 31 May in the early morning Roessler's friend, Captain Mayr von Baldegg, from the no. 1 Swiss Intelligence post in Lucerne, found himself to his great surprise in police custody. Of all the leading members of Radó's network still at liberty, apart from himself and his wife, who stayed put in their hiding place, there remained only Otto Pünter, who was still living at his home address in Bern.[25]

11 The Final Months

1

On 20 July 1944 the bomb planted by von Stauffenberg exploded; quite by chance it narrowly missed killing Hitler and consequently changing the course of history. Ten days earlier, before this incident had taken place, Gisevius had secretly left Zürich for Berlin; he was deeply involved in the anti-Hitler conspiracy and aware that its critical moment was at hand. His presence in the capital was essential when, following the death of the man who had been leading the country to disaster, the conspirators were to take over power. As a former official of the *Gestapo* and now of the *Abwehr*, and the highly trusted member of the *Black Orchestra*, after the successful coup he was to be appointed Special Adviser to the Head of State in matters of public security.[1]

Halina Szymańska, after having acted as a link between Gisevius and British Intelligence for four years, knew a great deal about the German underground movement and about the plot to kill Hitler. His removal had become absolutely essential because the Western powers were refusing to give the conspirators any binding promises until Germany had got rid of her dictator. A coup d'état would bring about a complete change in the current state of affairs and it would also provide irrefutable proof that the *Black Orchestra* was actually a reality and a force to be reckoned with. Although they were making no promises, the Western leaders were encouraging their activities: that same month, July 1944, Britain's Deputy Prime Minister, Clement Attlee, made a speech in the House of Commons along these lines, and Churchill himself expressed a similar opinion.[2]

This is why Gisevius had been passing top secret information to his Polish go-between, in the knowledge that it would immediately be conveyed to the British. Szymańska was aware of the importance of these matters, but she could not tell to what extent her German informant was personally involved in them. so she was astonished when he suddenly vanished. It was not until she saw the headlines in the Swiss newspapers that she realized that Gisevius's unexpected disappearance might be closely connected with the dramatic events at Hitler's 'lair'.[3]

The failure of the assassination attempt, which led to a great wave of arrests and executions, destroyed all the hopes of the millions of people living in the countries of central and eastern Europe bordering with the Soviet Union which depended on a coup d'état in Germany for their realization. The leaders of the *Black Orchestra*, intending to maintain the links between Germany and the West at all costs and to shield the country against the Red Army, had anticipated that, should the attempt to assassinate Hitler and take over power succeed, the German troops currently engaged in battle on the western front would surrender and could then be free to defend Europe's eastern flank. Gisevius's swift departure for Germany was connected with this very matter, for he was to go to France together with Carl Goerdeler to meet the newly-appointed commander of the western front, Field Marshal Günther von Kluge, who was at that time already in with the conspiracy movement, in order to convince him of the need for such an operation. The mission was a success; talks were also held with Field Marshal Rommel, and his agreement to the plan was obtained as well. However several days later he was seriously wounded when his motorcar fell target to an allied air attack.[4]

But the conspirators' entire scheme had to be suspended in mid-air when the Western leaders insisted that Germany surrender unconditionally. In addition to this it turned out that they had also drawn up their own plans for the future of Europe, first in Quebec in August 1943 and then in Teheran the following November-December, and that these took into account all of Stalin's demands. Nevertheless a small ray of hope still remained, since these sentiments could always undergo transformation following Hitler's death. In this case the political situation might alter, the threat of a separate peace treaty between Germany and Russia might disappear, and the West might consider the future of Europe in a more realistic manner. Such changes could have brought about a last minute reversal in the fate of Poland: although she had been the first to put up any resistance to Hitler, she was now destined to be handed over to her other bitter enemy, Russia. Under the new scheme, had the Western powers confirmed Poland's pre-1939 western frontier and rejected the Soviet claim to her eastern provinces, and thereby realized Allen Dulles's secret hopes (see chapter 8, p. 131), the Second World War would have ended with a more solid peace, with none of the tensions of the cold war or the continuous threat from Soviet Russia.

At that time, during those hot July days, no one knew yet what the immediate future held in store, but the opinions voiced at the Polish diplomatic mission in Bern and at the Polish consulate followed more or less the same line of reasoning; consequently the failure of the coup, which represented yet another victory for Hitler, caused an enormous impact and a total collapse of the faint hopes of the Poles. The diplomatic mission also served as a secret communication post through which information could be passed from occupied Poland to the West, so it was possible to find out how the situation there was developing: the Home Army was mobilizing its underground·forces, entering open battle and collaborating with the Red Army in fighting the Germans. This mode of action had been undertaken with certain aims in mind: it had been expected that the Soviet authorities would confirm that Poland had a right to territories that had belonged to her and which she was reclaiming from Germany, and that the administration of these provinces would be carried out by people within the conspiracy movement who had been prepared for this task by the Polish government, then in London. Unfortunately these expectations were never realized. As soon as the battle was over all Polish units would be disarmed; the Soviet Union would assume authority over the Polish provinces which lay to the east of the demarcation line established by the Molotov-Ribbentrop Agreement of 1939, and the Stalinist Polish Communists over those to the west of it.

The Red Army marched forward, and before the end of July 1944, when the Poles had scarcely had enough time to get over the shock of the unsuccessful attempt on Hitler's life, it had reached the Vistula river. On the evening of 1 August the Polish diplomatic mission in Bern received the news over the radio that the anti-German uprising had broken out in Warsaw. This was the Poles' last, desperate attempt to lay claim to the right to self-government and to enter into battle once again with the German invader, with the aim of liberating the capital by their own efforts, before the arrival of Soviet troops.

For many days Halina Szymańska ignored other matters, and all her thoughts were directed towards the fighting city. That was where her parents were—her mother was to be killed, her father survived—she had many sentimental links with Warsaw, and moreover, along with millions of Poles, she grasped the full significance of what it was all about. Would the insurgents be able to crush the Germans on their own? Would the Red Army come to their aid? Would the West intervene, in support of Polish self-determination? She waited to see what would happen in a state of great anxiety.[5]

2

Allen Dulles knew a great deal more about the circumstances surrounding Gisevius's departure, for he was well acquainted with the conspirators' plans. He had been observing their activities and encouraging their endeavours, and he hoped the critical moment would soon arrive. In contrast to official United States policy he would himself have preferred the West to have examined the possibility of co-operating with the Germans, once they had managed to rid themselves of Hitler. The Americans were placed in a much easier position than the Europeans with regard to this, for they had very little personal grievance against the Germans: their country had been neither occupied nor bombed, and the conflict in the Atlantic, in North Africa, Italy and France took the form of ordinary military confrontation, and was not to any extent an expression of uncontrollable animosity.

Unfortunately the conspirators' plans did not come off: Hitler was still alive, and in response to his orders the pursuit of all those who were in any way associated with the assassination attempt began at once. Gisevius was in Berlin at the time; he experienced several hours of terrible agony as von Stauffenberg attempted to save the situation by reacting quickly, but that same night he was forced to seek immediate cover, when the Nazis regained control.

The ramifications of the conspiracy movement were widespread; Gisevius was picked up by a diplomatic acquaintance and taken by car to the home of a friend of his who lived in Berlin, Hans Koch, where he concealed himself for a few days. It was too dangerous for him to remain in the area for too long however, and so he made his way, via a chain of acquaintances, among them Theodor and Elizabeth Strünck in particular, to the chief of the Berlin Criminal Police, Baron Wolf Heinrich von Helldorf, who was also in the conspiracy movement. His chauffeur who was a member as well, undertook to drive the fugitive (who attracted attention everywhere on account of his immense size) and his friends, at considerable risk to himself, to the home of another conspirator, Arthur Nebe, who was the head of the Criminal Bureau of the Reich and a major in the *SS*. He was himself in danger likewise, and as soon as Gisevius and the Strünck couple joined him he drove them out of Berlin in his car, taking the road to Potsdam, and then making for a village some 100 km from the capital, where they knew the local pastor.[6] The journey was very hazardous, for Hitler's fury had wide repercussions: there were checkpoints all over the place at which every passing car was made to stop. Everyone's papers had to be checked and dozens of questions were asked: where did the petrol come from, who had given permission to travel and to cross district boundaries, who had allowed the carrying of passengers, and so on. Fortunately for them Nebe was wearing the uniform of an *SS* oficer, and this ultimately caused all barriers to be lifted, but they had to submit their documents for control just the same, and no detail escaped the scrutiny of the inspectors. It looked as though the names of Gisevius, Nebe and the Strüncks had not yet been added to the list of those who were to be caught and placed under arrest.[7]

Unfortunately the pastor, scared by the recent events and depressed by the way the war was progressing, was unwilling to accept the risk of sheltering four people who were wanted by the police. He did however know another pastor, with a parish in a secluded village situated not far away, who might be able to give them some assistance. But on arriving there they found that this was no longer the case. This pastor was a man of great integrity and courage, prepared to take any kind of risk, but he was already sheltering a number of Jews, and he did not have room to take in anyone else. The situation was now critical: they had to decide there and then what to do next. They could always continue to look for a place to hide further on, in the country, but their chances of succeeding in this were negligible. The entire country was intersected by a network of police and military posts, there were very few able-bodied men in civilian clothes out and about, no newcomer escaped notice, and the number of people willing to accept the risk of confrontation with the Nazi authorities was dwindling. They took a daring decision, probably the only option available to them: they would return to Berlin and seek shelter in the bustling capital.

Arthur Nebe did not have any doubt that he must by now be a wanted man. He realized that his *SS* officer's uniform was no longer of any use to them: indeed it might even bring him to the special attention of the police. So he changed into civilian clothes, burned his

170

uniform, and got out the false documents he had prepared for such an eventuality. The group then split up: Nebe and Gisevius went one way, while Theodor and Elizabeth Strünck went another. The chances that they would ever see each other again were very slim; indeed Nebe and Theodor Strünck were caught, and executed.[8]

Hitler's vengeance extended so far that even young children and old folk, who could not have possibly been involved in the coup in any way, were seized. Several thousand people in all were arrested, and yet Gisevius miraculously managed to escape, completely by chance: despite his unusual physical appearance and the fact that he had remained in Berlin he was able to stay concealed for several months. He changed his address frequently and took advantage of the help offered him by various people, of whom only Hans Koch was later to be killed. He managed in addition to this to find a way of conveying to Switzerland the news that he was still alive. He asked Dulles to send some documents which would enable him to extricate himself from the deadlock to the secret address he provided.

Dulles set about organizing help at once. He despatched a messenger to Berlin to see Gisevius; after showing him the book which was the prearranged sign the man told him that someone else would be coming shortly to bring him what he had requested. Indeed a woman turned up one night soon afterwards and put an envelope containing a passport through the letterbox. The date by now was 20 January 1945. The impeccably forged document, which had been provided by the OSS in London, bore the name of Doctor Hoffman, a member of the *Gestapo*; a metal identification badge was enclosed with the passport. From now on everything flowed smoothly, although Gisevius had to move about a country which was until the end gripped in the iron claws of police control. Luckily for him the most severe storm of pursuit of members of the *Black Orchestra* had by now abated, and the heavy and continual air raids made the work of the security authorities more difficult and less effective. Travelling by train, on 23 January Gisevius reached the Swiss frontier, near Bodensee, and crossed over without any trouble, for his papers were in perfect order. He found himself in the small frontier town of Kreuzlingen, at liberty, and at last he was able to breathe easily.[9]

At the same time his superior, Admiral Canaris, one of the most prominent leaders of the *Black Orchestra*, stripped of his post and deprived of his liberty was locked up in a cell in a *Gestapo* prison, awaiting transfer to the concentration camp at Flossenbürg, where he was to be hanged on the gallows, on 9 April 1945.

3

The Swiss security authorities had separated two areas of their operations: the counter-intelligence service was responsible for the surveillance of people suspected of working for a foreign Intelligence service, establishing their addresses and the locations of the illegal radio transmitters, whereas either the federal or the local police were given the task of actually carrying out the arrests. This division of responsibilities was the cause of grave misunderstandings and errors; because the police were not allowed access to Intelligence secrets, they had no idea of who was working for whom or how they were related, and in their enthusiasm they often went too far. In order to be successful each arrest had to be preceded by a period of surveillance; this procedure often provided additional information and revealed the identities of people who were in contact with those under observation. Motivated by excessive zeal or perhaps even a desire to compete against the counter-intelligence service, the police sometimes overreached themselves and arrested people who should have been left alone.

This is exactly what had happened during the assault on the *Dora Group* with the arrest of Rudolf Roessler, who was after all working for Swiss Intelligence and who had official connections with the *Büro Ha* (see chapter 1, p. 14). An even more glaring error had been made with regard to Captain Mayr von Baldegg, a Swiss officer, who was the deputy head of the no. 1 Intelligence station in Lucerne.

Colonel Masson flew into a rage when he found out about this because he knew that both men had secret connections. The news of the arrests, which was taken up by the press, exposed this very important section of the Swiss Intelligence network and drew attention to it. It would have been better had it been possible to hush up the whole affair quickly, but under a democratic system such a course of action could not be contemplated; the Commander-in-Chief of the Swiss army, General Guisan, swiftly called together a military tribunal, which set to work as early as 3 June, examined the case, and acquitted Captain von Baldegg of all the charges. It ordered his release, which followed on 25 July, and it also decreed that he should be reinstated in his position as deputy head of the no. 1 Intelligence post, that his continued membership of the General Staff should be confirmed, and that he should be paid 800 francs by way of compensation.[10]

For Rudolf Roessler and Doctor Schneider the case was of a different nature, for neither was a member of the Swiss officer's corps, and Roessler did not even hold Swiss citizenship. It would have been hard to keep them in prison since they had rendered the local Intelligence network valuable services and they continued to be indispensable. Yet it would have also been hard to drop the charges against them without the authorization of a court ruling; their case was not as clear-cut as that of Captain von Baldegg's. The decision that was arrived at, following preliminary questioning, was that they should be released on bail; a moderate sum was quoted. Doctor Schneider was set free on 5 September, and Roessler the following day.[11]

The security authorities proceeded in a similar manner with the other members of the *Dora Group* who were in custody. The investigation continued for quite a while, but they were all released on bail, before the case ever reached the courts. Olga Hamel left prison on 7 June 1944, Margrit Bolli on 12 July, Foote on 8 September, and Rachel Dübendorfer and Paul Böttcher on 28 of the same month; Edmond Hamel alone stayed imprisoned for more than a year, and he was not allowed out until 7 July 1945. Böttcher, who was living in Switzerland illegally, was consequently sent to a refugee labour camp, to Eggiwil, where he remained until 27 July 1945.[12]

The material confiscated during the raids, principally from the Hamels, together with the investigation which had been carried out, enabled the police to establish quite a number of interesting facts and, in particular, some concerning the financial aspect of the whole *Dora Group*. Edmond Hamel did the book-keeping for Radó; from his figures it emerged that during the period from 21 April 1941 until 5 September 1943, practically right up to the end of its viability, Moscow paid out 300,000 francs for services rendered. This was a derisory amount, in relation to the significant results of the work that was being done and the great value of the reports being sent to the *Director*. This was so only because some of the people were working almost for nothing and had other sources of income. The couriers in *Pakbo*'s group, who had to pay for the cost of their travel themselves and for whom this was their sole occupation, received no more than 1,000 francs a month, whereas he was in no need of any money at all himself.[13]

Roessler's circumstances were altogether exceptional, because he was working for several people simultaneously and was receiving payment from a number of sources. The *Büro Ha* was paying him, with Doctor Wallner acting as intermediary, first 200, then 1,000, and finally 2,000 francs a month; the no. 1 Swiss Intelligence station, through Mayr von Baldegg, initially 250, and later 400 francs a month; and Moscow, via Dr Schneider, paid him a total of 700 francs in 1942, increasing to the sum of about 3,500 francs a month. Over and above this Roessler was also receiving 800 francs every month from allied sources, again by way of Dr Schneider. These were fairly large sums, and Roessler must have laboured hard in order to accomplish all that was demanded of him. The *Büro Ha* was receiving between 80 and 130 reports a month from him; the no. 1 post about 10 or 15, and Moscow and the Western allies were being sent first 70 and later on an average of 110 reports over the same period of time.[14]

Rachel Dübendorfer, despite being an agent of the Comintern, held in high regard in Moscow and decorated with the order of Lenin, was also working for the British, and consequently her monthly income was substantial. From these two sources, with Dr Schneider yet again acting as intermediary, she was until November 1943 receiving between 6,000 and 7,000 francs a month. She did however have to pay off her collaborators, and so out of the money she was getting each month about 4,000 to 5,000 francs went on expenses.[15]

With the initial arrests the possibility of continuing operating collapsed and the *Dora Group* was left with no financial support. The radio transmitters were gone, Radó was in hiding, and although valuable information was still being gathered there was no way of relaying it to Moscow. The *Director* was concerned only with information, and had no interest whatsoever in the fate of the people who had been supplying it and who were no longer of any use to him. He might perhaps have demonstrated some trace of human feeling, in the form of financial aid for concealing and rescuing the remnants of the fragmented network, were it not for the fact that Radó had contemplated seeking assistance from the British. This had provoked such anger in Moscow that the supply of money had immediately been cut off. They had no wish to finance work the results of which, incapable of being relayed to the headquarters in Moscow, would almost certainly be sold to the Western allies. This is what in fact happened, but on a small scale, and for modest financial benefit.[16]

Then, for a short period of time, Rachel Dübendorfer took the most important business of the declining network into her own hands. She had been at Radó's side right from the start, playing the role of controller on behalf of Moscow, and now that the moment of crisis had arrived she needed to increase her activity (see chapter 5, p. 58). Nothing could be accomplished without any money, so *Sissy* reached out to her old contacts and wrote to a friend of hers in New York. She in turn asked the Soviet Intelligence network in Canada, code-named *Giselle*, for assistance, and she succeeded in obtaining $10,000, which was dispatched to Switzerland via a firm which manufactured watches. The money was not much help however, for it was already too late; what is more, *Sissy* provoked Moscow's displeasure because, first of all, her action had been contrary to their purposes and, secondly, through her direct contact she had revealed the existence of *Giselle* to the Canadian authorities.[17]

4

All those in the *Dora Group* who had been arrested were released on bail, and only Edmond Hamel remained in confinement as the war approached its end. Sándor Radó continued living in his tiny room, together with his wife, and only from time to time, late at night, did he dare to go outside, to take a short walk. The fact that a number of people accused of espionage had been released on bail might have indicated that their crimes had not been very serious, but such an assumption would not necessarily have been correct. The security authorities were anxious to get to the leader of the whole set-up, and it is most likely that they had released those arrested in the hope that Radó would make an error, seek contact with them, and thereby fall victim to the agents who were observing those who had been released. The long period of enforced inactivity weighed heavily upon the immobilized Radó: almost nine months had elapsed since the loss of the last radio transmitter, in Lausanne. He knew that Moscow was still impatiently expecting further information, so he was keen to get in touch with the radio operators who were now free and to undertake an attempt to construct at least one transmitter. However, this time common sense prevailed; Radó rejected the idea, and reconciled himself to the fact that his work in Switzeland was now definitely over. He decided to leave as soon as he could the country where only arrest and interrogation awaited him. Perhaps he would succeed in making radio contact with Moscow again from elsewhere. [18]

Switzerland was now surrounded on all sides by German forces, but the situation was not identical everywhere; the most logical course of escape lay across the former frontier with unoccupied France, just south of Geneva. There, in the province of Haute-Savoie, the French partisans were active, and they were for the most part Communists. Radó decided to get in touch with them and to set out to join them. The Germans could not very well deal with them any longer: they were engaged in combat with invading Allied detachments in northern and in southern France.

Radó, despite his almost complete immobilization, was still in touch with the local Communists, principally with Léon Nicole and his son Pierre; through them he got in touch with Pünter, who then came along to his hiding-place. Pünter also thought that Radó ought to flee the country, since his own attempts to legitimize Radó's further stay in Switzerland had not been successful. This was the period, in the late summer of 1944, when Russia was to have established diplomatic relations with Switzerland, although negotiations were progressing with some difficulty. Pünter had hoped that the government would now regard espionage activities in the service of the Soviet Union with a greater degree of tolerance, but his attempts were confronted by a totally negative attitude. The matter had already been placed in the hands of the security authorities, and a number of arrests had followed: the rule of law governing illegal spying activities had to be applied. [19]

The Nicoles also assisted in making contact with the Communist partisans on the French side of the border. Radó gave them the address of his hiding-place, and in a short while a young major, who had plenty of experience in jumping the border, called to see him in order to formulate a plan. The scheme was put into effect on 16 September, a Saturday. The doctor in charge of the clinic to which Helena Radó had been taken during the first stage of her disappearance drove them to the tunnel through which ran the railway line linking the Eaux-Vives terminus in Geneva with the small town of Annemasse, which was strictly speaking a suburb of Geneva, although on the French side of the border. The rail link between Switzerland and unoccupied France had been severed as soon as the Germans had arrived, but once a week, on Saturdays, a locomotive passed through pulling a trailer loaded with containers of milk, which the French farmers had been supplying to Geneva for many years. The train driver, also a Communist, had been drawn into the plot, so on his return journey, when he caught sight of Radó, his wife, and the partisans who were escorting them, in the tunnel, he stopped the engine, and they clambered up into his cab. The locomotive then gathered speed, flew past the border post, and did not halt until they reached Annemasse, which was held by the partisans.[20]

The danger was in fact over now, but they needed to take care, however, for although the area was controlled by the French partisans it was nevertheless still under German occupation. Radó and his wife were driven to Annecy, where they were given a house to themselves and a few days in which to rest and regain the use of their legs. They were then taken by car to Lyons, which had just been liberated by the Americans, where they managed to obtain French passports, from a highly placed municipal official who was also a Communist. From there, together with a group of people from the politial bureau of the French Communist Party, they set out for Paris, in armoured cars. Bands of marauders, their origin unknown, roamed the highways, and they could have also come across small tightly-knit German units in flight. They finally reached the liberated capital of France on 24 September 1944.[21]

5

It may not be entirely apt to compare a spy network to a ship sailing the distant sea, but all enterprises in which individuals work together as a team under one leader do have something in common. In accordance with a timeless inflexible principle, the captain of a ship which is in danger will remain in command on the bridge until the final moment and he will be the last to leave the sinking vessel, sometimes perishing along with her. But in espionage affairs are conducted differently: they are always shrouded in mystery, everything is done secretly, and there is no place for deeds of heroism or grand gestures, although in essence the relationship between a leader and his men should be the same in this case as on a ship. Yet Radó's behaviour deviated wildly in this respect from the generally accepted principles: he abandoned his people, left Switzerland in secrecy, quickly crossed the still occupied provinces of France, and reaching complete safety arrived in Paris, to avail himself of all the privileges

177

freedom had to offer.

His network continued to exist however: with the exception of Hamel all the Swiss members had come out of prison, and although their movements were to a certain extent restricted and despite being kept under surveillance, they had regained some means of operating. Rachel Dübendorfer began cautiously to re-establish severed contacts, and brought about the first ever and, as it later turned out, the last meeting between Foote and Roessler. Prior to this Foote had met with Olga Hamel and with Pünter, who had himself already made contact again with Margrit Bolli. All of them knew that they were being watched—*Pakbo* avoided making telephone calls from home because the police were tapping the line—but they did not let this worry them unduly. The war had long since passed its critical point, the Germans were now fighting not for victory but for survival, and Switzerland was no longer threatened with invasion.[22]

In the course of the last few months when there had been no link with Moscow a large amount of interesting material concerning the eastern front and the substantial German losses during the first half of 1944 had mounted up at Pünter's. He had also received a great deal of information directly from Berlin regarding the gradual disintegration of the National Socialist movement. Dübendorfer was contemplating the possibility of constructing another transmitter, in the same way as Radó had, but she soon abandoned the idea as well, and together they came to decide that the intelligence in their possession should be conveyed to Paris, which was now liberated, where a branch of the Soviet Intelligence service had most likely already been established.[23]

Of all the candidates willing to undertake the expedition to Paris Alexander Foote was the most suitable since apart from his intelligence work, which was now over, there was nothing to keep him in Switzerland, and besides he was thinking of moving on anyway, although legitimate travel from a country surrounded on almost all sides by the Germans was impossible. The same local Communists who had helped to arrange Radó's escape got him in touch with the French partisans, and on 7 November he found himself on the French side of the border, just south of Geneva. The transport system was by now operating far more efficiently, and two days later Foote was already pacing the free French capital.[24]

In spite of the insurrection which had lasted for several days Paris remained virtually untouched, for the German military governor,

General Dietrich von Choltitz, going against Hitler's explicit orders, had not agreed to the barbaric destruction of the magnificent city. At the same time General Eisenhower, altering his plans, directed his attack, spearheaded by the French division commanded by General Jacques Leclercq, towards Paris. It was to him and to the insurgents that the German commander quickly surrendered the city, and on 24 August the whole of Paris was submerged beneath a sea of tricolor flags. In Warsaw, on the other hand, the situation was different: the Poles were struggling against the Germans simultaneously, unaided, while Russian divisions idly stood by on the eastern bank of the Vistula, a few kilometres from the centre of the city.

In Paris Foote sought the same contacts as Radó before him had and so it was inevitable that they should come across each other. They discovered the whereabouts of the Soviet Intelligence post, and they handed over all the outstanding reports which they had been unable to transmit to Moscow. The Hungarian consulate in Paris had by now been reopened and consequently Radó and his wife were able to obtain Hungarian passports. Making use of the contacts they had previously established they managed to have their two sons and Helena's mother brought over from Geneva to Paris.[25]

The war was to continue for a further six months, but since the liberation of Paris life there had gradually begun to return to normal. Diplomatic representations and Allied military missions were being established. The first Soviet aircraft, an American Dakota as it happens, landed at Paris on 23 November, bringing Maurice Thorez, the French Communist leader from safe hiding, along with Colonel Novikov, the commander of the Soviet military mission. The latter was to be responsible for the repatriation of Soviet citizens and for arranging passage to the Soviet Union for anyone else Moscow demanded to see as soon as possible.[26]

Several weeks later the same Dakota left Paris, carrying a dozen passengers, among them Leopold Trepper, Sándor Radó and Alexander Foote. Flying to Moscow by the shortest route, over Germany, would have been out of the question, and for this reason and on account of the limited range of aeroplanes of that period they made refuelling stops in Marseilles and Italy, and in North Africa, at an airport under American control. The next stage of the journey took them to Cairo the following day where there was a Soviet embassy which they all went to visit. All except Radó that is, but no one paid any attention to his absence, having assumed that he had probably gone to take a look at the fascinating old quarter of the city and had got buried there somewhere. The next morning the whole group assembled in front of the hotel to await the bus which was to take them back to the airport, and it was now that they all noticed that Sándor Radó was missing. They began to search for him: they looked in his room, where the bed had not been slept in, they questioned the hotel staff, they telephoned the embassy, all to no avail. Finally they made their way to the airport, and that afternoon the aircraft took off in the direction of Persia on the next stage of the journey to Moscow.[27]

6

The war in Europe had just finished and the old continent was still trying to get its breath back after nearly six years of terrible struggles; in Switzerland the military court was preparing with scrupulous precision to try a case. Four members of the now extinct *Dora Group* were about to appear before it: Rachel Dübendorfer (*Sissy*), Paul Böttcher (*Paul*), Christian Schneider (*Taylor*) and Rudolf Roessler (*Lucy*). They were all accused of conducting illegal military intelligence activities on behalf of a foreign government (Soviet Russia) against the interests of another foreign government (Hitler's Germany). The trial had to take place partly *in absentia*, for Dübendorfer and Böttcher had by now secretly left the country.[28]

A few months later, on 22 and 23 October 1945, the court (*Divisiongericht* 2B) convened in Bern, examined the case, and delivered its verdict. Rachel Dübendorfer was found guilty, and was sentenced to two years' imprisonment, a fine of 10,000 francs and five years' deprivation of citizenship. Paul Böttcher, also found guilty, was similarly sentenced to two years and a 10,000 franc fine, but because he did not hold Swiss citizenship he was deprived of the right of residence in the country for fifteen years. Although found guilty, Christian Schneider received a term of only thirty days in prison, which he did not have to serve, as his period in custody during the investigation had been taken into account. Rudolf Roessler, who had been defended by Dr Gerhard Schürch, was acquitted of all the charges. Indeed the court acknowledged that he had rendered Switzerland valuable services, and under Article 20 of the Criminal Code it completely exempted him from any punishment.[29]

Two years passed, and old affairs were revived yet again, although it seemed that it would have been best to forget the bygone war as soon as possible. On 30 and 31 October 1947 the trial of further members of the former *Dora Group* took place before the military court (*Divisiongericht* 1A) in Lausanne. This case was considerably harder to put together and more complicated in nature; the investigation had been protracted, and for this reason the preparation for the trial had taken more than two years. Besides, whereas in Bern the trial had been held in German, here it was conducted in French. This was an additional reason why the members of the *Dora Group* who lived in Lausanne were being tried separately.[30] The Chief Judge, Lieutenant Colonel Roger Corbaz presided, Major Pierre Loew took the role of Public Prosecutor, and the cryptologist Marc Payot was called upon to give evidence. There were six accused: Sándor Radó, his wife Helena, Alexander Foote, Edmond and Olga Hamel and Margrit Bolli. The three former were being tried *in absentia*, for they were no longer in Switzerland, but the others were attending the trial of their own accord and had defence counsels. Herzl Sviatzky was acting for Edmond Hamel, Albert Dupont for his wife, and Jacques Chamorel for Margrit Bolli.

The trial was taking place during the period when the initial honeymoon months of the coexistence of the East with the West were already over and the 'Cold War' was just beginning to set in for good. Consequently the court had to take care not to discuss openly any affairs which might unduly interest and excite public opinion. For this reason the most important witnesses, Captain Mayr von Baldegg, Rudolf Roessler and Dr Christian Schneider, were examined behind closed doors. The relationship between the Swiss Intelligence Service and the Soviet *Dora Group*, which collaborated with Moscow, was the sensitive issue.[31]

The Public Prosecutor, acting on behalf of the State, did not seek to attack the accused: he put forward the argument that although they had violated the rule of law regarding espionage and neutrality they had been acting in good faith and for a cause which they believed to be just. The defence advocates took the same line, and recalled besides that the accused had been gathering intelligence not from Switzerland but from Hitler's Third Reich, which no longer existed, and that their activities had been of benefit to Swiss security.

The court took these arguments into account, but found the accused to be guilty, and meted out sentences somewhat harsher than those resulting from the first trial two years earlier. Sándor Radó was sentenced to three years' imprisonment, a 10,000 franc fine and deprivation of the right of residence in Switzerland for fifteen years. Alexander Foote received two and a half years' imprisonment and an 8,000 franc fine, and he was deprived of the right to reside in Switzerland for fifteen years as well. Edmond Hamel was sentenced to twelve months' imprisonment and a 1,000 franc fine, and his wife Olga to seven months' imprisonment. Margrit Bolli was given ten months in gaol and ordered to pay 500 francs. The sentences of these three, all Swiss citizens, were suspended for five years.[32]

The situation postwar Europe found itself in then was so fraught, the economic problems impinged on everyday lives in every country and community so acutely, and the Cold War was causing such anxiety, that the Lausanne trial passed by unnoticed. In one country alone was it followed with particular diligence, and every detail of the public part of the proceedings was noted. It can also be assumed that the same eyes and ears were endeavouring to find out above all what was being said behind the closed doors. The country was Soviet Russia, and her interest was motivated not only by the fact that a group of people who had rendered her enormous services during the war were being tried.

Russia took a broader view of these matters which extended to a greater depth and encompassed the distant future. During the war, when she found herself siding with the Allies as a result of Hitler's attack, she was able to expand her Intelligence networks in a number of countries, either in the Allied camp or else neutral, without any considerable difficulty. At that time, when the defeat of Nazi Germany was the single most important objective, these networks did not receive any considerable attention and they were not pursued with nearly the same ruthlessness with which German agents were being hunted down. Soviet Russia took advantage of this and gradually squeezed her people into all the decision and management nerve-centres of her Western partners. As soon as victory over Hitler became a certainty the Kremlin immediately set about planning postwar operations. Pre-war planning had enabled Russia to acquire excellent agents from among the British intelligentsia: Guy Burgess, Donald Maclean, Harold 'Kim' Philby, Anthony Blunt, and others. In the United States they also managed to secure the services of a number of distinguished individuals. First of all there was Alger Hiss, and beside him Judith Coplon, who helped Stalin to obtain the secret of the atom bomb. These people were so well camouflaged that they survived for a number of years and continued to work for Russia for a long while, even after wartime operations were over. If their secret was discovered and if they either managed to escape to Moscow for refuge or were imprisoned, their place was always taken by others who had been recruited in similar fashion before or during the war. Some of the replacement agents were also eventually discovered and rendered harmless, while others still continue to work for Soviet Russia, but now that she is no longer an ally of the West there is no way of justifying their espionage on her behalf.

As a neutral country Switzerland has always been the focus of attention of various Intelligence Services on account of her central position, and for this reason Russia built up her network thus during the war with great expectations for it in the post-war years. The agents were excellent and had demonstrated what they were capable of during times of great hardship, and they could certainly be relied upon. But the plan collapsed, however, as a result of the two *Dora Group* trials. Their proceedings revealed the names of the principal agents upon whom the operation was founded, their connections were exposed, their methods discussed, and the verdicts had stated explicitly that they had been working for Soviet Russia.

Moscow took the trials and the verdicts to be deliberate provocation on the part of Switzerland, and they retaliated by creating great difficulties when talks began to re-establish diplomatic relations between the two countries which had been severed ever since the time of the Revolution and the fall of the Tsar. Their anger was directed not only against the Swiss authorities, but also against some of the accused. The behaviour of Sándor Radó and Rachel Dübendorfer had particularly enraged Moscow. After all both were choice agents, trained in the motherland of the proletariat, yet he had taken the liberty of seeking refuge and aid at a British diplomatic mission and she had brought about the exposure of the Soviet network in Canada.[33]

All the defendants in both trials were rendered permanently inactive, and the Moscow headquarters realized that none of them could ever be of any use to them in the same capacity, especially in Switzerland. But the Kremlin never gives up and will not consider that any territory is not worth operating in. The Intelligence network set up during the war undeniably ceased to exist but its place will have without doubt been taken by another, consisting of entirely new and unknown people, with excellent covers, who are getting ready for a new armageddon. Only then will they really come into their own.

Epilogue

It was with mixed feeling that Leopold Trepper fastened his safety belt as the pilot gave out that they were approaching Moscow and would be landing in a few minutes. The cordial greeting by the head of the Soviet mission in Paris, Colonel Novikov, the friendly smiles in the embassy in Cairo, the visit to the hospitable home of the military attaché in Teheran—had all lulled the alertness of an experienced agent. He was somewhat disturbed by Radó's sudden disappearance and the excitement displayed by Alexander Foote in this matter. After all the Hungarian had done a great job in Switzerland and could have only been expecting praise and promotion, and yet he had preferred to lose himself in the big city. Did he still consider that nothing had changed in Russia and that the *NKVD* could pick up anyone at will and wipe out all traces of him? No, war must have changed all that, especially after such a wonderful victory. Anyway had he really any choice? Radó knew that his wife and sons were safe in Paris, but he himself was in quite a different situation: his elder son had never been allowed to leave Moscow and his wife with the younger son, Edgar, had, on the clear instructions of their superiors, been forced to return there from Belgium in May 1940, just before that country was occupied by the Germans. He had not seen them for so long and had lived through so much during the last years that he could not hesitate.[1]

These unpleasant thoughts rolled away at the moment that the wheels of the aircraft touched down on the concrete runway and it began to lose speed. After all he had also done a good job and here he was returning to the country he had served so faithfully. In a moment he would see his dear ones and gather them into his arms.

All the passengers went down the steps and each of them, the same thoughts in their minds, started to look around. No, there were no families, no civilians at all, before them arose the silhouettes of several officers with impassive faces. Two of them took Trepper to a car, got in and it moved off in an unknown direction. He asked about his family and was told that they were all well and his wife was regaining her strength in a convalescent home. When would he see her and his sons? Very soon, but in the meantime he was being taken to a private apartment where he would be able to prepare his report on his wartime activities, in peace and quiet.[2]

On the following day, although he had indeed been given two rooms in the apartment of an officer's wife, interrogation began. It appeared that not a word he said was believed and that having taken orders from and being commissioned by the former head of the *Razvedupr*, Gen. Jan Berzin, was a great crime. Very soon the private apartment became a single cell in the infamous Lubianka prison and there the interrogations became more frequent and very disagreeable. All the accusations had the same trend: collaboration with the *Gestapo* and betrayal of the Soviet Union. The perspective was of long-term imprisonment, a concentration camp in Siberia or even death. From the Lubianka he was transferred to the very severe prison of Lefortovo, where the interrogation continued. He was sent back to the Lubianka for a short time and back again to Lefortovo. All the time he was subjected to never weakening pressure to confess to the crimes with which he was charged.

In June 1947 the Council of Three, the famous *Trojka* of those years, sentenced him to fifteen years for treason and spying. He defended himself vigorously, twice a month he wrote petitions to the prosecutor, which were in fact a serial history of the *Red Orchestra*, and still remained in solitary confinement in the Lubianka, where he had been finally imprisoned. After almost three years a similar council reduced his sentence to ten years, but what meaning did that have? During the years in his lonely cell he attained a certain kind of stoicism, which enabled him to survive in a comparatively equable state of mind. He also lost his naive faith in a political system which was supposed to be good in itself, only badly executed. He had no illusions, he knew that if he managed to last out to the end of the ten years of his sentence, he would be sent to a concentration camp in a far corner of Siberia. Unless there were some great changes in Russia.[3]

Fate decided that such changes took place just at this time. On 5 March 1953 Jozeph Stalin died, the absolute monarch of a huge empire, by whose will hundreds of thousands of people had been done to death in Russia and over 20 millions deported to Siberia. At once a

186

new wind blew through the country, there were revolts in the concentration camps and an uneasy Moscow began to send out commissions, sentences were revised and in some cases reduced, numbers of people were set free.

Leopold Trepper was given the right to appeal and did so with a positive result. Almost ten years had passed when in May 1954, cleared of all charges, he walked out through the gate of the prison to freedom. He immediately made for the half-ruined wooden house on the outskirts of Moscow where his family lived. His sons did not recognize him, his wife was away from home, nobody expected him for the police had told them that he had disappeared during the war.

By 1957 the whole family was in Poland, and years later, after various trials and tribulations, in November 1973 they were re-united in London. Trepper now lives in Jerusalem.[4]

Sándor Radó, although he had received instructions to go to Moscow, nevertheless of his own accord boarded the Soviet aircraft at the airport in Paris, which was to take him there. He was not forced to take this step for any family reasons, for his wife and sons stayed behind in France. He need not have reported to the Soviet authorities in France at all, but, like many others after the war, could have sought a safe spot in one of the Latin American countries. He behaved otherwise, found himself in the not too comfortable fuselage of a Dakota and from that moment stepped onto Soviet territory. It is hard to discover what his thoughts were as, during the flight, he talked to Trepper, Foote, several Soviet officers and an old Communist, Chliapnikov, who during the first post-revolutionary years had tried to set up independent trade unions in Russia, with the right to strike, and had barely escaped with his life by fleeing abroad. Now, this ordinary labourer, who for many years had lived and worked in Paris, charmed by the great Russian victory, at Molotov's personal invitation, was returning to the fatherland.[5]

This example should have been encouraging, the fact that Leopold Trepper was flying with him also made the decision easier, and the presence of Foote, whom he knew well, made for a relaxed atmosphere. Yet, when they found themselves in Cairo for a few days, Radó disappeared from the hotel and hid in the big city. There is nothing to tell what his intentions were, he himself is silent on this subject, so it can only be conjecture that he counted on help from the

British who in Bern had offered him asylum when he asked for it at the turn of he year 1943–44. If those were his hopes, he was to suffer a grave disappointment. These were the first post-war months, when the Western democracies considered that co-operation with Soviet Russia was possible and necessary, especially as she had been given everything she demanded. In the name of this co-operation, after sentencing many nations to slavery, they were now handing over to the Soviets people from the countries she had conquered, who had fought against Stalin and did not now want to find themselves in his hands. The Soviet embassy in Cairo immediately turned to the British authorities asking for help in finding the escaper and within a few days the military police handed him over to officers of the NKVD who had come specially from Russia.

In Moscow his fate was much the same as that of Trepper. Interrogation, accusations of collaboration with the Intelligence Service, of betraying state secrets, threats of death. His years of work for and great services to the Soviet Union, his very important intelligence achievements in Switzerland, all this faded in the face of one crime: contact with British intelligence. Moscow had entertained great hopes of its Western contacts and spy networks, deployed in these countries. Radó, by his irresponsible behaviour had ripped one of them asunder and destroyed all hopes of further, post-war work. He was threatened with death, finally he finished up with ten years of prison and concentration camp.

Like Trepper, he managed to survive this period, lived to hear of Stalin's death and was set free in 1955. After 36 years he went back to Hungary. His wife then joined him from Paris, but in a poor state of health and she died three years later. He himself returned at last to his beloved maps, was appointed professor at the university and a member of the Hungarian Land and Map Department in Budapest and from time to time visits the Department of Maps of the British Library, located in the British Museum.[6]

Rachel Dübendorfer and her friend, Paul Böttcher, met a similar fate. They were experienced, mature persons and had for years been engaged in work of a confidential nature, they knew Russia and her methods well, they had observed with dread Stalin's great purges and the deaths of many friends, and yet they were enticed into going to Russia. The same Trojka which had sentenced Leopold Trepper, judged them to be guilty of treason and collaboration with Western powers. Rachel's contact with the cell of the Soviet Intelligence in Canada, *Giselle*, was held against her. The court paid scant heed to their services and the results of their intelligence work for the Soviet Union. The sentence was twelve years of imprisonment.

They managed to survive ten years in the terrible conditions of a Siberian concentration camp and the Siberian winters. They were freed in 1955 and went to East Germany. Rachel died in Berlin in 1973.[7]

Alexander Foote came best out of the whole affair, perhaps because he was a Westerner, had never lived in Russia and the mentality of those who, in the face of reality, insisted that the Soviet system was good only the execution of it bad, was quite foreign to him. He flew to Moscow because he considered that to be the logical end of his many years of work on behalf of Russia. That pressure was brought on him to fly, neither astonished him nor aroused any suspicions. During the journey he had a moment of doubt when Radó suddenly disappeared in Cairo, but he soon chased away the dark thoughts.

In Moscow he was treated with great courtesy, although he was the one who might have been the most easily accused of being a double agent and collaborating with British Intelligence. It looks as if he was treated differently as there were plans for his future. Whereas Trepper, Radó, Dübendorfer and Böttcher, long-time Communists and utilized up to their limit as intelligence agents, could be considered as spent forces, Foote, little known and with only a comparatively short career in Russia's service behind him, might still be useful. A great asset was his perfect English, he did not have to pretend to be an Englishman— he was one. So, instead of being taken to the Lubianka, he was lodged with a Russian family, but under the constant guard of a man who was officially his servant. He was constantly visited by a good looking woman about forty in the uniform of a Red Army major, called 'Vera'. Apparently she had spent some years in Switzerland before Radó in the same capacity and during the war was in radio contact with him. He was interrogated for a considerable time, but the commission came to the conclusion that his wartime activities were genuine. He was asked a lot of questions about Rudolf Roessler and his network, but he was unable to say much on this subject for he knew practically nothing.

Foote was an experienced radio and morse operator, but he knew very little about intelligence work, so he was sent to a spy school. Here he distinguished himself by his quick progress and new tasks lay ahead of him. He was told at this time that Radó had been found in Cairo, put on trial in Moscow, sentenced and executed.[8]

In March 1947, when the first wave of euphoria and the hopes of a new, better world had passed over and when the 'Cold War' had started, Soviet Intelligence decided it was time to make use of the inactive Englishman. Foote was moved to East Berlin, given papers in the name of a German, Albert Mueller, and told that he had been appointed head of the Soviet Intelligence network in Mexico, where he was to concentrate on the United States.[9]

But he was no longer the same naïve, carefree young man who had gone off to the war in Spain as to a cricket match, and later lived through the bad years in the safety of Switzerland, absorbed by the secret affairs of intelligence work, which amused him. It is possible that this was only outward appearance, camouflaging a very discreet, clever man who was only playing the role of a light-hearted, happy-go-lucky individual. We don't know for sure, but one thing is certain: if Alexander Foote did go to Russia in good faith, his years of living there in the 'fatherland of the proletariat' must have opened his eyes to the real picture of life in that country. Here are his own words on the Intelligence Central Office in Moscow: 'It was entirely ruthless, with no sense of honour, obligation, or decency towards its servants'.[10]

When he found himself in Berlin and when he was told that he was to go to Mexico and start intelligence work against the United States, he made up his mind. On 2 August he got into the western zone of Berlin and reported to the military authorities in the British sector of the city.[11]

He died in August 1956 in the service of his own country.

The end of the war was very hard for Halina Szymańska. She had tried to serve the common cause to the best of her ability, by coincidence she had found herself at the centre of secret matters of great importance and knew a great deal more than those around her. Now, after the unsuccessful attempt on Hitler's life and the collapse of the Warsaw Rising, she almost broke down. There was no doubt that the whole of Poland was to be utterly in the power of Stalin, that the eastern provinces were defintely lost and even if some territory was gained from Germany, it would not be governed by Poles. It was already known how the Russians were behaving to the east of the river

Vistula. News was coming out of Poland of the mass arrests of soldiers of the Home Army, of the imposing of a Communist administration and of the complete Russian domination of the Polish Communist political authorities, put into power by Stalin. The collapse of the Warsaw Rising, given no help by the Red Army standing on the far bank of the Vistula, was further proof of the Russians' future attitude towards Poland. The conference at Yalta had already taken place (4–11 February 1945) and news had come through to the Legation that the fate of Poland had been finally sealed by the leaders of the three great powers. The German occupation was to be replaced by a Soviet one.

Nostalgia for her country and her family did not overrule her cool conjecture that return, especially from a diplomatic post, would certainly mean a Soviet gaol. Of her work for Canaris and the Intelligence Service it was better even not to think. Mrs Szymańska could not foresee the fate of Radó, Trepper and the others, in any case she knew nothing about them, but instinct told her that her work as a go-between in intelligence matters would place her in deadly danger.

She already had news of her husband, because immediately after he got out of Soviet hands the British authorities had told her and let her know that he was in the Near East (see chapter 7, p. 87). They had been in contact and now, after the armistice, she was expecting his arrival any day. Their reunion finally took place at Christmas, 1945, which they spent together in the family circle for the first time since 1938. The meeting, for which she had waited so long, was not a success. The long years of separation and anxiety, the different fortunes of war, all made for difficulties in adjusting to each other. However these were only the first impressions and they decided to leave Switzerland and go to Paris, where the colonel was at the head of the Polish Military Mission, sent from London. The eldest daughter, Ewa, stayed behind, because she was studying for her matriculation.[12]

However the attempt at living together was not successful and it became necessary to decide what to do in the future. Her heart pulled her towards Poland, but there could be no question of returning straight into the hands of the police, so Mrs Szymańska had to consider the agreement she had come to with the British in 1940. As well as the high wages which they paid regularly up to the end of the war, they had promised her then that if she should ever wish to settle in Great Britain with her children, this right was guaranteed with the extra condition that funds would be assured for their education if she were to die early. Now she decided to take advantage of this promise and applied to the British authorities in Paris. No difficulties were made, no obstacles put in her way, no bureaucratic delays. In the early autumn of 1946 she arrived in London with her daughters. Thanks to her war-time savings she was able to make a home for herself, began to work and placed her two younger girls in an Anglo-French convent just outside London. A new life had to be made far from her own country. [13]

The unpleasant conversation which General Guisan had with Dr Karl Kobelt after his two meetings with Schellenberg and the resolution passed by the *Bundesrat*, in which he was reprimanded (see chapter 7, p. 116), finally closed the whole affair, without further consequences. When he died, 200,000 of his former soldiers followed his coffin to the grave on 12 April 1960. The country considered that the General had served its cause well and thanks to his 'active neutrality' had saved Switzerland from a German attack, much suffering and colossal destruction. [14]

But for Brigadier Roger Masson his meetings with the SS general had a more unfortunate sequel. In September 1945 he gave an interview to a reporter from the *Chicago Daily News* and told him about his meetings with Schellenberg. Thanks to this a top secret, known only to the highest ranking political and military authorities, ceased to be a secret. This was taken up by two members of the Swiss Federal parliament, the radical M. Dietchi from Basel and the social democrat Walter Bringolf from Schaffhausen, who attacked the brigadier, stating that he had exceeded his authority and demanding an enquiry. They carried their point and the case was handed over to Judge Couchepin, who began to study it in October 1945 and in January of the following year gave his opinion. Roger Masson was completely cleared of all suspicions and wrongful actions.

The judge's opinion left no room for doubt, but the affair had made its mark and Masson never recovered from it. People were divided into two camps: some defended Masson, others attacked him. He could not defend himself for he was bound by the secrecy of his service even after he had left the army and gone into retirement. He died in 1967 an embittered man. [15]

A similar fate befell Captain Hans Hausamann, who had directed the *Büro Ha* during the whole war and kept it going with his own money, thereby rendering great services to Swiss Intelligence. After the war he became, like Masson, the object of attacks accusing him of contacts with the Nazis and of playing a questionable role in the Schellenberg affair. He did not lie down under these accusations and brought several lawsuits. The first was in 1945–6 against Captain Haefeby; the second, during the same years, against the editors of *Der Tat*, Dr Kummer and Dr H.R. Schmidt; the third, in 1947–8, against the editors of *Freien Volk*, F. Schwarz and F. Salzmann. It then turned out that he had had only fair-weather friends during the war, when he was useful. In those years he had been of great service to Allen Dulles, whom he had met regularly in Zürich and to whom he had handed over much important information. Now, when in the course of the last trial he needed a testimony to his real work during the war and to the importance of the documents he had received from Germany, Dulles, in a letter of 28 July 1947, refused him such a testimony. Hausamann withdrew completely from all public and state affairs and for a number of years kept a photographic shop in Zürich. He died on 17 December 1974[16]

Major Max Waibel is also dead. During the last months of the war he did the allies a great service when he contacted Allen Dulles with his Italian friends towards the end of February 1945 and was instrumental in arranging the talks in Ascona, which hastened the armistice and saved the lives of many soldiers and civilians. An important part in this was played by the General of the *Waffen SS*, Karl Wolff, who paid no heed to Hitler's orders and started talks with the Americans. To this end he even made a secret journey to Switzerland in mufti.[17]

Major Waibel also finished his intelligence service a very disappointed man and painfully affected by the behaviour of the government, which transferred him from an important position in intelligence to the diplomatic service and sent him to Washington as a military attaché of the Swiss legation. In 1954 for a short time he became head of armaments for the Swiss infantry. After leaving the service he gave himself over to his beloved horse riding, organizing and running clubs for children, and rode a great deal himself. He also went on to the board of directors of a private bank, unaware that this bank was engaged in illegal and dishonest transactions. When this became common knowledge Max Waibel, after trying to repay the shareholders, took his own life on 21 January 1971.[18]

The other eminent members of the intelligence networks in Switzerland disengaged themselves without any serious difficulty, except for the trials already mentioned. Otto Pünter (*Pakbo*), who escaped arrest and trial altogether, went back to journalism and was even chairman of the Swiss Union of Journalists for some time. Now, advanced in years and retired, he does a lot of social work. The Hamels returned to their former occupation and now enjoy the quiet life of old age. Margrit Bolli got married.

Walter Schellenberg served National Socialism to the very end—among his other duties he had to arrest Admiral Canaris—but at the same time he managed to put himself in such a position that when the Third Reich collapsed, he was able to save his own skin. As one of the chief figures in the security forces, which were responsible for numberless crimes, he well knew what might await him after the war. He therefore got in contact with a former President of Switzerland, Jean-Marie Musym, with the object of saving those remaining Jews still alive in camps in Germany, and with Count Folke Bernadotte, who on behalf of the Swedish Red Cross was trying to get permission from the Germans to transport political prisoners from the concentration camps to neutral countries, above all to Sweden. He maintained these contacts with the knowledge of Himmler, who also hoped to be able to seize power at the last moment, come to an agreement with the Western Allies and, while saving the remnants of the collapsing Third Reich, save his own life.[19]

Thanks to this Schellenberg was helped by the Swedes and on 6 May, forty-eight hours before the armistice was declared in Europe, he got to Stockholm. He was there officially on a peace mission, but his mediation turned out to be unnecessary. The Germans capitulated, Hitler was dead, Himmler had disappeared,* Admiral Dönitz's government was only an ephemeral stop-gap and Schellenberg asked for asylum. He was given it thanks to the intervention of Count Bernadotte, whom he had helped to get a certain number of Scandinavian political prisoners out of German hands.[20]

His stay in Sweden was however short, for the allied authorities demanded his extradition, so in June 1945 he found himself back in

*He was captured by the Allies and committed suicide.

Germany, and in January of the next year he gave evidence as a witness in the Nuremberg Trials. Later he spent two years in Great Britain where he underwent treatment for gall-stones and where he was interrogated by the Intelligence Service. He was taken back to Nuremberg and in January 1948 came up before an American military tribunal with twenty other Germans, not the chief leaders of the Third Reich. The charges included planning a war of aggression, crimes against humanity and belonging to a criminal organization. The court found Schellenberg guilty of belonging to the *SS* and *SD*, but not guilty on the other counts and at the same time took into consideration his efforts to save concentration camp prisoners. The court must certainly have also borne in mind his indirect contact with Allen Dulles, his journeys to Sweden and Switzerland and his attempts at mediation in the peace talks. He was sentenced to six years imprisonment including his confinement since June 1945. It was one of the lightest sentences.

Schellenberg spent only a comparatively short time in prison, where he underwent a severe operation. Soon after it, in June 1951, by an act of grace, he was set free. He then got in contact with his wartime associate, Roger Masson, and appealed to his generosity. Masson seems to have remembered him as someone worthy of help, for he facilitated a secret entry into Switzerland and introduced him to a friend, Dr Lang, who hid him not far from Romont. However the Swiss police very soon found him and ordered him to leave the country, so he crossed the Italian frontier and settled in the small town of Pallanza, on Lake Maggiore. There, with the help of a German journalist, he began to write his memoirs, but the work was constantly interrupted by a liver complaint, from which he had suffered since childhood. He died in a clinic in Turin on 31 March 1952, aged barely forty-one.[21]

In Wesemlin, a suburb of Lucerne, Rudolf Roessler still lived in a modest flat. He had decided not to leave Switzerland and return to Germany, although Hitler was no longer alive. Every day, as of yore, he went to his firm, *Vita Nova Verlag*, and every evening he went back home, avoiding social contacts and conversation.

To those around him it might have seemed that the war period had been forgotten and that after his trial in 1945 Roessler was interested only in his publishing firm and would settle down to a peaceful old age. Yet no. In November 1953 a new trial took place and Roessler again stood up in court accused of working for Czechoslovak intelligence. This time he was in danger of deportation, for he was still stateless and the state prosecutor demanded it, but the court refused the demand.

Roessler once again decided to stay in Switzerland, but his life became empty and meaningless. More and more his thoughts turned to the past and he lived with the memories of former days. This was also because, in spite of his own intentions, he had become an object of great interest. Journalists, publicists and historians constantly appeared at his flat in Lucerne and at his place of business. From the time of the first trial the wartime spy activities of *Lucy* were no longer secret and everyone was curious to know who had been the agents sending information from the centres of decision of Hitler's Third Reich. Numerous questions turned on these same code-names: who was *Werther*? Who were *Teddy*, *Stefan*, *Anna* and *Olga*?

Rudolf Roessler, however, stood firm, just as during the most hectic years of war. He remained silent and no persuasion, no plea, no sum of money nor guile could open his lips. He died in Lucerne in 1958 and only a few people followed the funeral to the cemetry in Kriens. Among them was his oldest friend, Xaver Schnieper and his son. To him, to this young boy, Roessler just before his death is said to have divulged the secret and told him from whom and by what means he had received his priceless information during the war. He probably also told him under what circumstances and after what length of time the secret could be revealed, but fate decided that this should never happen. A year after Roessler's death Schnieper's son died in a road accident.[22]

So what really happened? Were *Werther*, *Teddy*, *Stefan*, *Anna* and *Olga* real people, or were they born in the imagination of this mystery man? Was there any connection between them and the informants of the *Wiking Linie*, did some foreign intelligence send this top secret information to Lucerne, or was it conveyed to him in a subtle manner by the British Intelligence Service thanks to the breaking of the secret of *Enigma*?

We will probably never know the answers to these questions.

Notes

Chapter 1: Secret Preparations

1 Jerzy Budkiewicz, interview, Arolsen, 24 August 1972.
2 James Joll, *Europe Since 1870*, London, 1973, p. 389.
3 Christian Vetsch, *Aufmarsch gegen die Schweiz*, Olten and Freiburg, 1973, p. 9.
4 Pierre Accoce and Pierre Quet, *La Guerre a été Gagnée en Suisse, 1939–1945*, Paris, 1966, pp. 55–8.
5 Hans Rudolf Kurz, *Nachrichtenzentrum Schweiz*, Frauenfeld and Stuttgart, 1972.
6 Karl Lüönd, *Spionage und Landesverrat in der Schweiz*, vol. I, Zürich, 1977, pp. 64–5.
7 Kurz, p. 12.
8 Ibid, p. 15.
9 Edgar Bonjour, *Geschichte der Schweizerischen Neutralität*, Basel and Stuttgart, 1970, vol. V, p. 95.
10 Alphons Matt, *Zwischen allen Fronten*, Frauenfeld and Stuttgart, 1969, pp. 14–17.
11 Ibid, p. 14.
12 Ibid, p. 15.
13 František Moravec, *Master of Spies*, London, 1975, pp. 58 and 181–6.
14 Werner Rings, *Schweiz im Krieg, 1933–1945*, Zürich, 1974, p. 354. Also: Kurz, p. 30.
15 Accoce and Quet, p. 81.
16 Xaver Schnieper, recorded interview, Lucerne, 18 September 1977. Also: Accoce and Quet, pp. 82–3.
17 Accoce and Quet, pp. 86–8. Also: Otto Pünter, *Der Anschluss fand nicht statt*, Bern and Stuttgart, 1976, p. 103. Also: Wilhelm von Schramm, *Verrat im Zweiten Weltkrieg*, Düsseldorf-Wien, 1967, p. 19.
18 The word *Eidgenössishes* has a long tradition in Switzerland, going back to the fourteenth century when Wilhelm Tell fought against the Hapsburgs for Swiss independence.
19 Accoce and Quet, pp. 66–7.
20 Kurz, p. 30.
21 Ibid, pp. 30–1 and 112 (foot-note 17). Also: Pünter, pp. 102–3.
22 Kurz, pp. 31–2. Also: Pünter, p. 103. Also: Von Schramm, p. 19. Also: Bonjour, pp. 98–9.

Chapter 2: Foreign Intelligence Services

1   Kurz, pp. 24–5.
2   David Irving, *The Mare's Nest*, London, 1964, p. 13.
3   Lüönd, p. 72. Also: Moravec, p. 121.
4   Lüönd, p. 72.
5   Ibid, pp. 74–8.
6   André Brisant, *Canaris*, pp. 152–9.
7   Lüönd, pp. 75–6.
8   Ibid, pp. 72 and 77.
9   Ibid, p. 46.
10 Public Record Office, London, file DEFE 3/1, ZTP 770, 20.5.1941.
11 Pünter, pp. 105–6. Also: Lüönd, p. 73.
12 Lüönd, pp. 100–1.
13 Henri Michel, *The Shadow War*, London, 1972, p. 311. Also: Lüönd, p. 101.
14 Vojtech Mastny, 'The Czechoslovak Government-in-Exile during World War II: an Assessment', p. 5. Also: W. Barker, 'H.M.G. and the Czechoslovak Government in Exile during the Second World War', pp. 1–2. Also: Moravec, p. 164.
15 Tadeusz Szumowski, 'Po upadku Pragi', *Kierunki*, Warsaw, Cracow, No. 20, 19.5.1968, p. 10 and Nr. 21, 26.5.1968, p. 10. Also: Moravec, pp. 159–61.
16 Moravec, p. 177.
17 Barker, pp. 3–5.
18 Mastny, pp. 6–11. Also: Barker, p. 5.
19 Barker, pp. 5–6.
20 Matt, p. 219.
21 Józef Garliński, *Poland, SOE and the Allies*, London, 1969, pp. 33–4.
22 Ibid.
23 Ibid.
24 Studium Polski Podziemnej, London, file 5.2.8., Bern.
25 Stanisław Appenzeller, a letter to the author, 18.8.1979.
26 Armia Krajowa w Dokumentach, London, 1970, vol. I, pp. 275–6.
27 SPP, file 5.2.8., Bern.

Chapter 3: Various Residents

1   Sándor Radó, *Codename Dora*, London, 1977, p. xi
2   Pünter, p. 120.
3   Radó, pp. xii–xx.
4   Ibid, pp. 4–5.
5   Ibid, pp. 6–12.
6   Ibid, pp. 13–18.
7   Ibid, p. 19.
8   Hermann Langbein, *Die Stärkeren*, Wien, 1949, p. 39.
9   Pünter, a letter to the author, 10.1.1980.

10 Ibid.
11 Pünter, pp. 104–6. Also: Kurz, *Nachrichtenzentrum* . . . , p. 118.
12 Pünter, a letter to the author, 10. 1. 1980.
13 Pünter, pp. 106–8, and his letter to the author, 28. 10. 1980.
14 Ibid, pp. 108–9.
15 Aleksander Bregman, *Najlepeszy sojusznik Hitlera*, 4th edn, London, 1974, pp. 104–5.
16 Pünter, p. 120.

Chapter 4: Two Orchestras

1 Heinz Höhne, *Codeword: Director*, London, 1971, p. 1.
2 Ibid, pp. 3–4.
3 Ibid, pp. 4–5.
4 Ibid, pp. 6–23.
5 Ibid, pp. 23–4.
6 Ibid, pp. 31–2.
7 Ibid.
8 Józef Kiermisz, a letter to the author, 5. 7. 1979.
9 Leopold Trepper, *The Great Game*, New York, 1977, p. 11.
10 Ibid, p. 11.
11 Ibid, p. 14.
12 Ibid, p. 24.
13 Höhne, pp. 44–5.
14 Ibid.
15 Trepper, pp. 30–2.
16 Höhne, pp. 45–6.
17 Ibid, p. 43.
18 Trepper, p. 97.
19 Höhne, pp. 41–8.
20 Ibid, p. 37.
21 Schramm, pp. 41–2.
22 Höhne, pp. 138–42.
23 Ibid, pp. 119–20.
24 Ibid, pp. xv and 55.
25 Trepper, pp. 255–6.
26 Radó, pp. 34–6.
27 Karl Heinz Wildhagen and others, *Erich Fellgiebel*, Hannover, 1970, pp. 283–288. Also: André Brissaud, *Canaris*, London, 1973, pp. 112–5.
28 Hans Royce, Erich Zimmerman and Hans-Adolf Jacobsen, *20 Juli 1944*, Bonn, 1961, pp. 28–35. Also: Brissaud, pp. 112–5.
29 Fest, pp. 539–41.
30 Ibid, p. 559.
31 Ibid, pp. 559–60. Also: Brissaud, pp. 115–17.

Chapter 5: War and Action

1   Radó, p. 36.
2   Ibid, pp. 32–4. Also: Kurz, p. 52.
3   Ibid, pp. 44–5.
4   Alexander Foote, *Handbook for Spies*, London, 1964, 2nd edn., pp. 9–51. Also: Kurz, p. 52.
5   Radó, pp. 58–62. Also: Kurz, p. 54.
6   F. H. Hinsley, *British Intelligence in the Second World War*, vol. I, London, 1979, p. 185. Also: Frederick W. Winterbotham, *The Ultra Secret*, London, 1975, pp. 80–1.
7   Höhne, pp. 60–1.
8   Pünter, p. 115.
9   Ibid, pp. 105–8.
10 Radó, p. 55.
11 Kurz, p. 118, foot-note 59.
12 Lüönd, p. 87.
13 Ibid, p. 88.
14 Kutz, pp. 31–2.
15 Ibid, p. 112, foot-note 21.
16 Lüönd, p. 88. (He says that the interview was carried out by a journalist from Zürich, Ludwig A. Minelli, and that this was the only interview granted by Schneider's widow.) Also: Pünter, p. 124.
17 Kurz, p. 34 and 112 (foot-note 22). Also: Radó, p. 58.
18 Trepper, p. 97.
19 Ibid, p. 53.
20 Ibid, pp. 63–6.
21 Ibid, pp. 68–9.
22 Ibid, p. 75.
23 Ibid, pp. 83–5. Also: Kurz, p. 52. Also: Pünter, p. 123.
24 Ibid, pp. 70–1. Also: Höhne, pp. 59–62.
25 Kurz, p. 52. Also: Radó, pp. 114–15.
26 Radó, pp. 114–15 and 130–1.
27 Kurz, pp. 35–6.
28 Ibid, p. 36. Also: Lüönd, p. 92.
29 Schnieper, recorded interview, Lucerne, 11.12.1979. Also: Radó, pp. 295–6.
30 Accoce and Quet, p. 80.
31 Kurz, p. 113, foot-note 28.
32 Schramm, p. 73.
33 Höhne, pp. 234–47.
34 Kurz, p. 36. Also: Bonjour, p. 103.
35 Bernd Ruland, *Die Augen Moscaus*.
36 Reinhard Gehlen, *The Gehlen Memoirs*, pp. 87–8.
37 Schramm, p. 178.

38 Royce, Zimmermann and Jacobsen, p. 39.
39 *Der Spiegel*, 16.1.1967.
40 Schramm, pp. 350–63.
41 Gustave Bertrand, *Enigma*, Paris, 1973. Also: Ronald Lewin, *Ultra Goes to War*, London, 1978. Also: Józef Garliński, *Intercept, Secrets of the Enigma War*, London, 1979.
42 Peter Calvocoressi, *Top Secret Ultra*, London, 1980. Also: Edward Crankshaw, 'How reluctant Russians helped to break the Enigma', *The Observer*, 27 July 1980.
43 Constantine Fitzgibbon, *Secret Intelligence in the 20th Century*, London, 1976, pp. 277–8.
44 Garliński, *Intercept*, p. 55. Also: Patrick Seale and Maureen McConville, *Philby, the Long Road to Moscow*, pp. 143 and 165–7.
45 Seale and McConville, p. 167.
46 Anthony Brooks, interview in London, 23.1.1980.

Chapter 6: Canaris

1 It was Lieutenant-Colonel Hartwig from the *Abwehr* (Höhne, *Canaris*, London, 1979, p. 362).
2 Halina Wiśniowska (primo voto Szymańska), authorized interview in London, 14.6.1979.
3 Czesław Madajczyk, *Polityka III Rzeszy w okupowanej Polsce*, Warsaw, 1970, vol. I, pp. 64–72.
4 Wiśniowska, interview, 14.6.1979.
5 Ibid.
6 Ibid.
7 Ibid.
8 Ibid. Also: Victor G. Farrell, a letter to the author, London, 8.3.1980.
9 Ibid.
10 Kurz, recorded interview, Bern. 4.12.1979. Also: Bundesarchiv, Bern, Landesverteidigung 1848–1950, vol. 5, section 27, document No. 10022.
11 Wiśniowska, interview, 14.6.1979.
12 Ibid.
13 Wiśniowska, interview, 28.8.1979.
14 Hans Bernd Gisevius, *To the Bitter End*, London, 1948, p. 452. Also: Allen Welsh Dulles, *Germany's Underground*, New York, 1947, pp. 126–7.
15 Gisevius, p. 452. Also: Brissaut, pp. 22–3.
16 Gisevius, p. 453.
17 Wiśnowska, interview. 28.8.1979.
18 Ibid.
19 Ibid.
20 Ibid.
21 Bradley F. Smith, *Reaching Judgement at Nuremberg*, London, 1977, p. 349.

Chapter 7: The Most Secret Contacts

1 Kurz, pp. 60–1. Also: Accoce and Quet, p. 24.
2 Alan Bullock, Introduction to *The Schellenberg Memoirs*, London, 1956, p. 12. Also: Kurz, p. 66.
3 Matt, pp. 226–7. Also: Kurz, p. 66.
4 Lüönd, vol. II, p. 70.
5 Kurz, p. 61.
6 Accoce and Quet, pp. 38–9.
7 Ibid, p. 27.
8 Kurz, p. 61.
9 Accoce and Quet, p. 44.
10 Ibid, p. 31.
11 Ibid, p. 30.
12 Walter Schellenberg, *The Schellenberg Memoirs*, London, 1956, pp. 68–70.
13 Ibid, pp. 82–98. Both British officers remained throughout the whole of the war in a German concentration camp.
14 Accoce and Quet, pp. 35–6.
15 Ibid, pp. 40–1.
16 Bob Edwards and Kenneth Dunne, *A Study of a Master Spy* (Allen Dulles), London, 1961, pp. 45–6.
17 Kurz, pp. 73–4.
18 Bonjour, p. 101.
19 Schramm, pp. 95–8.
20 Schellenberg, pp. 322–9.
21 Helmut Maurer (a German, former subordinate of Canaris), a report made to the Swiss Intelligence on 21 February 1950. Bundesarchiv, Bern, Landesferteidigung 1845–1950, Volume 5, section 27, number 9923. According to him these documents were in the hands of the *Gestapo*. The head of the German criminal police and high ranking *SS* officer, Arthur Nebe, who was in the conspiracy with Admiral Canaris, got hold of the documents and gave them to the admiral, who hid them. Also: Kurz, recorded interview, Bern, 4.12.1979.
22 Lüönd, p. 72.
23 Kurz, interview, 4.12.1979.
24 Matt, pp. 193–5. Also: Kurz, interview, 4.12.1979. He stated that he is the only man alive who knows the names of the informants of the *Wiking Linie*, but that he cannot give them because of their families in Germany. Also: Pünter, p. 138.
25 Kurz, pp. 72–3.
26 Major Bracher, Swiss counter-espionage report of 12 March 1943 on the meeting between Gen. Guisan and Gen. Schellenberg in Biglen, 3 March 1943, and in Arosa, 6 March 1943. Bundesarchiv, Bern, Landesverteidigung 1848–1950, Volume 5, section 27, number 10022.

27   Bracher, report.
28   Ibid.
29   Lüönd, volume II, p. 70.
30   Bracher, report.
31   Ibid.
32   Ibid.
33   Bundesarchiv, Bern, document No. 10022.
34   Bracher, report.
35   Kurz, interview, 4.12.1979.
36   Karl Kobelt, notes from a conversation with Gen. Guisan about the meeting
     with Schellenberg and official letter on the instructions of the *Bundesrat*.
     Bundesarchiv, Bern, document, No. 10022.
37   Kurz, p. 70.
38   Ibid, pp. 70–1.
39   Accoce and Quet, p. 66.
40   Kurz, *Dokumente des Aktivdienstes*, Frauenfeld, 1965, p. 129.

Chapter 8: Allen Dulles

1   J. Garliński, Poland . . . , pp. 19–23.
2   Calvocoressi and Wint, *Total War*, London, 1972, pp. 277–8.
3   Rhodri Jeffreys-Jones, *American Espionage*, New York and London, 1977, pp.
     165–9 and 172–9.
4   Lüönd, pp. 105–6.
5   Dulles, *Germany's* . . . , p. xi.
6   Dulles, *The Craft of Intelligence*, New York, 1963, p. 7.
7   Kurz, *Nachrichtenzentrum* . . . , p. 59.
8   Ibid. Also: Lüönd, p. 105.
9   Kurz, *Nachrichtenzentrum* . . . , p. 59.
10   Dulles, *The Craft* . . . , p. 27.
11   Höhne, *Canaris*, p. 482.
12   Garliński, *Intercept*, p. 131.
13   Fest, p. 665.
14   Dulles, *Germany's* . . . , pp. 37–9.
15   Gisevius, p. 476.
16   Dulles, *The Craft* . . . , pp. 203–4.
17   Gisevius, pp. 476–7.
18   Edwards and Dunne, p. 44.
19   Dulles, *Germany's* . . . , pp. 130–1.
20   Ibid, p. 170.
21   Ibid, pp. 131–4.
22   Wiśniowska, interview, 14.6.1979.
23   *SPP*, file 5.2.8, despatch No. 8925, 30.9.1942.
24   Appenzeller, undated report in French about his activities in Switzerland

during the war, and his letter to the author, 30.1.1980.

25 M.R.D. Foot, *Resistance*, London, 1976, pp. 218–19. Also: Dulles, *The Craft* . . . , pp. 82–3.

26 Dulles, *Germany's* . . . , pp. 131–2.

27 Cave Brown, p. 311.

28 Dulles, *Germany's* . . . , p. 140.

29 Ibid, pp. 147–9. Also: Fest, p. 701.

30 Fest, p. 701. Also: Schellenberg, p. 357.

31 Höhne, *Canaris*, pp. 486 and 510.

32 Maximilian Egon Hohenlohe, report on the meeting with Dulles, Berlin, 30.4.1943. Documents of Department VI of the *RSHA* (Edwards and Dunne, pp. 29–33).

33 Ibid.

34 Fest, p. 701.

Chapter 9: A Year of Successes and Danger

1 Höhne, *Codeword:* . . . , pp. 153–203. Also: Radó, p. 147. Also: see Chapter IV.

2 Ibid, p. 213.

3 Ibid, pp. 204–17.

4 Ibid, pp. 218–20.

5 Ibid, p. xiii. Also: Leopold Trepper, *The Great Game*, p. 168.

6 Ibid, pp. 220–7.

7 Ibid, pp. 223–5.

8 Ibid, p. 232. Also: Trepper, pp. 276–8.

9 Schramm, p. 85.

10 Radó, p. 151.

11 Schramm, p. 353.

12 W.F. Flicke, *Agenten Funken nach Moskau*, Kreuzlingen, 1954, p. 328.

13 Radó, p. 181.

14 Flicke, p. 310.

15 Radó, p. 176.

16 Pünter, p. 148.

17 Radó, p. 209.

18 Calvocoressi and Wint, pp. 478–9.

19 Schramm, pp. 95–8.

20 Garliński, *Intercept* pp. 35–7.

21 Radó, p. 170. Also: Schramm, pp. 350–64.

22 Max Waaser (former employee of the SD in Stuttgart), report deposited 30.8.1946, Bundesarchiv, Bern, document No. 9960.

23 Schramm, p. 251. Also: Accoce and Quet, pp. 278–9.

24 Ibid, pp. 252–4.

25 Foote, pp. 72–3.
26 Schramm, pp. 253–6.
27 Radó, pp. 105–6. Also: Schramm, pp. 287–8.
28 Accoce and Quet, p. 198.
29 Schramm, p. 282. Also: Radó, pp. 122–3.
30 Radó, p. 147.
31 Ibid, pp. 147–8 and 192–5.
32 Kurz, *Nachrichtenzentrum* . . . , pp. 77–8. Also Radó, p. 123.
33 Radó, pp. 119–21.
34 Flicke, pp. 324–6.
35 Radó, pp. 168–9.

Chapter 10: Pursuit

1 Kurz, *Dokumente* . . . , pp. 85–7 and 130–2.
2 Ibid, p. 131.
3 Schramm, *Verrat* . . . , pp. 248–9.
4 Ibid, p. 333. Also: Schramm, 'Die rot-weisse Kapelle', *Frankfurther allgemenie Zeitung*, 13.12.1966.
5 Kurz, *Nachrichtenzentrum* . . . , p. 77. Also: Radó, pp. 245–6.
6 Ibid, p. 79. Also: Radó, pp. 251–4. Also: Rings, pp. 363–5.
7 Radó, pp. 251–2.
8 Ibid, p. 254.
9 Ibid. Also: Pünter, *Der Anschluss* . . . , pp. 161–2, and his letter to the author, 28.10.1980.
10 Kurz, *Nachrichtenzentrum* . . . , pp. 61–2.
11 Radó, pp. 255–7.
12 Pünter, *Der Anschluss* . . . , p. 162. Also: Radó, pp. 261–2.
13 Kurz: *Nachrichtenzentrum* . . . , p. 83. Also Flicke, pp. 377–9; Radó, pp. 261–263.
14 Ibid, p. 84. Also: Radó, pp. 263–6.
15 Bonjour, vol. V, p. 101.
16 Radó, pp. 264–6.
17 Ibid, pp. 270–1. Also: Schramm, *Verrat* . . . , p. 296.
18 Foote, p. 125. Also: Radó, pp. 271–2.
19 Radó, p. 277.
20 Pünter, *Der Anschluss* . . . , p. 162.
21 Radó, p. 275.
22 Kurz, *Nachrichtenzentrum* . . . , p. 79. Also Radó, pp. 279–80.
23 Ibid, pp. 80–1.
24 Radó, p. 281.
25 Kurz, *Nachrichtenzentrum* . . . , pp. 81–5.

Chapter 11: The Last Months

1   Dulles, *Germany's* . . . , p. 181.
2   Ibid, pp. 140–1.
3   Wiśniowska, recorded interview, London, 13.2.1980.
4   Dulles, *Germany's* . . . , pp. 140 and 175–6.
5   Wiśniowska, interview, 13.2.1980.
6   Gisevius, pp. 569–76.
7   Ibid, p. 576.
8   Ibid, pp. 577–8.
9   Ibid, pp. 579–90. Also: Dulles, *Germany's* . . . , p. 141.
10 Kurz, *Nachrichtenzentrum* . . . , pp. 84–5.
11 Ibid, p. 81.
12 Ibid, pp. 77–81.
13 Kurz, *Nachrichtenzentrum* . . . , p. 80. Also: Pünter, *Der Anschluss*, p. 163.
14 Bundesarchiv, Bern, document No. 10110, Polizeidienst, Bern, 19.1.1944: Radó und Konsorten.
15 Kurz, *Nachrichtenzentrum* . . . , p. 81.
16 Ibid, p. 94. Also: Foote, pp. 134–5.
17 Ibid, p. 124, foot-note No. 110. Also: Flicke, p. 401.
18 Radó, pp. 282–3.
19 Pünter, *Der Anschluss* . . . , p. 164. Also: Kurz, *Nachrichtenzentrum* . . . , p. 87.
20 Radó, pp. 285–6.
21 Ibid, pp. 287–9.
22 Ibid, pp. 289–9.
23 Pünter, *Der Anschluss* . . . , pp. 164–5.
24 Radó, p. 290–1.
25 Ibid, pp. 291–2.
26 Trepper, p. 329.
27 Ibid, pp. 330–1.
28 Kurz, *Nachrichtenzentrum* . . . , p. 87. Also: Pünter, *Der Anschluss* . . . , pp. 165–6.
29 Ibid, pp. 87–8. Also: Pünter, pp. 165–6.
30 Kurz, a letter to the author, 27.2.1980.
31 Kurz, *Nachrichtenzentrum* . . . , p. 88. Also: Pünter, pp. 166–7.
32 Ibid, pp. 88–9. Also: Pünter, pp. 166–7.
33 Ibid, p. 94.

Epilogue

1   Trepper, pp. 97, 108 and 332–3.
2   Ibid, pp. 333–4.
3   Ibid, p. 368.
4   Ibid, pp. 384–408.

5   Ibid, pp. 330–1. Chliapnikov was taken to prison straight from the airport and later sent to a camp in Siberia.

6   Radó, pp. 297–8. Also: Pünter, *Der Anschluss* . . . , p. 165.

7   Foote, p. 159.

8   Ibid, pp. 141–59.

9   Ibid.

10 Ibid, p. 142.

11 Ibid. Also: Pünter, *Der Anschluss* . . . , p. 165.

12 Wiśniowska, recorded interview, 13.2.1980.

13 Ibid.

14 Accoce and Quet, p. 311.

15 Kurz, recorded interview, 4.12.1979.

16 Bundesarchiv, Bern, file No. 27, documents No. 9845, 9846, 9847 and 9864.

17 Lüönd, Vol. I, pp. 112–13 and Vol. II, pp. 89–95.

18 Ibid, Vol. I, pp. 113 and 116.

19 Schellenberg, pp. 428–454. Also: Matt, p. 288.

20 Bullock, p. 14.

21 Ibid, pp. 16–17.

22 Schnieper, recorded interview, Lucerne, 11.12.1979.

Select Bibliography

Archival sources

1 Archives

Bundesarchiv-Militärarchiv, Freiburg, West Germany.
Bundesarchiv, Bern, Switzerland.
Public Record Office, London.
Studium Polski Podziemnej (Polish Underground Movement—1939–45—Study
Trust), London.

2 Unpublished documents, reports and statements

Abwehr documents from Stuttgart on intelligence activity against Switzerland,
1939–1945. *Bundesarchiv*, Bern, file 27: *Landesverteidigung* 1848–1950, vol. 5,
document no. 9960.
Angebliche Verbindungen Hausamanns mit dem engl. Geheimdienst, Bundesarchiv . . . , doc.
no. 9841.
Appenzeller, Stanisław, undated report in French about his activities in Switzerland
during the last war.
Ausländische Militärattachés in der Schweiz, Bundesarchiv . . . , doc. nos 9803 and 9836.
Barker, William, 'H.M.G. and Czechoslovak Government-in-Exile during the
Second World War'. Lecture given during a conference on Governments Exiled
in London during the Second World War, London, October 1977.
Bracher, Major, report of 12.3.1943, *Zusammentreffen General Guisan mit SS-General
Schellenberg und SS-Major Eggen im Gasthof Bären in Biglen an 3.3.1943 und in
Arosa am 6.3.1943, Bundesarchiv* . . . , doc. no. 10022.
Brooks, Anthony, interview in London, 23.1.1980.
Chapman, John W.M., German Intelligence reports on Switzerland, 1939–1944,
Brighton, 1979.
*Falschmeldunge und Gerüchte aus Italien betr. englische Fliegerstützpunkte in der Schweiz,
1940, Bundesarchiv* . . . , doc. no. 9973.
Farrell, Victor C., an interview, London, 26.9.1980.
French documents from La Charité-sur-Loire (copy), *Bundesarchiv* . . . , doc. no. 9932.
Hausamman's court cases, *Bundesarchiv* . . . , doc. nos 9845, 9846, 9847, 9864.
Hohenlohe, Maximilian Egon, report on a meeting with Dulles, Berlin, 30.4.1943,
documents of Department VI of the RSHA.
Identified intelligence officers and agents of the enemy states (England, USA,
Russia) who have been incorporated as members of diplomatic and consular

missions, High Command of the Armed Forces, Berlin, 6.8.1942.

Intelligence from enemy radio communications (Enigma), Public Record Office, London, file DEFE/3/1.

Italienische Spionage in der Schweiz, 1927–1945, Bundesarchiv . . . , doc. no. 10050.

Kobelt, Karl, notes from conversation with General Guisan, 12.3.1943, *Bundesarchiv* . . . , doc. no. 10022.

Kurz, Hans Rudolf, recorded interviews, Bern, 22.9.1977, 4.12.1979.

Mastny, Vojtech, 'The Czechoslovak Government-in-Exile during World War II: an Assessment'. Lecture given during a Conference on Governments Exiled in London during the Second World War, London, October, 1977.

Maurer, Helmut (former subordinate of Canaris), report made to the Swiss Intelligence on 21.2.1950; his opinion on Schellenberg and the document on La Charité-sur-Loire, *Bundesarchiv* . . . , doc. no. 9923.

Nachrichten und Berichte über Deutschland und die deutsch bezetzten Gebiete, 1939–1945, *Bundesarchiv* . . . , doc. no. 9932.

Polish secret outpost in Bern for liaison with occupied Poland, *Studium Polski Podziemnej*, London, file 5.2.8, Bern.

Polizeidienst, Bern, 19.1.1944, Radó und Konsorten, Bundesarchiv . . . , doc. no. 10110.

Reisen von Oberstbrigadier Masson zu Schellenberg nach Deutschland, 1943, *Bundesarchiv* . . . , doc. no. 10020.

Rejewski, Marian, *Reminiscences of my work in the cipher office of the Second Bureau of the General Staff in 1930–1945*, Bydgoszcz, 1967 (in Polish).

Report on Schellenberg, Eggen and others, 1942–45, *Bundesarchiv* . . . , doc. no. 10019.

Russische Geheimsender in Genf und Lausanne, 19.2.1945, Bundesarchiv . . . , doc. no. 10110.

Schnieper, Xaver, recorded interviews, Lucerne, 18.9.1977, 11.12.1979.

Stellungen und Truppenbewegungen and der Italian/Schweiz Grenze während des Krieges, 1939–1945, Bundesarchiv . . . , doc. no. 9972.

Waaser, Max (former employee of the SD in Stuttgart), report deposited 30.8.1946, 'Tätigkeit des deutschen Spionageabwehr in der Schweiz', *Bundesarchiv* . . . , doc. no. 9960.

Waibel, Max, the activities of the Austrian secret organisation 05 in Switzerland, 1945, *Bundesarchiv* . . . , doc. no. 9922.

Wiking Linie, Bundesarchiv . . . , doc. no. 10020.

Wiśniowska, Halina (primo voto Szymańska), authorized interviews, London, 14.6.1979, 28.8.1979, 13.2.1980.

3 Letters to the author

Appenzeller, Stanisław (France), 26.6.1979, 18.8.1979, 23.10.1979, 30.1.1980.

Chapman, John W.M. (Brighton), 7.2.1979.

Farrell, Victor C. (London), 8.3.1980.

Kiermisz, Józef (Israel), 5.7.1979.

Kurz, Hans Rudolf (Bern), 28.5.1979, 29.10.1979. 4.1.1980, 27.2.1980.
Meyer, Walter (Thun, Switzerland), 26.4.1979.
Pünter, Otto (Bern), 10.1.1978, 22.11.1979, 10.1.1980, 28.10.1980.
Rohwer Jürgen (Stuttgart), 13.3.1980.

4 Other letters

Dulles, Allen Welsh (USA)   to Hans Hausamann, 28.7.1947.
Guisan, Henri (Switzerland)   to Karl Kobelt, 20.5.1942.
Hausamann, Hans (Switzerland) to Karl Kobelt, 1947.
Kobelt, Karl (Switzerland)   to General Guisan, 6.4.1943, 29.11.1943.
                                                    to Rev. Paul Vogt, 21.9.1944.
Lützelschwab, W. (Switzerland) to Karl Kobelt, 23.6.1943, 28.8.1943.
Vogt, Paul (Switzerland)   to Karl Kobelt, 5.9.1944.

Books and Articles

Accoce, Pierre et Quet, Pierre, *La Guerre e été gagnée en Suisse*, Libraire Académique, Perrin, Paris, 1966.
Armia Krajowa w dokumentach, 1939–1945, vol. I, Studium Polski Podziemnej, London, 1970.
Arsenijevic, Drago, *Genève appelle Moscou*, Paris, 1969.
Astley, Joan Bright, *The Inner Circle*, Hutchinson, London, 1973.
Bonjour, Edgar, *Geschichte des Schweizerischen Neutralität*, Basel and Stuttgart, 1970.
Borer, Ernst R., *Spionage*, Neptun Verlag, Kreuzlingen, 1975.
Boveri, Margret, *Treason in the Twentieth Century*, Macdonald, London, 1961.
Boyle, Andrew, *The Climate of Treason*, Coronet Books, London, 1980.
Brissant, André, *Canaris*, Weidenfeld and Nicolson, London, 1973.
Buchheit, Gert, *Die deutsche Geheimdienst*, List Verlag, München, 1966.
Bullock, Alan, Introduction to *The Schellenberg Memoirs*, Deutsch, London, 1956.
Calvocoressi, Peter, *Top Secret Ultra*, Cassell, London, 1980.
—— and Wint, Guy, *Total War*, Penguin, London, 1972.
Cave Brown, Anthony, *Bodyguard of Lies*, Harper and Row, New York, 1975.
Colvin, Ian, *Canaris, Chief of Intelligence*, Mann, Maidstone, 1973.
Crankshaw, Edward, 'How reluctant Russians helped to break the Enigma', *The Observer*, 27 July 1980.
Dulles, Allen, *The Craft of Intelligence*, Harper and Row, New York, Evaston and London, 1963.
—— *Germany Underground*, Macmillan, New York, 1947.
Edwards, Bob and Dunne, Kenneth, *A study of a Master Spy (Allen Dulles)*, Housmans, Publ., London, 1961.
Farago, Ladislas, *The Game of the Foxes*, Hodder and Stoughton, London, 1972.
Fest, Joachim, *Hitler*, Weidenfeld and Nicolson, London, 1977.
Fitzgibbon, Constantine, *Secret Intelligence in the 20th Century*, Hart Davis, MacGibbon, London, 1976.

Flicke, W.F., *Agenten funken nach Moskau*, Verlag 'Welsermühl', München, 1957.
—— *Spionagegruppe Rote Kapelle*, Neptun Verlag, Kreutzlingen, 1954.
Foot, M.R.D., *Resistance*, Eyre Methuen, London, 1976.
Foote, Alexander, *Handbook for Spies*, Museum Press, 2nd edn., London, 1964.
Garliński, Józef, *Intercept, Secrets of the Enigma War*, J.M. Dent and Sons, London, 1979.
—— *Poland, SOE and the Allies*, Allen and Unwin, London, 1969.
Geheime Kommandosache, Vol. I and II, Verlag Das Beste, Stuttgart, 1969.
Gehlen, Reinhard, *The Gehlen Memoirs*, Collins, London, 1972.
Gheysens, Roger, *Aventuriers de l'historie les espions*, Elsevier Sequoia, Brussels, 1973.
Gisevius, Hans Bernd, *To the Bitter End*, Jonathan Cape, London, 1948.
Hinsley, F.H., *British Intelligence in the Second World War*, Vol. I, H.M.S.O., London, 1979.
Howard, Michael, *The Mediterranean Strategy in the Second World War*, Weidenfeld and Nicolson, London, 1968.
Höhne, Heinz, *Canaris*, Secker and Warburg, London, 1979.
—— *Codeword: Director*, Secker and Warburg, London, 1971.
Irving, David, *The Mare's Nest*, Kimber, London, 1964.
Jeffreys-Jones, Rhodri, *American Espionage*, The Free Press, Macmillan, New York, 1977.
Joll, James, *Europe since 1870*, Weidenfeld and Nicolson, London, 1973.
Kahn, David, *Hitler's Spies*, Hodder and Stoughton, London, 1978.
Kessel, Albrecht von, *Von anderen Deutschland*, Atlantis Verlag, Zürich, 1947.
Kimche, Jon, *Spying for Peace*, Weidenfeld and Nicolson, London, 1961.
Kozaczuk, Władysław, *Bitwa o tajemnice*, 2nd edn., Ksiazka i wiedza, Warsaw, 1969.
Kurz, Hans Rudolf, *Dokumente des Aktivdienstes*, Verlag Huber, Frauenfeld, 1965.
—— *Nachrichtenzentrum Schweiz*, Fraunfeld and Stuttgart, 1972.
Langbein, Hermann, *Die Stärkeren*, Wien, 1949.
Lewin, Ronald, *Ultra Goes to War*, Hutchinson, London, 1978.
Liberak, Stanislas, *Témoignages*, La Metze, Sion, 1978.
Lüönd, Karl, *Spionage und Landesverrat in der Schweiz*, Vols. I and II, Ringier, Zürich, 1977.
Madajczyk, Czesław, *Polityka III Rzeszy w okupowanej Polsce*, Vol. I, Państwowe Wydawnictwo Naukowe, Warsaw, 1970.
Masterman, John C., *The Double-Cross System in the War of 1939 to 1945*, Sphere, London, 1973.
Matt, Alphons, *Zwischen Allen Fronten*, Verlag Huber, Frauenfeld and Stuttgart, 1969.
Michel, Henri, *The Shadow War*, Deutsch, London, 1972.
Moravec, František, *Master of Spies*, The Bodley Head, London, 1975.
Navarre, Henri, *Le Service Renseignements, 1871–1944*, Plon, Paris, 1978.
Neave, Airey, *Saturday at M.I.9*, Hodder and Stoughton, London, 1969.
O'Donnell, James P., *The Berlin Bunker*, J.M. Dent and Sons, London, 1979.

Paillole, Paul, *Services Spéciaux* (1935–1945), Robert Laffont, Paris, 1975.

Penrose, Barrie, Leitch, David and Knightley, Phillip, '"A grotesque smear" say top spy-masters', *The Sunday Times*, London, 20.1.1980.

Pünter, Otto, *Der Anschluss fand nicht statt*, Verlag Hallweg, Bern and Stuttgart, 1976.

Radó, Sándor, *Codename Dora*, Abelard, London, 1977.

Rings, Werner, *Schweiz im Krieg, 1933–1945*, Ex Libris Verlag, Zürich, 1974.

Rohwer, Jürgen und Jäckel, Eberhard, *Die Funkaufklärung und ihre Rolle Im 2. Weltkrieg*, Motorbuch Verlag, Stuttgart, 1979.

Royce, Hans, Zimmermann, Erich and Jacobsen, Hans-Adolf, *20. Juli 1944*, Berto-Verlag, Bonn, 1961.

Ruland, Bernd, *Die Augen Moskaus*, Schweizer Verlaghaus, Zürich, 1973.

Schellenberg, Walter, *The Schellenberg Memoirs*, Deutsch, London, 1956.

Schramm, Wilhelm von, 'Die rot-weisse Kapelle', *Frankfurter allgemeine Zeitung*, 13.12.1966. *Verrat im Zweiten Weltkrieg*, Düsseldorf-Wien, 1967.

Seale, Patrick and McConville, Maureen, *Philby: the Long Road to Moscow*, Hamish Hamilton, London, 1973.

Smith, Bradley F., *Reaching Judgement at Nuremberg*, Deutsch, London, 1977.

Speer, Albert, *Inside the Third Reich*, Weidenfeld and Nicolson, London 1970.

Szumowski, Tadeusz, 'Po upadku Pragi', *Kierunki*, Warsaw, Cracow, 19.5.1968, 26.5.1968.

Terry, Anthony and Knightley, Phillip, 'The housewife who spied for Russia', *The Sunday Times*, London, 27.1.1980.

Thomas, Hugh, *The Murder of Rudolf Hess*, Hodder and Stoughton, London, 1979.

Trepper, Leopold, *The Great Game*, McGraw-Hill, New York, 1977.

Vetsch, Christian, *Aufmarsch gegen die Schweiz*, Walter-Verlag, Olten und Freiburg, 1973.

Villemarrst, Pierre de, *L'espionnage soviétique en France, 1944–1969*, Nouvelles Editions Latines, Paris, 1969.

Whiting, Charles, *Spymasters*, Dutton, London, 1976.

Wildhagen, Karl and others, *Erich Fellgiebel*, Im Selbstverlag, Hannover, 1970.

Williams, Neville, *Chronology of the Modern World, 1763–1965*, Penguin, London, 1975.

Winterbotham Frederick W., *The Ultra Secret*, Futura, 1975.

Periodicals

Bulletin de l'Amicale des Anciens Membres des Services Speciaux de la Defence Nationale (quarterly), France.

Frankfurter allgemeine Zeitung (daily), West Germany.

The Guardian (daily), London.

Kierunki (weekly), Warsaw, Cracow.

The Listener (weekly), London.

Neue Züricher Zeitung (daily), Zürich.

The Observer (weekly), London.

Sphere (weekly), London.

Der Spiegel (weekly), West Germany.

Stern (weekly), West Germany.

The Sunday Times (weekly), London.

Tribune de Genève (daily), Geneva.

Tribune de Lausanne (daily), Lausanne.

Index

Index

Index

Index

Index